S0-CBJ-785

ON THE EAST–WEST SLOPE

ON THE EAST–WEST SLOPE

Globalization, nationalism, racism and discourses on Central and Eastern Europe

By Attila Melegh

Central European University Press
Budapest New York

Published in 2006 by
Central European University Press

An imprint of the
Central European University Share Company
Nádor utca 11, H-1051 Budapest, Hungary
Tel: +36-1-327-3138 or 327-3000
Fax: +36-1-327-3183
E-mail: ceupress@ceu.hu
Website: www.ceupress.com

400 West 59th Street, New York NY 10019, USA
Tel: +1-212-547-6932
Fax: +1-646-557-2416
E-mail: mgreenwald@sorosny.org

ISBN 963 7326 24 3 (cloth)
978-963-7326-24-0

Library of Congress Cataloging-in-Publication Data

Melegh, Attila.
On the East–West slope : globalization, nationalism, racism and discourses on Eastern Europe / By Attila Melegh.—1st ed.
p. cm.
ISBN 9637326243
1. Europe, Eastern—Politics and government—1989. 2. Europe—Foreign relations—Europe, Eastern. 3. Europe, Eastern—Foreign relations—Europe. 4. Europe—Economic integration. I. Title.

DJK51.M46 2005
940.56'1—dc22

2005018537

Printed in Hungary by
Akadémia Nyomda,
Martonvásár

Table of Contents

List of Tables

Acknowledgements

I have been helped by many institutions and individuals while researching and writing this book. Without them I would not have been able to accomplish this task.

The book is partly based on more than forty narrative interviews. I would like to express my gratitude to the interviewees for their willingness to set time aside for me and for my narrative type of interview. There is a sense in which they are the heroes and the co-authors of this book, but unfortunately their names cannot be revealed due to the sensitive nature of the analysis. Nonetheless, my gratitude to them could not be greater. However, I have also had "normal" help.

First of all I am grateful to the Research Support Scheme for providing a generous scholarship and additional funds for traveling to the United States and to Russia. Their support and flexibility have been vital. I am extremely grateful to József Böröcz, who as a very good friend not only encouraged me from the beginning that ideas such as those developed below can be fruitful and important, but who as head of the Hungarian Institute at Rutgers University also provided a suitable base for my research in the States. His comments and my discussions with him have been crucial. His intellectual contribution cannot be formalized into sentences and quotations. In Moscow the Institute of International and Economic and Political Sciences of the Russian Academy of Sciences arranged the institutional backing I needed for entering the country and doing research there. I am very grateful to Svetlana Glinkina at this institute and also to Alexei Miller, both of whom helped me greatly with organizational matters. Miller also opened my eyes in many ways with regard to current social and political developments in Russia. The help of my former teacher Zoltán Sz. Bíró was also essential in finding contacts in Russia, and in personal conversations he has gave me an extremely fine analysis of Russian society. I must also mention János Mátyás Kovács, who, despite being in a constant debate with me, generously supported my applications and kindly provoked me by his editorial comments on various Hungarian research papers I had written. I am also grateful to the EUSSIRF project of the European Union, which allowed me to spend 3 weeks at the Library of the London School of Economics to finalize my manuscript. My debt to Anna Loutfi is also enormous. She found time for revising the manuscript before submission from a linguistic point of view and she did so with great sensitivity. My gratitude cannot be greater toward László Löb as a precise, careful editor of the book who has made the text "real" at the end of the process.

There have been friends who always found time to read and to comment on my writings. Many ideas have emerged from such discussions with Éva Kovács. As an old friend she has taught me several things, including the technique of narrative interviews, and ours have been extremely enlightening. Eric Kaldor has graciously allowed me to use one of his interviews and has also made extremely valuable comments on my texts. Claude Karnoouh has proved a very good friend in writing comments on my texts and translating some into French: his critical thinking has made a definite and characteristic imprint on my text. Without Sorin Antohi's help and intellectual encouragement this book could not have been finished: his help as a reader and friend has proved to be vital. Conversations with Mahua Sharkar have offered me perspectives beyond Eastern Europe and ideas for the future, which are so much needed when a work has been finished. The comments of Judit Bodnár, Gyula Benda and Péter Őri have also become an integral part of my thinking. In addition I owe a great deal in various ways to Elwood Carlsson, Roman Iourev, Balázs Krémer, Mária Adamik, Viola Zentai, Miklós Haraszti, Ákos Szilágyi, András Barabás, Miklós Hadas, Zsolt Spéder, Katalin Kovács, Dezső Dányi, László Hablicsek, Emese Lafferton, Katalin Orsolya Németh, John Clement, Irina Tyiskina, Zsuzsa Farkas. I would like to thank Adrienn Hegyesi for her work in the research on public discourses on migration and helping me in many ways when preparing the final manuscript. During the work Katalin Zalatnai left our world voluntarily because she did not feel well among us. She proved a great help typing interviews. Her memory should be with us when this book is read. During my research I also had the opportunity to work with talented and hard-working students. Among them I am extremely grateful for the interest and comments of Vera Várhegyi, Dóra Mester, Katalin Dancsi, Vera Tömkő. I also owe much to my students at the Central European University. Among them Salome Asatiani and Adrian Brisku have become friends providing full emotional and intellectual support. I have partly written these texts for younger "East Europeans" like them who have not fallen into the traps of discursive arrangements offered to them in our new era. Gergely Baics has also become a friend and with his interest in the work a major force in making me persevere.

During the whole work my wife Virág Erdős, an extremely sensitive writer, inspired me with her precise insights into the mechanisms of our current social life. She very much shares my desire to understand how aggression and exclusion have become so dominant in today's East European societies. Apart from listening and finding texts for me she also allowed me to leave my family behind and to concentrate on my research. I can only wish that the outcome were as good as her contribution to it. My parents and my in-laws have also been very helpful. They have constantly supported me in all possible ways even in very difficult periods. Many thanks to them. I also admire my children Máté and Bálint for their patience and emotional support. This book is dedicated to them as future readers and critics. They will be able to judge its true value.

The list could be continued to include many other people who played a role in my research on the East–West dichotomy. Once again the only words I have are words of gratitude. But one thing should be said very clearly. None of those above can be held responsible for the outcome of my research. The responsibility is solely mine.

Preface

I. The Paradox of Central and Eastern Europe?

The dominant discourse on Central and Eastern Europe in and outside the region confronts us with a paradox. Central to this discourse is the interpretation of the events of 1989 and the subsequent social and political development presenting a hope/chance for a "return to normalcy." Here normalcy means the "West," a combination of ideals such as "diversity," "freedom," "democracy" and "market economy," This "Europeanization," prescribing radical "westernization" and "normalization," supposedly meant the end of a distinct "Eastern" category in Europe, or at least the rapid evaporation of its unpleasant connotations and a gradual "reintegration" of Europe. But paradoxically, at least in the short run, this "normalization" has led to extremely "abnormal" and partly unexpected disintegrative tendencies around the shifting borders of "Europe." Federal structures and states collapsed creating geopolitical uncertainties, harsh disputes over minorities and territories evolved, and in some cases ugly and devastating civil and international wars were conducted, hindering the return to "normalcy" and thus the hoped-for disappearance of the East–West divide. It is still with us and only the level of "Easterness" or "Westerness" is debated with regard to different, geographically and politically understood contexts.

The political disintegration, the wars and the "rise" of nationalism have been rarely explained by the emerging new socio-political framework, i.e. global capitalism and the European Union. The arguments tend to fall back instead on essentialized and scaled "Eastern" characteristics of the region. The "abnormal" phenomena have been either understood as the "return of the past," i.e. the reproduction of the inherited "Eastern" structures and sociopolitical reflexes, or they have been dismissed as the "necessary" but "unpleasant" costs of getting back to the "normal" path of Western development.[1] Thus on the one hand there has been widespread talk of the reappearance of "Balkanic political leprosy," "murderous" nationalism, the "burden of history," "tribal collectivism," "ancient East–West divide" or "old wine in new bottles," to quote just some of the most frequently used terms suggesting that "East is East".[2] On the other hand, as compared to the blood-wine-disease focus, from institutional actors such as the EU and the World Bank to prominent "East Europeanist" intellectuals there is lamentation about the difficulties of transplanting certain "Western" practices or getting beyond certain developmental phases in Central and Eastern Europe. In this genre of "developmental" or "transitional" thought there are ideas of necessary "modernization", "hybridity", and it is argued that Central and Eastern Europe has some "unfinished business" and the "ten–fifteen years" of transition are still going "on" within the newly accessing "Eastern" parts of the European Union or beyond.[3] Alternatively, in the case of the primeval nationalism, it is claimed that the Central and East European states are still in a "state-building" and "nation-building" phase, whereas most West European states have entered an essentially "post-nationalist" era.[4]

That the above interpretations, narratives or discourses are highly problematic is not a new discovery. Attacks on them have been manifold, and at times devastating.[5] This book is not a new attempt to refute or to deconstruct this mythology directly. The point of my analysis of East–West discourses is not that the above understanding of political and social development is Eurocentric or teleological, or that categories like Central and Eastern Europe are socially and historically constructed and can serve as a basis for hegemonic discourses.[6] The question for us is rather how these "East–West slopes" based on the idea of gradually diminishing civilization toward the "East" enable the translations of "liberal humanitarian utopias" onto a global scale and how the related identity structures actually operate and transform themselves into social and political action or individual narratives in the context of Central and Eastern Europe. Even within this broad area, my prime focus is not on the social and political behavior of actors at the extreme positions (the "West," EU versus poor "Third World" states), but of those who are delegated by the discourse into a mid-way position on the slope, or who imagine themselves in that locus. Geographically and socially this position is not fixed in the discourses being analyzed, but the institutional and non-institutional actors of the former "Eastern Bloc" are prime examples and therefore provide the main target of my analysis.

II. The concept of this book

This book is organized around three major problems. The first is the issue of historical change in East–West discourses from a modernizationist type to a new/old civilizational one and the relevance of this discursive change in the collapse of state socialism in Central and Eastern Europe. The second is the role and functioning of this new/old discourse of civilizational slope at the end of the 20th century. In particular this entails an attempt to understand why Central and Eastern Europe necessarily turns "ugly" (racist, xenophobic and nationalistic) under a global pattern of Westernization understood in the framework of the civilizational slope. Thirdly the book looks for an interrelationship between discourses and narratives, that is to say the ways in which institutions or individuals attach themselves to cognitive structures such as the East–West slope. My aim is to examine not only how we can imagine ourselves on the slope, but also how these narratives and their interrelationship can be categorized.

1. Changes in discourses

One of the main arguments of this book is that around 1980 there was major shift in discourses, which is analyzed in chapter 1. The con-pts of "Central Europe" and "Europe" emerging in both popular d scholarly analyses of the early 1980s mark the collapse of one dis-rse and the arrival of a new/old one. The reinvention of these con-s was not some kind of historical accident whereby intellectuals " and "West" returned to concepts that had been forgotten for 30 ears. Rather these concepts had been suppressed in a discursive, ldian sense. During that period of 30–40 years there had been se of rival modernities or "cold war" competition, conceptu-rgely in terms of quantitative and ideological differences. This e appeared as something "real" and did not lend itself to self-. Around the early 1980s, still within a teleological frame-e was a shift to a qualitative-regional schema. The discursive shift was evident in the "now-classic" texts on the concept of Central Europe and post-totalitarianism. They were all relying on the idea of the collapse of the modernizationist-progress discourse and the (re) vitalization of a new/old conceptual framework. All this facilitated the collapse of state socialism and the reallocation of political power both within socialist countries and in the international community.

The same historical shift is addressed in chapter II, where I follow the development of population discourses on "East" and "West" in both "East" and "West." I use new archival-documentary material from influential American and Hungarian intellectuals, policy makers and demographers to trace "local" racist discourses of qualitative population development to "global" modernizationist ones (which suppress but in some way still carry certain elements of previous cognitive structures) and to analyze the shift to the new/old qualitative-regional discourses of population changes. It is of some significance that, as compared to the prewar discourses, those of the 1980s and 1990s show a definite interest in incorporating Eastern Europe into an overall non-Western category. Furthermore the tracking of East–West exchanges and the mutual reflection of "local-global" discourses on each other provide a critical insight into the "paradoxical" rise of "Eastern" racism.

The marks of qualitative East–West discourses can also be shown in the spatial imagination of global actors such as multinational corporations, major research and development foundations and international newspapers, discussed in chapter 3. There it turns out that, counter to the idea of a unified world and deterritorialization cherished by th literature on globalization, the globalization processes bring back lor suppressed civilizational projects with regard to the region, a retu which clearly fits into the idea of discursive change around the 198

2. The role and functioning of East–West discourses in the late 20th century.

In chapters 2 and 3 I attempt to find a way out of the above lib adox by analyzing how the idea of gradual Westernization on West slope leads to disintegrative processes in Central and Europe and these unwelcome processes cannot be explaine belatedness or their prevailing "Eastern" traits. What is th ic (the sociology) of this slope sequenced by geo-cultural

I will examine this not at the extreme points, where the perspectives, behavior and the identity of the West and that of the "least developed" countries have been widely discussed in recent postcolonial and cultural studies, but in the mid-way points of "half Western, half Eastern" countries.

It seems that the main mechanism has already been outlined by Sorin Antohi's linkage of mimetic competition, the "failures of political identity" and disintegration in Eastern Europe or by concepts such as "nesting Orientalism" pioneered but never fully and systematically elaborated by Bakić-Hayden (Antohi 2000; Bakić-Hayden 1995). According to these ideas, then, the essence of the present dominant discourse of an East–West slope prescribes the gradual Westernization of different areas of the world and a drive to climb higher on the East–West slope. This upward emancipation leads to a mechanism designated in this book as movement on the slope or perspectives on the slope, which invites a grotesque chain of racisms or Orientalisms between different public actors, depending on the position and perspective they adopt on the above slope. In this chain everybody finds more "Eastern" actors or social arrangements that can be scapegoated for the failure to move upward on the slope or toward "liberal-humanitarian" ideals. In some other perspectives on the slope the Orientalism of the actor positioned higher or at the top of the slope is used to legitimize East–West exclusion further down the global civilizational scale. Conversely it is possible to construct a "Western, liberal, Jewish colonizer" who is aiming at the total subordination of the local population. This East–West game makes the internal political fights in Eastern European countries very fierce, while it can also lead to strange international conflicts between the states themselves, destabilizing the region and inviting Western intervention as exemplified by the disintegration of Yugoslavia.

3. Discourses and local narratives.

How do we as individuals relate to this slope? By what kind of narratives and narrative identities can we attach ourselves to this East–West slope if we cross the designated East–West borders? How do we reproduce these patterns by way of our own life histories? These are the questions of the concluding chapter of the book, in which we can follow the individual translations of the East–West slope and of the East–West paradoxes projected on us.

Two months of field research have produced forty-five narrative interviews in the United States, Hungary and Russia with people involved in East–West relations. The interviewees included representatives of multinationals or "emerging" "Eastern" business people investing heavily in the United States; academics who were also working on the social and economic problems and processes of the "other" region or who had simply moved across the border and taken long-term teaching assignments on the other side; employees of major international foundations and non-corporate actors engaged in philanthropic activities related to Central and Eastern Europe; political experts and one senior military figure.

The main assumption behind chapter 4 is that, besides providing meaning through temporality, narratives are also our prime means of "weaving" ourselves into East–West discourses. They are critical intermediaries in the materialization and reproduction of the power arrangements concerned. This reproduction by way of narrative identities is interpreted through hermeneutic analyses of the different narratives. The narratives cross each other or meet at the "border." "Easterners" speak about their activities related to the "West" or Central Europe and "Westerners" about their activities with regard to Eastern or Central Europe. This allows us to interpret not only the techniques used in creating a story for a Hungarian researcher in the East–West context, but also the role of the interviewees' position on the East–West slope and the possible consequences of "interactions" or the "dialogue" between the different actors.

From the types of the narratives and the reflection of the "Eastern" narratives on the "Western" ones it turns out that paradoxically the discussion between those who still rely on "cold war" patterns ("the children of the cold war" as one of the interviewees put it) have a much greater respect for each other's culture, then those trapped in the "dialogue of the deaf" between "nomadic," or "global traveler" versus "nationalist" types. Thus see again that the identity structure resulting from global Westernization creates conflicts contradicting the original assumptions of the proposed gradual "enlightenment" in the region. This seems to be the real paradox of Central and Eastern Europe or any other would-be "Western" region of the world.

Notes

1 For the categorization of "comparative" analyzes of non-Western developments see: Böröcz 2003, chapter 1. For nationalism and this very useful division of arguments see: Rupnik 2000.
2 These terms appear in different sorts of texts from newspaper articles to scholarly analysis. Here I will only mention some of the authors who rely on such ideas with regard to Eastern Europe: Judt 1996; Glenny 1992; Tismaneanu 1999, 2001; Gross 1999; Fisher-Galati 1992; Richards 1999. For a critical overview of these terms see also Appadurai 1996; Burgess 1997 and Todorova 1997.
3 This modernizationist analytical angle is maintained basically by the whole genre of transition literature and all the major international institutional actors managing the "transition" including the EU, World Bank and EBRD, but it has been reformulated even more eloquently by many intellectuals preoccupied by the translation of the institutionally promoted "global design." For institutional actors see chapter III of this book, while for intellectuals among others see Chirot 1999, 2001; Kovács, J. M 1999, 1999a; Ash 1999–2000; Ramet 1999.
4 See among others: Bideleux and Taylor 1996; Rupnik 2000.
5 There are a number of critical attempts for historical, sociological to political analyses. See among others: Tamás 1999a; Burgess 1997; Todorova 1997; Neumann 1999; Böröcz-Kovács 2001; Böröcz 2000.
6 See among others: Amin 1989; Said 1978; Böröcz 2000; Böröcz and Kovács, 2001; Böröcz, 2005; Wallerstein 1991, 1997; Appadurai 1996; Neumann 1999; Todorova 1997; Antohi 2000; Wolff 1994; Mignolo 1998, 2000; Spivak 1990.

CHAPTER 1

Liberal Humanitarian utopia and Eastern and Central Europe

1.1. On the slope. Introductory examples of East–West discourses in the late 1990s

From the early 1980s the geopolitical and geocultural imagination has been recaptured by the idea of a civilizational or East–West slope providing the main cognitive mechanism for reorganizing international and socio-political regimes in the Eastern part of the European continent. In this radical "normalization" and "transition" process almost all political and social actors "East" and "West" identify themselves on a descending scale from "civilization to barbarism," from "developed to non-developed" status. This discursive structure appears in very different forms and areas of knowledge and is utilized by very different speakers ranging from the European Union to restaurant owners, but in each case the concept of a "sliding scale of merit" with regard to Eastern and Central European countries as members of the former so-called socialist block[1] (Glenny 1992, 236). To further conceptualize this cognitive order of differentiation let us take some introductory examples "East" and "West":

> On July 12, 2000, the Italian daily *La Stampa* published an interview with Giuliano Amato, the prime minister of Italy at the time, who, arguing heavily against putting the EU candidate Eastern and Central Europeans into *"quarantine,"* felt outraged because of the delaying tactic of the European Union with regard to the "Eastern enlargement." As he put it, when the East European nations expressed their wish to belong to Europe the EU told them: "Yes, you are European, but only of mixed blood." And this answer showed him that "with this we [Europeans] accept some responsibility for communism" (MTI, Hungarian News Agency, press archive, 07/13/2000).

The same racial descending scale appeared in April 2001 in a narrative interview conducted by me and analyzed in details in the last chapter of this book. In this report a Walloon professor living in St. Petersburg reflected upon the day when she met her Russian husband in Moscow:[2]

> It was a very, very beautiful day. And it was a discovery of Russian for me, of Russia, and I think, like everybody in the beginning, I didn't feel myself a foreigner here * I think for everybody it's the same because... especially because the people look like us * there is no difference. Of course there is un petite Slav, but they are white, they are very different, like, like in Europe, there is black hair, there is blond hair, everything, and * we look not very different. And especially now because the clothes are the same. Ten years ago * it was all of this very Soviétique, and * until now anyhow the people know in one second that you are not, you are not Russian. * Before it was enough to look at the shoes, but you know this because you were living in Hungary. I think it is for you very familiar.

On October 23, 1998 Mr. Orbán, the newly elected Hungarian prime minister was interviewed by Business Week, a Budapest-based English language weekly, with regard to the economic damage arising from the financial turmoil of August 1998 in Russia. In this interview he established another type of descending scale with regard to the progress toward a fully-fledged market economy:

> The Hungarian market is not an emerging market anymore, it is a converging market. ... The crisis in Russia is deep, and we will have to live with the situation for a long time. But I am quite confident that investors realize the difference between NATO and soon-to-be European Union members—such as Hungary, the Czech Republic, and Poland—and Russia. And they will make a clear distinction in the future. Investors will come back—more than who left—and Hungary and Poland will be the stars for them over the next two years (*http://www.businessweek.com/bwdaily/dnflash/oct1998/nf81023e.htm*, accessed: July 27, 2001).

In 1996, analyzing the European integration and the "East European" disintegration process, the director of the Centre of Russian and East European Studies at University of Wales and his co-author came up with the following conclusion concerning the disintegration process in "Eastern Europe" and its post-communist transformation toward "Western" ideals:

> An even more important consequence of these East–West divergences is that East European politics is seriously "out of phase" with West European politics, and this constitutes another crucial hindrance to pan-European integration. Fundamentally, the East European states are still in a "state-building" and "nation-building" phase, whereas most West European states have long since completed (or exhausted) their state-building and nation-building projects and have moved essentially post-nationalist era (Bideleux–Taylor 1996, 285).

In October, 2000, in a restaurant called Sydney Bar, a menu gave advice to guests looking for food or drink in downtown Bucharest, Romania. Among items like "Bloody Mariana," "Bucharest Road Kill," "Where the Hell Am I" and "Castro's Revenge" the following hierarchical evaluation could be read with regard to legality in different areas of Europe:

> Wallaby toasted
> "We'll-al-be-toasted" is our standard reply to the often asked question "why isn't there a Sydney Bar in a Western Country?" With our uniquely inoffensive menu destined to battle with those western lawyers (whom we are sure do not sue in lei) we definitely see a conflict of interest. 60,000 lei

In 2001 Péter Nádas, one of the most renowned and finest Hungarian writers of Europe today, published a short article in a liberal Hungarian Weekly on "Training Practices of Freedom." This article became something of a cult piece among the Hungarian intelligentsia and is worth quoting more extensively due to its dense hierarchical vision of Hungary and Europe put into civilizational terms:

> Yet it does not take just ten years—it takes well over two hundred to change a nation's most singular characteristics …

While the person was talking I was standing in front of my bookcase in an attempt to compile a list of books s/he should not miss by any chance. I was going to suggest them accessible books to enhance their image of Hungary. It was no easy task since Hungarians excel in quite a number of fields, self-knowledge, however, not being one of them. They had written on the Swedish, the Italians and maybe on Norwegians as well and had come to Budapest to carry on with their peculiar undertaking.

The compilation of the list required information about what languages they could read.

In answer to my question they casually turned away from their heart-to-heart conversation only to return to it a moment later. "European languages" they said. They probably did not name them to avoid making a show of their brilliance and to avoid later embarrassment owing to their boasting. They laughed instead, as if clearing up the flotsam and jetsam of their modesty.

It is unfair to identify a single person with the country or people of the person's origin. I, for one, am Hungarian but this has no significance for others. My own self does, however. A person is always more than his people or his country—yet no matter how great a master of words somebody is, that person will still know less than his mother tongue.

As regards them, it was never a worry that I might indecently identify them with their nation. Any master of vivisection observing them will find delicate junctions of individualism and egotism, well worth scrutinizing. And then, in principle, they should be considered French, not German. Furthermore, I could not have identified them with the Germans since in those days the Germans had two peoples, two countries and two German languages simultaneously. One of their two countries always smelled of insufficiently burnt lignite, it was like a rotten egg—while the other was saturated with the scent of detergents and fabric softeners used in compulsive overdoses. As a matter of fact, there was much to be scented and washed away. To avoid the self-destructive obsession of sterilization must have been as tough a task in one country as surviving two successive dictatorships without going insane in the other.

I do not want to talk big but to me, the old Bundesrepublik [Federal Republic] compares to Goethe. Not, however, to Hölderlin or Kleist or Büchner.

Let me tell you what I am thinking of: I am talking about the country's face, poetry, and history, about the great process of individualization which has been carried through in the past fifty years by the worthiest of Germans in the Bundesrepublik, though they had to cut themselves into pieces and then put themselves together again. …

I should describe the toilet in the first class car of the fast train connecting the town of Zalaegerszeg with Budapest [in Hungary]. I would thereby be fulfilling a long-time obligation of mine as a human being as well as a citizen of Hungary and, last but not least, as a writer. From the aesthetic point of view this is no easy task. It would of course be all too simple just to get into a train toilet and put down everything I see like a clerk. Then I would be entangled in stylistic problems. Narrative prose would apparently solve the problem with similar ease. This would involve my approaching and describing a rather distinct toilet that does not actually exist in nature, making use of my decades-long experience. Should the latter be the case, I might unwillingly embellish the massive reality of this toilet.

It is thirty-nine years now that I have been traveling along this route. I have been using it on a regular basis for sixteen years. Ever since I can remember I have not given up hope.

It will be better, it will please the eye—the day will come when facilities will be used for their original purpose because my countrymen will learn how to use them. …

In a democracy, things happen by the people, not to the people. You act. Now I feel obliged to declare bankruptcy. And with this bankruptcy the Head of State has nowhere to appeal to.

Either we discuss this rather simple logistical problem, then we embark upon an agreement, clean up and repair things—or there is no solution (translated by András Barabás, accessed 2003.03.21).

The first thing to be noted in the above examples is that the "authors" do not see themselves actually creating differences, but merely feel that they are bringing something to the surface. Nádas speaks about national and "personal" characteristics which cannot be changed in a short period of time. The "author" of the "inoffensive" menu also clearly assumes knowledge of a difference between a hellish place like Bucharest and the "West." It is certain (it is "destined") that in the "West" lawyers would sue a restaurant with such arrogant pieces as the one above. It is also openly assumed in the text that in Romania the authors of the menu are allowed to do so. Amato, the Italian prime minister, directly refers to the categorization of an institution, namely the European Union, as sending out an implied message of half-Europeanness. The Walloon woman evokes the special, lower value whiteness of Eastern and Central Europeans as a civilizational level with which the interviewer—put into the same category—should be familiar. The then prime minister Orbán is "quite confident that investors realize the difference," that is to say the fact is so obvious that one only has to refer to it. The problem is simply one of clarification. The same lack of control appears in the idea of "these East–West divergences" and the complaint about the lack of "hygiene" in Hungary in spite of the freedom and democracy that have been achieved. That is to say, all our authors draw upon packaged, ready-made "facts of differences" as available references.

This reliance on externally and historically given differences, in addition to the used or evoked and partially overlapping, partially contradictory geocultural categories, always assumes some kind of axis with two end points: "East" and "West," "white" and "not white," "cleanliness" and "dirt," "emerging" and ready or "fully developed," "nationalist" and "post-nationalist" aspects which unite all the texts above. That is to say spaces, countries, people and regions are put on some kind of a ruler along which they can be moved or along which they are moving. The *reduction* or *localization* of differences, the definition of the *coordinates* and the *distances* all form part of some kind of a metonymic *mapping* exercise, both in the geographical and in a cultural sense (Antohi 2002, 20). Categories are not only set up, but are also put into a *hierarchical* order, that is to say the scale possesses some superior and inferior points, or at least the differences are positioned above and below a certain line.

More concretely the mapping exercises based on "given" differences aim at establishing "in-between," transitional categories, gray zones which are problematic, insecure and vague. The menu item, "Where the Hell am I?" might refer to being nowhere, but possibly also to being on a borderline, where localization is problematic. Mixed blood means half one type, half not that type (Böröcz and Kovács 2001, 35). "Un petite Slav" or "Sovietique" means whiteness, but of a different, lower quality. A "converging" market is an in-between category among fully developed and emerging markets. And "Eastern Europe" is still in a "state-building" and "nation-building" phase" or it is just "quarantine," a place where people are temporarily put for the purpose of observing them in their movement to "hygienically safe" places. Writing not about freedom but the "trainings of freedom" the Hungarian writer Nádas builds his whole narrative upon a metaphor of being on the road, on train or being in transition between "East" and "West" in a geographic and cultural sense. The key issue is locating and establishing borders between larger categories, and this *border mechanism* guides the actors and the speakers in their texts.

The constructed textual borders cannot be put into any kind of a fixed geographical pattern outside the "West." In the words of the title of a book written by an emigrant Hungarian sociologist, in these texts "There is West, but not East" (Ankerl 2000). In our examples Hungary can be placed in the category of "purely" Eastern European and "real Western" or between the emerging markets and the developed ones etc. The point seems to be not an emerging fixed geographic or regional pattern, but rather the use of racist and other types of negative markers, like "emerging," "still nation-building," "Slav" (Neumann 1999, 206–207). These markers and the attempted localizations are then the focus of the fight over categories.

The fight adds a tone of hysteria, embarrassment or fear to the texts. There are two interrelated regulatory practices within these textual worlds. First we are in a "twilight" zone, in an era of fear and danger. Ghosts or lingering memories of major catastrophes characterize this location as an object of the texts. Second the border constructed is a point at which, or the scale where, countries and people become disconnected. This point of ambiguity, together with some value hierarchies, suggests possible and at the same time unfinalized (conditional and contextualized) exclusion, or in the revealing phrase of Böröcz "contingent closure" (Böröcz 2003a, 128, 230–254).

Such exclusion mechanisms mean that those dissatisfied with the location along the non-privileged side of the border try to cross it by way of certain verbal maneuvers. The then Hungarian prime minister,

Orbán wants to change the classification of the Hungarian economy as an "emerging market" and to take it out of a class related to crisis. He actually invents a new title in order to distinguish Hungary from Russia and to push Hungary closer to the "most developed" areas. Nádas, who is most embarrassed by the Hungarian "reality" on the train and especially the uncivilized behavior of fellow Hungarians, makes a demonstrative announcement that they should use the toilet in a proper manner and thereby start the cleaning process which will move them further up the ladder of civilization.

The speakers on the other side of the "floating" border are also tantalized by this "contingent closure" and would like to see an upward movement as soon as possible. The Walloon lady distances herself from her husband who is not "proper white," but says that much has changed in the previous ten years: clothes, for instance, are now the same everywhere. Amato is afraid of accepting some responsibility for communism and that is why he wants to move some countries out of the danger zone, the era of in-between. Via their inbuilt teleology the scholarly discussions on nationalism also wish to move the East European countries out of the "nation-building" phase and push them into the "post-nationalist" phase. However, it is important to note that looking down the slope might involve vested interests in keeping the "inferiors," "down," as evidenced by the Sydney Bar menu in Bucharest. Moving Romania out of the backward category would mean that then the open despicability of the place might be challenged.

The above examples can be interpreted either as a proper or as a distorted representation of reality. In either case they deserve careful analysis since it seems that most of the political and social changes in Eastern and Central Europe have been institutionalized in accordance with this cognitive pattern. The most obvious example of this is the "Eastern enlargement" of the European Union, a process which, according to Böröcz, is not only imagined in this slope manner, but is actually managed accordingly if the published EU reports legitimizing decisions on starting the accession negotiations with the countries concerned are analyzed retrospectively (Böröcz 2001). To show the legitimacy of this argument and the links to our examples it is enough to quote the Copenhagen criteria announced in 1993.

In 1993, at the Copenhagen European Council, the Member States took a decisive step towards the current enlargement, agreeing that "the associated countries in central and eastern Europe that so desire shall become members of the European Union." Thus, enlargement was no longer a question of "if" but "when." Here too, the European Council provided a clear response:

"Accession will take place as soon as an applicant is able to assume the obligations of membership by satisfying the economic and political conditions required."

At the same time, the Member States designed the membership criteria, which are often referred to as the Copenhagen Criteria.

As stated in Copenhagen, membership requires that the candidate country has achieved:

stability of institutions guaranteeing democracy, the rule of law, human rights and respect for and protection of minorities;

the existence of a functioning market economy as well as the capacity to cope with competitive pressure and market forces within the Union;

the ability to ta.ke on the obligations of membership including adherence to the aims of political, economic and monetary union.

has created :

the conditions for its integration through the adjustment of its administrative structures, so that European Community legislation transposed into national legislations implemented effectively through appropriate administrative and judicial structures (http://europa.eu.int/comm/enlargement/intro/criteria.htm23 March, 2002).

It can clearly be seen that the EU enlargement process is not imagined as a negotiation between the assigned political body of the EU and certain nation states, with a deadline to be met, but as a timeless *process* (the question being when) of achieving certain capacities like the "stability of institutions guaranteeing" humanitarian liberal ideals such as the "rule of law," "human rights" etc., or the "existence" of a "functioning market economy" or the "capacity to cope with" certain "pressures within the Union." Even at first glance it can be seen that the criteria are vague and imply processes with no real end. Any country in the world can be found to be lacking some of the required conditions (for instance the guarantee of human rights) and therefore the process becomes merely a question of "translating" these ideals into a multidimensional slope and measuring countries accordingly. This inevitably leads to hierarchies not only between EU countries and the applicants, but also between the applicants themselves, as we have seen. Furthermore the selection method is entirely at the discretion of the issuer of criteria. The socio-political implications of these "redundant," "overdetermined" and in many respects "substantive" translation methods have been eloquently analyzed by Böröcz with regard to the behavior of the EU in this slope situation as follows:

> This has far-reaching implications for the nature of the statehood of the European Union as well as the politics of state-making and remaking in Europe today. Within the EU, "eastern enlargement" is widely seen and commonly portrayed as a mission civilisatrice. In the words of a British commentator: "if redrawing the map of Europe is effectively about extending the territorial coverage of the rules of law and norms of civil society, this is equivalent to the projection through much of central and eastern Europe of the code Napoleon, this time without the blood-shed and with legitimacy." The questions this leaves the observer with, then, are the same as raised by the inclusion of what used to be the German Democratic Republic in the legal and administrative structures of the Federal Republic of Germany a few years ago: Is it possible to establish the rule of law through substantive and overdetermined means? Furthermore, even if it is possible, what are the implications of that for the legitimacy of the process and the structures created thereby (Böröcz 2001)?

Good questions. The writing of this book has been very much inspired by such paradoxes particularly concerning interpretations of the above cognitive patterns as they relate to Eastern and Central Europe and asking how they fit into the structures revealed by studies on colonial-postcolonial patterns or East–West dichotomies. First I will argue that Karl Mannheim's concept of liberal humanitarian utopia is a relevant notion. Then, with regard to Eastern and Central Europe, I will try to summarize and partially reinterpret some of the key findings of literature on coloniality and East–West discourses on the basis of the previously discussed patterns and utilizing the concept of liberal humanitarian utopia.

1.2. Liberal utopia versus Orientalism and coloniality

1.2.1. East–West discourse as liberal humanitarian utopia

All the textual mechanisms in the above texts add up to an overarching cognitive pattern establishing a civilizational slope. As a structure of mentality this civilizational slope is strikingly similar to the "*liberal humanitarian utopia*" introduced by Karl Mannheim. The addition of some postcolonial insights to this originally Eurocentric concept clarifies elements of the cognitive structure mentioned above and its social function.

In his classical piece "Ideology and Utopia" Mannheim sought to find a way out of the history of political ideas and "partial ideologies" to describe wider, "total" cognitive systems and to link them to a particular social structure. He calls these wider cognitive structures "total ideologies," among which there are patterns "incongruous with the state of reality within which they occur." This incongruence is to be understood not as containing "transcendental," "mythical" or "metaphysical" elements, since all ideologies carry such parts, but elements which, "when they pass into conduct, tend to shatter, either partially or wholly, the order of things prevailing at the time" (Mannheim 1936, 173). These revolutionary models are the utopias.

On the basis of "historical time-sense" Mannheim identifies four utopias, one of which is the "liberal humanitarian utopia" linked to the period between the Enlightenment and the 1920s when Mannheim wrote his classic piece. Mannheim characterizes the former type of utopia in the following manner:

> The utopia of liberal humanitarianism, too, arose out of the conflict with the existing order. In its characteristic form, it also establishes a "correct" rational conception to be set off against evil reality. This counter-conception is not used, however, as a blueprint in accordance with which at any given point in time the world is to be reconstructed. Rather it serves merely as a "measuring rod" by means of which the course of concrete events may be theoretically evaluated. The utopia of the liberal-humanitarian mentality is the "idea." This,

> however, is not the static platonic idea of the Greek tradition, which was a concrete archetype, a primal mode of things; but here the idea is rather conceived of as a formal goal projected into the indefinite future whose function is to act as a mere regulative device in mundane affairs (Mannheim 1936, 197).

The "belief that reality moves continually towards an ever closer approximation to the rational" almost perfectly describes the dominant discourse on Eastern and Central Europe illustrated by the above examples, including that of EU accession.

First, it suggests the idea of an ongoing transition (progress or evolution as pointed out by Mannheim) to an ideal social form postponed into the indefinite or localized out of the reach of the "locals." Second, it also contains the idea of "perfection" and "civilization," which is a movement upwards on the slope and in the qualitative level of social behavior (see also Elias 1994). Third, it focuses on the idea of scaling and measurement and the associated linear conceptions of difference or change. Fourth, it introduces the idea that such concepts are not correct or incorrect descriptions of some kind of reality, but texts and concepts which actually change the existing "order of things" and make "reality" or, in Mannheim's words, regulate "mundane affairs." And last, due to the above traits it also reflects a highly normative mode of thinking, which, being at the same time extremely flexible, tends toward expansion or the incorporation of new objects into its discursive machinery.

Mannheim's concept nonetheless lacks the idea of qualitative borders on the slope and the racist or functionally racist constructions of these points. It seems then that Mannheim maintained a Eurocentric perspective. His main focus was the understanding of European developments as having universal validity, and he made Weberian references to "Oriental" experiences merely for the sake of static comparisons. Thus it is very important to consider how examples of East–West discourses and their interpretation as a liberal utopia fit into studies on postcolonial and colonial cognitive patterns, preoccupied as they are with qualitative-racist borders and exclusions. Here I will argue that Mannheim's idea of liberal utopia and the methodology behind it can be reinterpreted in such a way that it incorporates "coloniality" and the related findings of this literature. Actually it seems that the idea of a civilizational slope can provide a solution for the debates on the link between discourses on Eastern and Central Europe and colonial and postcolonial ones.

1.2.2. Concepts of knowledge production

Several major concepts and related methodological approaches have dominated the studies on knowledge production with regard to the non-Western world in the last two decades. These include ideas of discourse, the imaginary, ideology, identity formation and narrative. The idea of a civilizational slope interpreted as a liberal utopia can be harmonized with the concept of discourse and narrative, and especially of the imaginary, but it does not fit into the concept of ideology and identity formation. But let us examine the concepts one by one.

Most systematically elaborated by Michel Foucault, the idea of *discourse* is certainly a key element. Foucault's idea of the concept and his concrete examples made a great impact on Said's analysis of Orientalism and, through Said's work, on the whole genre of postcolonial and colonial cultural studies. In fact the later studies can be understood as translations of Foucault's ideas into a field positing Europe against non-Europe that was ignored by the founder himself (Stoler 1995, 59–60). As Said argues:

> He [Foucault] seems unaware of the extent to which the ideas of discourse and discipline are assertively European and how, along with the use of discipline to employ masses of detail (and of human beings), discipline was used also to administer, study, reconstruct—and then subsequently to occupy, rule, and exploit—almost the whole of the non-European world...The parallel between Foucault's carceral system and Orientalism is striking (Said 1978a, 117–118).

Discourse analysis as understood by Foucault refers to the understanding of rules and regularities in the creation/dispersal of objects, subjects, styles, concepts and strategic fields, and thereby reveal why certain "statements" and not others are made, and how these statements are related to each other. As Foucault put it:

> Whenever one can describe between a number of statements such a system of dispersion, whenever, between objects, types of state-

> ments, concepts, or thematic choices, one can define a regularity (an order, correlation, positions, and functionings, transformations) we will say, for the sake of convenience, that we are dealing with a discursive formation (Michel Foucault 1972, 38).

Thus in a discourse there is some kind of an order of knowledge, which creates and absorbs "statements" or systems of statements. These orders by way of the web of objects or styles are the grids and acts of power. Such "disciplining" discourses are also truly historical as they come into existence at a certain point in time and then disappear. It is important to note that these changes are linked to social and political relations and institutional arrangements but are not explained by them (Foucault 1972 1974, 1991a; 1999; Neumann 1999; Said 1978a; Goldberg 1990; Racevskis 1983, 90; Kiss 1996; Bakić-Hayden 1995; Wolff 1994).

It seems that the East–West slope interpreted as liberal utopia implies some kind of a discourse since it focuses on rules for statements. Thus, as with a discourse, we are tracing the transformation of certain rules into social reality by creating certain critical ideas out of the confrontation between rational ideals and "evil reality" and the measurement of the distance between them. This confrontation is not reduced to certain areas of knowledge (history writing, public attitudes etc.) and thus, as do discourses, it crosses all boundaries of forms and spheres of knowledge. It also lacks the idea of "author" and maintains the linkage between cognitive and social structure, which is so important for Foucault's analysis. Thus Mannheim's liberal utopia and the East–West slope revealed above can be reinterpreted as a discourse and can therefore be fitted into the relevant findings in cultural studies which apply this concept.

A structuralist version of a "post-structuralist" (or, as claimed by Foucault, non-structuralist) discourse analysis, namely the idea of asymmetric counter-concepts, provides additional insights into the working of the East–West slope and harmonizes well with the interpretation as a liberal utopia (Koselleck 1985, 159–196). "Asymmetrical" or universalist binary counter-concepts as self-designations deprive the "other" of some kind of essential trait, such as being a member of some kind of "universal" community. As Koselleck put it:

> This kind of self-definition provokes counterconcepts, which discriminate against those who have been defined as the "other". ...Thus there are a great number of concepts recorded which function to deny the reciprocity of mutual recognition. From the concept of the one party follows the definition of the alien other, which definition can appear to the latter as a linguistic deprivation, in actually verging on the theft. This involves asymmetrically opposed concepts (Koselleck 1985, 160–161).

The methodological status of these concepts is once again not that of a description of reality or a self-reflection, an identity. The concepts shape our social reality or more precisely they are meant to intervene in our reality on behalf of a political action. In Koselleck's words again: "Concepts employable in a particularly antithetical manner have a marked tendency to reshape the various relations and distinctions among groups, to some degree violating those concerned, and in proportion to this violation rendering them capable of political action" (Koselleck 1985, 162).

Ideas such as cleanliness, whiteness, Europeanness or being post-nationalist, which reveal the East–West slope in our examples are such asymmetrical totalizing concepts, which in themselves hinder positive identification through lack of a relevant trait. In addition, the slope, by depending on asymmetrical concepts like those above becomes the translation or representation of the political character of these binary oppositions. Thus the semantic structuralist idea of asymmetrical counter-concepts comes in handy for our analysis.

In analysis of the East–West slope interpreted as a liberal utopia, as an alternative approach to discourse analysis the concept of the *imaginary* is also helpful. Like Mannheim's concept of "total ideology" the imaginary is understood as the sum of ways in which a culture perceives and conceives the world or areas within it (Glissant quoted by Mignolo 1998, 2000 23; Bakić-Hayden 1995; Goldsworthy 1998, 1999; Csizmadia 2001). The imaginary is also a socio-historical concept which describes how different cultures cognitively structure the world (e.g. by continents, commercial routes or by setting up the categories like 1st world, 2nd world or 3rd world or mental maps, for instance in tourist guide books, Böröcz 1996, 44–51). Furthermore these structures are not pure images, or "true" or "false" representations but "world views" inherently linked to some social systems like the "modern/colonial world system" or the capitalist world system. It is to be noted that as a hegemonic *Weltanschauung* originating from the Enlightenment and linked to the hierarchical and unequal modern world system Wallerstein's analysis of a singular, universal civilization fits also into the idea of the "imaginary" or that of utopias (Wallerstein 1991, 215–230; Böröcz 2003 91–92; Wolff 1994, 8–9; Mignolo 2000, 23–24).[3]

In all the above methodological attempts, including that of liberal utopia, there is the clear shadow of the concept of ideology in its Marxist interpretation. Both Foucault and Mannheim rejected that concept and invented their diverging methods of analysis as an alternative to the idea of ideology understood as something that has its own development and in particular as forms of knowledge linked to particular social groups (Foucault 1972, Mannheim 1936). But it seems that regardless of the dominance of "non-ideological" concepts such as discourse or the imaginary the concept of ideology is resurfacing in the analysis of East–West dichotomy or coloniality. In one of the most critical books on relevant "Western" cognitive structures Amin bluntly argues that "Eurocentrism" is not a paradigm, not ethonocentrism, not a theory, but the "ideological framework of capitalism" (Amin 1989).

Behind the choice between ideology and discourse the crucial issue seems to be the problem of domination or hegemony of certain patterns and resistance to them. Most of those who accept the implications of discourse see no real way out of the imposed hegemonic patterns, while those who opt for ideology are able to conceptualize methods of breaking up the hegemonic mode of thought. As Rätzhel puts it:

> To say that a certain way of thinking is linked to a certain way of living and acting is not the same as to say that economic structures determine the way in which people think. ... When Marx suggests that the "ruling ideas are always the ideas of the rulers" this is not to imply that other ideas do not exist, that there are no practices of resistance and no competing ideas (Rätzhel 1997, 62).

Wallerstein and Amin are even more explicit (Wallerstein 1997; Amin 1989). They openly declare that the capitalist social formation or modern world system in its European form is not eternal and therefore the relevant cognitive patterns of Eurocentrism are not eternal either. It is a particular formation, both historically and philosophically, and this is the starting point for rejecting the liberal-humanitarian type of utopian universalism which serves the purposes of domination and exclusion:

> And if we are to do that we have to recognize that something special was indeed done by Europe in the sixteenth to eighteenth centuries that did transform the world, but in a direction whose negative consequences are upon us today. We must cease trying to deprive Europe of its specificity on the deluded premise that we are thereby depriving it of an illegitimate credit. Quite the contrary. We must fully acknowledge the particularity of Europe's reconstruction of the world because only then will it be possible to transcend it, and to arrive hopefully at a more inclusively universalist vision of human possibility, one that avoids none of the difficult and imbricated problems of pursuing the true and the good in tandem (Wallerstein 1997, 106–107).

Overall Mannheim's concept of "total ideology" and that of the imaginary seem, even in this later question of historicity and hegemony (the beginning and end of "Eurocentrism" and its dominance), to offer a convenient solution, which maintains the "totalitarianism" of such cognitive patterns, but neither pushes it too far in world history nor simply waits for the unpredictable collapse of the discourse.

Beyond the conceptual framework of discourse, the imaginary or ideology, another alternative methodological approach for understanding the hegemony of the above Eurocentric cognitive patterns is to say that they are linked to the formation of *collective identities* that are "functionally" somehow unavoidable or necessary (Said 1978, 7; Neumann 1999, 3–4, 207–243). The need for designating community boundaries leads to the search for "others." The location of this *alter ego* group can be changed, but for historical and semantic reasons these "others" tend to be fixed spatially and especially in the content of differences.

This effort of looking at the formation of collective identities is probably the most systematic attempt to break away from the discursive and "totalized" cognitive patterns and generally goes hand in hand with the idea of stereotypes and ethnocentric explanations (Todorova 1997, see footnote 1 above). First, the notion of identity assumes some kind of *self-identification* since it refers to ideas about ourselves (Neumann 1999, 209). Even if patterns are not coming from us, as an escape from uncertainty, there is the option of dressing up in clothes offered to us (Neumann 1999, 207–42; Baumann 1996). Thus there are collective actors who, by setting up "boundary markers," clarify the borders of the community.[4]

Second, this approach assumes that there is some kind of structural stability in such identities extending across very long periods of time. The best example of this ahistoricity is Neumann's analysis. Although he sees important historical changes in the process of collective identity formation and historically links, for instance, the "European" and Russian identities, he nonetheless fixes certain relationships such as that with the "Turkish other" in which there is a continuity between medieval perceptions and, say, those of the 18th century.

> In addition, the time of reconquest and empire was seen by many as a reincarnation of the old religious war—a continuation of the Crusades. What is interesting to note, however, is the increased use of the Greek term "barbarian" to describe "the Turk," as opposed to the strictly religious notion of the "infidel" or "non-believer." This change in terms would seem to fit with the growing secularization of the state system that had begun at Westphalia and is yet another reminder that the phenomenon of the Easterner as Europe's other predates the coming of Christendom and Islam. In other words, civilization, defined by criteria such as "humanity," "law," and 'social mores," seemed to supplant religion in Europe's external differentiation from non-European communities What took hold was a set of "intercultural relations" between Europe and "the Turk," relations that drew a sharp distinction between civilization and barbarism (Neumann 1999, 52).

Thus there are patterns that "supplant" each other and maintain some kind of "functional" link in history, even at the cost of assuming that the "Turks" are the same.

Third, authors following this line generally assume that not only does the "we" group exist, but so does the other group. Therefore, instead of looking at how a discursive order creates us we have to analyze a *dialogical* process, in which identities are formed by interactions of different groups and agents. Easterners have a definite impact on us: not only do we constitute them but we are constituted by them as well. With this approach the "other" receives a definite role as opposed to the passive role it is portrayed as having by discursive and hegemonic patterns. As Neumann puts it: "Since it is a pervasive theme of this literature that the formation of the self is inextricably intertwined with the formation of its other and that the failure to regard the others in their own right must necessarily have repercussions for the formation of the self" (Neumann 1999, 35).

The particular use of the "East" is the essence of this dialogical approach. Instead of just saying that there is a need for an abstract "Other," the dialogical approach describes the content of the imagination by reflecting the two actors' ideas onto each other. The argument is that: "Without the other, Bakhtin insisted, the subject actually cannot know either itself or the world, because meaning is created in discourse, where consciousnesses meet" (Neumann 1999, 13).

On the basis of our examples such an approach would mean that the civilizational slope and positions along it are somehow negotiated; independent subjects meet in a "discourse." Our examples do not allow us to answer this question directly, but the very idea of slope and asymmetry excludes the possibility of some kind of a discussion between more or less equal partners. Instead, a whole array of studies suggesting the hegemonic status and universalizing character of these patterns demonstrates that those on the lower part of the slope, in Böröcz's words, those "on the sideline," have no chance to formulate an autonomous perspective. Wallerstein puts it succinctly:

> The problem is structural. In an historical social system that is built on hierarchy and inequality, which is the case of the capitalist world-economy, universalism as description or ideal or goal can only in the long run be universalism as ideology, fitting well the classical formulation of Marx, that the ruling ideas are the ideas of the ruling class. But if this were all that universalism was, we would not be discussing it today. Universalism is a "gift" of the powerful to the weak which

> confronts the latter with a double bind: to refuse the gift is to lose; to accept the gift is to lose (Wallerstein 1991, 217).

In a sharp analysis of the relationship between the European Union and its applicants including Hungary, Böröcz not only demonstrates the working and institutionalization of the civilizational slope, but also directly addresses the problem of communication between the two actors (Böröcz 2000, 2001). He finds that during the submission of the application for membership the two partners do not even address each other as equals and one of the partners actually does not exist as a communicative actor. In his analysis, relying also on Bakhtin's ideas, Böröcz puts it thus:

> Hence, the addressivity of the two documents is completely asymmetrical. The Hungarian side treats the European Union as a subject by speaking directly and unambiguously to it. The European Union, in contrast, treats the Hungarian side as either an object or a locative adverb, but never as a subject" (Böröcz 2000, 861).

These are "dialogues" with only one subject ("dialogue with itself") and therefore we have to reject the idea of some kind of a dialogical identity formation with regard to the civilizational East–West slope.

As a last alternative approach, the idea of an overarching "grand," "global" or collective narrative is also applied in the analysis of East–West dichotomies or discourses.[5] Böröcz relies on the concept of modernization narrative with an unfolding story of those appearing in the top position. Mignolo use the term "global design" as opposed to "local histories" meaning a story "celebrating" the "occidental achievement of universal value" exemplified by Weber's much quoted introduction to "The Protestant Ethic and the Spirit of Capitalism" (Mignolo 2000, 3–4). On a national or regional level Neumann also points out the role of narratively "constructed" identities and the need for "as if stories." According to him the self (the political self) cannot be completely erased by the discursive formations and context-dependent, contingent identity formations. Interestingly he argues that narratives are the frameworks in which we combine different discursive elements:

> I would like to suggest that the making of selves is a narrative process of identification whereby a number of identities that have been

> negotiated in specific contexts are strung together into one overarching story (Neumann 1999, 218–19).

On this basis, the East–West discourse as a liberal, humanitarian utopia can be easily interpreted as a narrative. In fact it is nothing but an ongoing narrative of transition, putting differences into temporal order by way of translation using a "measuring rod." This essential story building technique, which is also the method of universalization and expansion, is most clearly summed up by Böröcz in his analysis of the main ways in which teleological modernization operates in terms of "comparison" (Böröcz 2003, 28–100).

1.2.3. East–West slope and coloniality

As we have seen above, in terms of methodology the East–West slope revealed in our examples and interpreted as a liberal utopia fits well into the methodological mainstream of the literature on East–West discourses. The only approach incompatible with this idea is that of understanding such relationships in terms of a dialogue of collective identities, which has never really gained ground in this field of study. But what about the content of the relevant cognitive patterns? Can we explain coloniality on the basis of a civilizational slope? To what extent can the East–West civilizational slope, also found in historical studies on Eastern and Central Europe, be linked to colonial or postcolonial patterns? In general it seems that coloniality has relevance, but it needs careful analysis especially in the light of the heated arguments about this issue (among others Wolff 1994; Todorova 1997, Bakić-Hayden 1995; Goldsworthy 1998). But first let me clarify what I mean by coloniality.

In my understanding coloniality is not essentially some form of physical territorial occupation and direct exploitation. By coloniality I mean a system of power understood as a complex form of domination, including the hierarchical classification of the populations of the planet, the reformulation of local concepts of space and time, the export of sexual energies into the "East," the "imperial gaze" and most importantly the *colonization of consciousness*. This latter point can be summed up as "an energy and a machinery to transform differences into values" and as the consequent "subalternization" of knowledge and societies (See among others Mignolo 1998, 2000; Said 1978; Erlmann 1999; Comaroff and Comaroff 1992; Williams-Chrisman 1994).

Darcy Riberio provides a very a good summary of the colonization of the mind:

> In the same way that Europe carried a variety of techniques and interventions to the people included in its network of domination...it also introduced to them its equipment or concepts, preconcepts, and idiosyncrasy that referred at the same time to Europe itself and to the colonial people. .... Even the brighter social strata of non-European people got used to seeing themselves and their communities as an infrahumanity whose destiny was to occupy a subaltern position because of the sheer fact that theirs was inferior to the European population (quoted by Mignolo, 2000, 13).

The East–West slope interpreted as a liberal utopia can easily lead to the colonization of the mind and the subalternization of non-western societies and cultures. The universalizing concepts of "Europeanization" are asymmetrical enough to silence all those somehow denied membership of that "universally valid" community. As our examples show, on such a "sliding scale of merit" no one should want to be out of "Europe" and the social and value patterns it represents or, more precisely, is aligned with. This asymmetry alone and the emerging asymmetrical binary oppositions are powerful enough to deny a "real existence" to those who are in a midway or bottom position on such a scale.

To see the importance of asymmetry as an essential element of "colonial" or "Orientalist" patterns it is enough to glance at 20th century Hungarian or Central European social history, which has struggled with concepts such as "pretended capitalism," "non-real bourgeoisie" or "distorted," "uneven development" (Melegh 1994).[6] We can even read accounts of the "unreality" of local social arrangements. As in the following quote from one of the best-known and certainly one of the most influential Hungarian social and political thinkers, István Bibó. He has been much praised for establishing the major traits of "European social development" during the international debate on the concept of Central Europe (among others Keane 1988). The "distress of East European small states" in comparison with the "West" is an integral aspect of his analysis:

> This means that nations living in this region lacked what was naturally, clearly, precisely and concretely present in both the everyday

> life and community consciousness of nations in Western Europe: A reality in their own national and state framework, a capital city, a harmony between economy and politics, a unified societal elite etc. In Western and Northern Europe the political rise or decline of one's country, the growth or diminution of its role as a great power, and gaining or losing of colonial empires could have been mere episodes, distant adventures, beautiful or sad memories; in the long run, however, countries could survive these without fundamental trauma, because they had something that could not be taken away or questioned. In Eastern Europe by contrast, a national framework was something that had to be created, repaired, fought for, and constantly protected, not only against the power factors existing in the dynastic state, but also from the indifference exhibited by a certain portion of the country's own inhabitants, as well as from the wavering state of national consciousness (Bibó 1991, 38–39).

This passage, emerging out of an extremely sophisticated idea of a civilizational slope, clearly shows the process of subalternization, the "silencing" of the local society and its local history. Bibó not only defends the undisturbed moral and social superiority of the "Western nations," regardless of the "beautiful or sad memories" of the colonial period, but also actually denies the inner and outer "reality" of local nationhood. In the normative "Western mirror" it does not exist, it is fabricated, imbalanced. Hungarian local history suffers under the heavy weight of the universally valid "West," whose dominance constrains the imagination at the lower points of the slope. By attaching normative statements such as "harmony" or "unified" to the upper points of the slope, Bibó's text provides a perfect example of how differences can be transformed into values by the machinery of the liberal utopia in a process that is coloniality itself. In other words this is a pattern, greatly supported by the "Western" imaginary of social development. Thus there can be no doubt that coloniality as a system of power internalizing the hierarchical visions of social development is relevant to an examination of East–West discourses on Eastern and Central Europe as practiced in and outside the region.[7] However, the problem is a little more complicated and in this regard it is necessary to take a closer look at the arguments for and against the use of colonial and postcolonial patterns in the case of Eastern and Central Europe since the 18th century.

1.2.4. East–West slope, racism and Orientalism: the case of Central and Eastern Europe

Since the mid eighties there has been a growing interest in the question of discourses on Eastern and Central Europe (Wolff 1994, Todorova 1997, Goldsworthy 1998, 1999; Neumann 1999; Böröcz 1996, 2000, 2001, 2003; Böröcz and Kovács, 2001; Antohi 2000; Bakić-Hayden 1995; Kideckel 1996; Dancsi 2001; Mester 2001; Melegh 1994, 1999, 2002, 2004, 2003, 2004). Regarding one aspect of the problem there is complete consensus. All the authors argue that Eastern, Central and South Eastern Europe represent a separate category in the Eurocentric imaginary of the world and all agree that the non-Western part of Europe is understood as a transitional category between the "real" "East" and "West." This is most eloquently put by Wolff in his book on "inventing Eastern Europe," in which, perfectly describing the ideas of the slope, he argues that there is a continuous scale which links "East" and "West": "Eastern Europe [in the 18th century] was located not as the antidote of civilization, not down in the depths of barbarism, but rather on the developmental scale that measured the distance between civilization and barbarism" (Wolff 1994, 13).

In his analysis of the discursive process of inventing Eastern Europe in the 17th and 18th centuries, Wolff implicitly argues that there was no real difference between Orientalist, cognitive colonial techniques and those used in the case of Eastern and Central Europe. There were mapping processes, there was the idea of the "possessing" Eastern and Central Europe, sexual exploitation and even racial categorization. Although Eastern and Central Europe exists higher up on the developmental scale, Wolff does not demonstrate any essential differences in the forms of Western cognitive rule with regard to Eastern and Central Europe in the 18th century (as compared to the Middle East analyzed by Edward Said). Historically only differences in the scale of the slope have been operational with many implications for the lives of people living at the bottom end of the civilizational slope.

The same link to Orientalism is found in the 1990s in the case of the Balkans by Bakić-Hayden, who, with important implications for the sociology of the East–West slope, introduced the idea of "*nesting Orientalism*":

> The gradation of "Orients" that I call "nesting Orientalisms" is a pattern of reproduction of the original dichotomy upon which Orientalism is premised. In this pattern, Asia is more "East" or "other" than Eastern Europe; within Eastern Europe itself this gradation is reproduced with the Balkans perceived as most "eastern"; within the Balkans there are similarly constructed hierarchies. I argue that the terms of definition of such a dichotomous model eventually establish conditions for its own contradiction (Bakić-Hayden 1995, 918).

As noted above, Böröcz found the same "civilizational slope" discourse in the 1990s in the communication between the European Union and Hungary. But in comparison with the above implicit statements, Böröcz goes one step further and openly declares the validity of colonial processes with regard to Eastern and Central Europe:

> A fascinating feature of the official exchange between Hungary and the EU is the "Western" side's reversion to the colonial topos of discovery. Just as colonial discovery involved, according to Anne McClintock, a "journey to a far-flung region, asking the local inhabitants if they know of a nearby river, lake or waterfall, paying them to take one there, then "discovering" the site, so, too the European Union "obtains" information as new knowledge and expresses it as a "discovery." …The issuance of a questionnaire to the native governments of the central and east European states, requesting information about the political, economic, sociolegal, and cultural landscape in their countries, and the presentation of this information as a discovery by denying subjectivity to the natives, bears striking resemblance to this ethos of colonial discovery (Böröcz 2000, 870).

In his latest piece Böröcz describes the European Union as a reformulated empire replacing previous individual West European empires, which in the "Eastern enlargement" process introduces straightforward imperialistic arrangements (Böröcz and Kovács 2001)

The same type of framework is offered by Goldsworthy in writing on the "imperialism of imagination" in the "textual" or "imaginative" colonization of the Balkans, mainly during the 19th century. She also argues for cognitive colonization or, more precisely, she also works with a colonial narrative framework. In her view the process begins rather early, with the formative period is the 19th and early 20th centuries, but it continues into the period of "media imperialism":

> The process of literary colonisation, in its stages and its consequences, is not unlike real colonisation. It begins with travel writers, explorers and adventurers undertaking reconnaissance missions into an unknown area. They are gradually followed by novelists, playwrights and poets who, in their quest for new plots and settings, rely just as frequently on research through atlases and timetables as on direct experience. By this stage the capacity of the new land to feed the ever-hungry mother country—and to make nabobs of those with the wits and ruthlessness to exploit it—is well established. Once "mapped," new territories are further appropriated by the writers of popular fiction, who delineate the final shape of the imaginary map and secure their stakes as surely as European colonists secured newly surveyed parcels of land in America, Australia or New Zealand. Their need to visit or know the area they describe is, at this stage, relatively remote and the "authenticity" they aim to achieve is one which fulfills the desires and fantasies of the reader. At this point they and their collaborators in the film industry can begin the full commercial exploitation of the appropriated territory (Goldsworthy 1998, 2–3).

In her polemical and powerful book Todorova also relies on the idea of the slope. For her the major images of the Balkans portray a region located low on a civilizational scale. However, in contrast with the authors cited earlier she disagrees on the use of Orientalism and colonialism, describing the transitory character of the Balkans and at the same time rejecting the idea of a continuous scale between the categories of "civilization and barbarity" and its discursive implications: "It is my thesis that while Orientalism is dealing with a difference between (imputed) types, balkanism treats the differences within one type" (Todorova 1997, 19).

In one sense Todorova is supported by Neumann, who, covering the history of different "Eastern others," but especially that of Turkish and Russian ones, also talks about a "marginal" European type clearly separable from non-European ones: "If 'the Turk' really became what we may call a marginal or liminal other in the guise of 'the sick man of Europe,' we have in the case of Russia a European other that, I will argue, has been marginal all along" (Neumann 1999, 63).

> Such "liminal" cases are those where the "self and the other overlap" and this capacity to recognize each other as such is tied to "certain external bodily similarities" (cf. Anne Norton, Neumann 1999, 8–9). Thus these "others" are border line cases but in certain physical characteristics they are the same. The descending scale is not continuous, but divided by race.

Kideckel offers an interesting "third way" with regard to Eastern and Central Europe by inventing the special term "*categorical Orientalism*" which refers to a temporal Orientalism, that is to say a new Orientalism after a subalternization process. Here the possibility of climbing on a liberal scale is clearly sustained:

> In Categorical Orientalism subjects retain their voice, though those voices that devalue their own lives or at least those aspects of them organized by the state, have the greatest credence. Furthermore, the devaluation of Eastern Life is not because "they" are totally different, but rather because "they" have fallen into difference over time … The categorical Orientalist holds out the possibility of redemption for the fallen through capitalism, democracy, civil society, privatization and the like (Kideckel 1996, 30).

Thus alongside the agreement on some kind of "in-between" status of Eastern and Central Europe and the existence of East–West slopes that are historically extremely resilient there are important differences of opinion with regard to the validity of colonial or Orientalist discourses. What conceptual and methodological issues underlie these disputes?

To begin with it seems that different lines of argument are not due to differences between the historical periods and regions under analysis. Although Wolff writes about the invention of "Eastern Europe" in the eighteenth century, Todorova and Goldsworthy are preoccupied with the late nineteenth and the twentieth century history of Balkanology, while Böröcz, Bakić-Hayden and Kideckel write about the 1990s.

Neumann covers almost all areas and all periods. He actually quotes texts by Gibbon or Herder as scrutinized by Wolff or Todorova. Thus the difference in opinions is not due to different periods or sources, unless we say that the texts quoted reflect different discourses, a plurality which would not go against the grain of discourse analysis. It seems instead that different methodologies and different judgements explain the diverging opinions.

As a starting point Todorova says that, in contrast with Said's Orientalism which stresses the fluidity of the borders of the Orient, the edges of the Balkans are clear. Here Goldsworthy disagrees, stating that there has been much ambiguity in the definition of the Balkans, especially around the inclusion of certain countries like Hungary (Goldsworthy 1998, 2–7). According to Wolff the discourses on Eastern Europe were vague with regard to its borders in the 18th century and Eastern Europe historically had no clear borders in the period of its invention. In the eighteenth century geographers and scholars constantly redrew its eastern, northern and southern borders (Wolff 1994: chapter 4). Thus, as we will also see in chapter 3 of this book regarding the maps of global actors, the almighty power of redrawing maps and setting new borders has always been practiced with regard to Eastern and Central Europe, and cartographic categories such as Eastern Europe or the Balkans have always lacked clear borders, especially as one moves away from the "West." In this respect I will argue throughout this book that the fluidity of borders is one of the most important traits of East–West slopes.

In Todorova's work gender issues are also raised. While Orientalism is a discourse in which the represented area is characterized by "female penetrability" and introduces an element of "lust," in the case of the Balkans this gendered vision is either not relevant, or in the discourse the represented area acquires male traits: "Unlike the standard orientalist discourse, which resorts to the metaphors of its objects of study as female, the balkanist discourse is singularly male" (Todorova 1997, 15).

This point is valid, but it does not address the portrayal of these regions as sexually "abnormal" in the "Western mirror." For instance in the New York Times in the mid 1990s the legal and cultural protection of female employees in Poland and Hungary is portrayed as incomplete and sexual abuse is shown to be widespread (Melegh 1999). Furthermore Wolff points out that elements of "lust" prevail and the region is "possessed" sexually by people like Casanova, who buy young female slaves for the sake of complete sexual and social control (Wolff 1994, chapter II). Thus although there is sexual ambiguity in the discourse, the basic elements are not missing and cultural differences are formulated through gendered lenses. The important point seems to be the setting up of civilizational differences by way of the coordinates of sexuality.

With regard to the relationship between Orientalism and discourses on Eastern and Central Europe Todorova has also argued that while Orientalism treats the Ottoman Empire as being at the same level socially (one ruling class versus another ruling class), the "East end of Europe" is imagined as a kind of lower class without any ruling classes:

> Whereas the treatment of Islam was based on an unambiguous attitude toward religious otherness (ranging from crusading rejection to enlightened agnostic acceptance), there was an ambiguous attitude toward the Ottoman polity that invited a very distinct class attitude of solidarity with the Muslim Ottoman rulers. This was in stark contrast to the poor and unpolished, but Christian, upstarts, who have been described in a discourse almost identical to the one used to depict the Western lower classes, a virtual parallel between the East End of London and the East End of Europe (Todorova 1997, 18).

This claim, while raising a highly interesting point in the "othering" processes, is not without problems. Although it is true that Eastern and Central Europe and the Balkans are portrayed as lower classes, this pattern is not universal. Eastern and Central Europe has also been invented with regard to their ruling classes. In the previously quoted work of István Bibó, even the elites have been inferiorized as part of their societies.

Yet it is not clear whether or not Orientalism is applicable in the case of Eastern and Central Europe. It seems that the question can only be answered by focusing on the racism found supporting the discourses of Orientalism and colonial, postcolonial patterns (among others Said 1978, Goldberg 1990). In our introductory examples racist language and racist scaling appear in the discourse of the East–West slope. Amato spoke about "mixed blood." There were references to "quarantine" and "whiteness." The same could be seen in the narrative of the Walloon woman on her Russian husband. Thus we have to ask to what extent they are inherent or functional in the East–West discourses on Eastern and Central Europe interpreted as a liberal utopia.

Todorova and Neumann have pointed out that Balkanism or the "use of the Russian other" has suggested negative treatment within one type based on the issue of color and body. Todorova declares: "On the other hand, despite the presence of the theme of racial ambiguity, and despite the important internal hierarchies, in the final analysis the Balkans are still treated as positioned on this side of the fundamental opposition: white versus colored, Indo-European versus the rest" (Todorova 1997, 19).

Historically, this argument may be correct and certainly in the heyday of imperialist racism the peoples of Eastern and Central Europe and the Balkans were not unambiguously presented as being racially non-white. Nevertheless, it must be noted that in the late 19th century the founders of scientific racism such as Gobineau saw Eastern and Central Europeans as being racially inferior to "civilized people" on a racist scale, just like our Walloon lady with regard to her Russian husband:[8] "The Russians, Poles and Serbians… even though they are far nearer to us than the negroes, are only civilized on the surface; the higher classes alone participate in our ideas, owing to the continuous admixture of English, French and German blood"(Gobineu quoted by Burgess 1997, 51).

However, the flexibility of racist codes and discourses has also been raised in other ways. Many of the authors found that in the inferiorization of Eastern and Central Europe on a civilizational slope there is a "functional" racism or cultural racism in operation (Burgess 1997, 195–198). In concrete terms this implies the working out of cultural essentialist categories which refer to characteristics of members of a designated group. They function as "old wine" in new bottles, which then becomes the element of blood or genes so important to racist discourses.[9] In the words of Tony Judt, an influential "British" liberal intellectual, there are "ancient" differences between "long time" European countries and lands "in the process of becoming" (Judt 1996, viii, ix, 60).

Even Todorova, an opponent of applying patterns of Orientalism and racism to Eastern and Central Europe, sees "politically correct" exclusion at work in "Balkanism." At the end of her book, paradoxically and interestingly, she argues that Balkanism in the 1990s can function as a comfortable *substitute* for a much criticized "racist" Orientalism and Eurocentrism:

> By being geographically inextricable from Europe, yet culturally constructed as "the other" within, the Balkans have been able to absorb conveniently a number of externalized political, ideological, and cultural frustrations stemming from tensions and contradictions inherent to the regions and societies outside the Balkans. Balkanism became, in time, a convenient substitute for the emotional discharge that orientalism provided, exempting the West from charges of racism, colonialism, eurocentrism, and Christian intolerance against Islam. After all, the Balkans are in Europe, they are white; they are predominantly Christian, and therefore the externalization of frustrations on them can circumvent the usual racial or religious bias allegations. As in the case of the Orient, the Balkans have served as a repository of negative characteristics against which a positive and self-congratulatory image of the "European" and the "West" has been constructed. With the reemergence of East and orientalism as independent semantic values, the Balkans are left in Europe's thrall, anticivilization, alter ego, the dark side within (Todorova 1997, 188).

Thus it seems that Eastern Europe might appear as being functionally on the side of the colonial or racial Other. We must therefore be prepared to accept that weighing and measuring countries, societies and people according to a liberal utopia of descending civilizational scale allows the appearance of Othering structures functionally related to Orientalist or racist discursive statements and structures. Furthermore, such structures can easily be vitalized in the fight for fixing borders on the slippery civilizational scale, especially by those who see this as a last resort to achieve a higher position in the imaginary of the world. This positioning game of would-be "Western" "Easterners" in the "East" will be analyzed in detail later in the context of East–West population discourses, European integration and individual narratives.

But before we look at the different perspectives of actors located at a lower point of the slope, we should look at the substantial changes in the East–West discourses of the late 1970s in order to see the variations within the discourses of liberal humanitarian utopia.

1.3. From modernization discourses to qualitative/civilizational discourses

1.3.1. The discourse of rival modernities

On the basis of the above general arguments about the discourses of liberal humanitarian utopia we should not assume that there has been no change within the discourses on Eastern and Central Europe. In the late 1970s there was certainly a general shift within the discourses leading to discursive statements such as those analyzed above. It can be asserted that the idea of an East–West civilizational slope was reborn after 30 years of discourses of rivaling modernities or modernizationist quantitative/ideological slopes. This change replaced one type of teleological, Eurocentric discourse about the world and within Eastern and Central Europe with another not seen for at least three decades.

Almost until its collapse the "Eastern" block was seen as something very "real" and "concrete," whose geographical boundaries were very clear. This "reality" was embedded in a discourse of modernization and progress. Within this discourse everything was understood in terms of ideologies and a related quantitative "competition" between different systems. Socialism versus capitalism, "backwardness" versus "superiority," "progress" (toward socialism or a modern economic system, for instance) "modernization," "industrialization" and "catching up" were the key concepts formulated in the framework of global competition of blocks and the incorporated nation states. There were "real" regions in Europe, real collective actors and real walls between them. The link between the sense of "reality" and the categories mentioned above cannot be shown better than by the title of a recent conference paper by Daniel Chirot, the author of the influential book *The origins of backwardness in Eastern Europe* (Chirot 1989, 1991). Focusing on the spread of a "modern, liberal, Western, democratic, individualistic, capitalist way of life" this recent "nostalgic" and with regard to the new "postmodern" anthropological approaches overtly critical paper bears the title "Returning to Reality: Culture, Modernization and Various

Eastern Europes" (Chirot, 2002). Here "returning to reality" is not just another phrase for saying that Eastern and Central Europe has achieved "normalcy," but it is also a witty remark suggesting that we return to talking about "real" things such as economic progress.

What happened to this sense of reality longed for by Chirot? How was it lost and how should we interpret this "reality?" Was the socialist Eastern European block really more real? Or were the observers just not reflective enough? The answer seems to lie less in the ignorance of the observers or the actual "reality" of the Eastern block than in the change of discourses. It appears that around the late 1970s an old/new civilizational discourse replaced a modernizationist discourse as a thesis. This old/new discourse constituted the world less as a competition between "real" powers fighting in terms of quantitative economic and military capabilities, but as a descending slope of regional cultures. In this change Eastern and Central Europe was thus vastly reconstructed as an object of the dominant discourses and this shift in the discourses and in the integrated power relations might have had a definite role in the "disintegration" or "decomposition" of Eastern and Central Europe.

Until the 1970s Eastern and Central Europe, or rather the socialist block, was placed in a discourse of modernization and a grand narrative of progress appearing sometime after the second world war (Böröcz 2003, 76–89, Kuczi 1992). This discourse, promoted in both the "East" and the "West," produced, in the main, hard, "real" "comparative" statistical facts on population development and economic growth as well as on the production level of the different countries and different branches of industry and agriculture. These "concrete" facts were clearly linked to the measurement of military capacity in assessing the possible outcome of a war. This discourse appears clearly in the reports of such organization such as the CIA, where the main aim of the espionage is the production of "real facts" on Soviet modernization (*www.cia.gov/csi/books/index.html* accessed on 10/10/03). In a recent collection of some declassified documents most of the reports deal with new computer and "automation" technologies, industrial capacities, pipelines, energy production etc. till in the early 1980s they were replaced by assessments of ethnic conflicts and religious dissent. The application of the same discourse on both sides is generally described as a "cold" war, although actually it was more like a discursive war over the measurement of progress embedded in a framework of competition between two political systems.

The modernizationist "reality" discourse was coupled with a discourse on something "unreal": the negative utopias of total power such as the "brave new world," "big brother," "animal farm" etc. The combination of this discourse on ideology and the modernizationist one provided the basis for the establishment of a wide network of East European Studies departments and institutes after the Second World War. This additional discourse on totalitarianism also had a history and following the analysis of Rupnik, we can even establish two discourses with regard to totalitarianism (Böröcz 2003, 88–89; Rupnik 1990; Csizmadia 2001, 136–45; Bence 1993).

The first initiated in the 1950s focused on the total centralization of the social and economic system, which was based on the rule of one party. This rule was understood as a totally centralized "tyrannic" rule which led to the total atomization of the individual subjects, the consequent total destruction of individual subjects and the creation of "mobs" looking for public repression (Arendt 1975; Orwell 1983; Kohn 2001). Thus totalitarian society became a collectivist power much to be feared by polities in the "West."

This was followed by a second debate in the late 1960s, which was a substantial break with the original ideas. At that time the popularity of the above concepts declined radically in the "West" and the debate on totalitarianism actually continued in Eastern and Central Europe. This new debate on totalitarianism among East European dissident thinkers deserves special attention, because the criticism coupled with the emergence of the idea of Central Europe shows very clearly the change form modernizationist to civilizational discourses referred to above.

1.3.2. Havel's greengrocer and the idea of Central Europe: Post-totalitarianism and discursive vacuum in the early 1980s

The "Eastern" version of totalitarianism, that is to say that formulated by authors in the target area of the debate, is interesting from several points of view. First, the authors sensed great social and political changes regarding the establishment of discursive power in the "East" (and the "West"). Second, the social system was portrayed as less of a closed barracks, prison or isolated fortress in which new types of human beings (Homo Sovieticus) were created under totalitarian pressure. Instead, totalitarianism became a rather airy political power in which direct repression through the central political machinery, the propaganda system and the military, which had earlier formed the cores of political power, gave way to a subtle web of lies which deterred everyday people, like greengrocers, from "living in truth" (Havel 1985; Ash 1986, Bence 1993, Csizmadia 2001, 136). The crucial point here is that the dissident thinkers of Eastern and Central Europe increasingly envisaged some kind of discursive "totalitarianism" which became less and less real due to the less and less visible political and ideological controls. In the literature this was exemplified by the ideological lip service of a Czech greengrocer, who, without any ideological belief, put out a banner in his shop window telling the proletariat of the world to unite.

This story, written by the dissident Havel, is emblematic because in it the discourse of progress is declared to be "empty." Without any motivation the greengrocer displays the banner with a key slogan of Marxist progressivism as an act belonging to the web of small "lies." Thus totalitarianism became more and more discursive, maintained only by a dominant mode of speech. Political control was in the heads of the people. The wall in the head (die Mauer im Kopf), as they put it in the debates on post-totalitarianism (Ash 1986, Konrád 1984, Karnoouh 2003).

Regardless of what we think about these analysis it seems that texts like Havel's indicated the change in discourses and their collective "subject." As the debate on totalitarianism shows, around the early 1980s the previous discursive system of modernization and progress collapsed or withdrew and was allowed to see itself as only a "discourse" (Karnoouh 2003).

On the "Eastern" side, in the case of Hungary, this change in the discourses has been clearly demonstrated, not only on the basis of texts written by political thinkers, but also in party documents, experts' analysis and newspapers. Two Hungarian political scientists, Kuczi and Csizmadia have documented in detail changes to vocabulary, themes and subjects in political discourses in Hungary from the late 1970s to the early 1980s (Kuczi 1992; Csizmadia 2001, 41–71). Political debates were less and less about the reforms of socialism and more and more about how to adapt the country to the "West"—portrayed normatively. Csizmadia has even shown that the emerging new discourse has been the basis of new constellations of social and political power into which new social groups could be incorporated in state-socialist Hungary:

> ...the texts, debates, opinions dealing with the role of Western Europe first came together as a latent and then as a more and more public discourse and this discourse probably became one of the most characteristic traits of the 1980s... these views were not only written down or told, but they transformed public life and the whole system (Csizmadia 2001, 135, translated by A. M.).

This new discourse, combining new objects, subjects and styles, thematized the emptiness of previous social and political categories, most notably the so-called "socialist block" and its contingent "cold world order," dividing Europe into two parts, as well as the related progress (modernization) narrative. It also (re)introduced new categories such as the "West" and the idea of Central Europe (Ash 1986, Schopflin–Wood 1989, Kuczi 1992, Csizmadia 2001, Bozóki 1999, Karnoouh 2003).

The emergence of the idea of Central Europe also reveals the discursive transition process described above on several levels. First, Central Europe was defined with reference to a set of "untrue" "false" discourses. Kundera in his seminal essay on the tragedy of Central Europe speaks about Central Europe being a hijacked "West" forced into the alien category of "East." According to him Central Europe is: "situated geographically in the center, culturally in the West and politically in the East" (Kundera 1984, Antohi 2000, 64–65). Central Europe is discursively hijacked at the moment it is imagined to be divided into two opposing categories politically and culturally. Second, the idea of Central Europe was a category which came to life like Sleeping Beauty. Ash, Schopflin and all the major authors of the debate repeated the "fact" of not hearing about the idea of Central Europe for decades either due to historical sins or due to political censorship (Ash 1986; Schopflin–Wood 1989). Accordingly "Central Europe" first disappeared from political, historical and cultural discussions after the second world war when it was politically awkward and then reappeared in the late 1970s and early 1980s. Third, even after its rebirth ontological problems remained (see also Dancsi, 2001). Schopflin has spoken of the "ghost" of Central Europe. Timothy Garton Ash has asked revealingly in his New York Review of Books essay: "Does Central Europe exist?" Or as György Konrád put it: "Compared to the geopolitical reality of Eastern Europe and Western Europe, Central Europe exists today only as a cultural-political anti-hypothesis (eine kulturpolitische Antihypothese)..." (quoted in Ash 1986).

The existential ambiguity is probably a clue to the new discourse in this discursive "transition" process. Central Europe did not exist because it had to clean itself of some historical-moral sins (e.g. the Holocaust, but also communism and totalitarianism). Timothy Garton Ash for instance, after a reference to the non-existence of Central Europe in the present tense, argued that it suffered the fate of Nineveh and Tyre, two morally corrupt cities, one destroyed by God and one forgiven by Him (Ash, 1986). This moral handicap can be located in the task of "whitening" Central Europe (losing the colors of red and brown) before it could be publicly accepted and then fixing the region in a clearly inferior position. Central Europe was seen as kind of a released prisoner on probation.

An exclusion mechanism is also apparent in portrayals of its ambiguous ghost-like character. Central Europe at the border of existence, on a mythological level, suggests a twilight zone. In this arena there are semi-human creatures, which are, to some extent like us, but on the other hand morally and physically corrupted and presenting a danger to "normal" individuals. Ash clearly spoke about a dark forest full of wizards and witches:

> an endlessly intriguing forest to be sure, a territory where peoples, cultures, languages are fantastically intertwined, where every place has several names and men change their citizenship as often as their shoes, an enchanted wood full of wizards and witches, but one which bears over its entrance the words: "Abandon all hope, ye who enter here, of ever again seeing the wood for the trees" (Ash, 1986).

The last crucial point in this emerging discourse is that the borders of Europe and Central Europe cannot be fixed and the inclusion of more and more "Eastern" countries becomes extremely problematic (Antohi 2000, 66). Danilo Kiš, the Yugoslavian writer, was very clear about this, arguing that it is difficult to speak about Central Europe as a "homogenous geopolitical and cultural phenomenon":

> With no precise borders, with no Center or rather with several centers, "Central Europe" looks today more and more like the dragon of Alca in the second book of Anatol France's Penguin Island to which the symbolist movement was compared: no one who claimed to have seen it could say what it looked like. To speak about Central Europe as a homogenous geopolitical and cultural phenomenon entails risks. Even if we might agree with Jacques Morin's affirmation that Europe is "a concept without borders," the facts oblige us to remove from this concept the part of the European continent, with the exception of Austria, that under the name of Mittel-Europa organically belonged to it (Neumann quotes Danilo Kiš's Variation on the Theme of Central Europe: Neumann 1999, 144–145).

Another prominent dissident thinker, the Hungarian Mihály Vajda, has also asked for serious investigations with regard to drawing the Eastern borders of Central Europe (Vajda 1986). In his essay on the problem of Russia's Europeannes, he asks: "Who excluded Russia from Europe?" The answer is Russia itself, which means that the guilty party should first prove its Europeanness, if that is at all possible. In a sense this new discourse then can be understood only as a constant border fight over "Eastern Europe" and an attempt to push parts of it out (Neumann, 1999, 206–207, 107–112). In other words the idea of Central Europe is linked to the hierarchization of Eastern Europe, with practical consequences for the more "Eastern" parts of Europe such as Russia and the Balkans. Concerning later developments Todorova has rightly observed:

> To summarize, the third round in the development of the Central European idea after 1990 witnessed its entry from the politics of culture into political praxis. Far from becoming a region-building notion, it was harnessed as an expedient argument in the drive for entry into the European institutional framework. It is during this stage that the Balkans first appeared as a dichotomical opponent, sometimes alongside with, sometimes indistinguishable from Russia. This internal hierarchization of Eastern Europe was born out

of political expediency, but in its rhetoric it feeds on the balkanist discourse (Todorova 1997, 159–160).

We can safely argue, then, that discourses on Eastern and Central Europe changed dramatically in the 1980s, with the old, "realist" modernizationist/ideological discourse that set up quantitative scales being replaced in the process by a new discourse decomposing the Eastern block into several regions with ambiguous borders and placed in a "sliding scale of merit," the sociology of which is our primary problem. In order to see how these discursive changes occurred in specific spheres of knowledge and how these East–West discourses have shaped social life, let us now look at the way 20th century "Eastern" and "Western" discourses on population interact with each other in the framework of civilizational slopes with the interim period of modernizationist discourses dominant between the Second World War and the 1980s.

Notes

1 In the book I refer to Eastern and Central Europe as the group of countries which belonged to the so-called socialist block. This term is used as a neutral category since, given the subject matter of the book, I definitely want to avoid playing the discursive game of drawing "Eastern" and "Central" European borders. I use "East" and West when I refer to the discourse and the claimed position within.

2 * stands for a break in the interview text by uttering "er" or stopping.

3 Nonetheless Todorova's expression of "imagology" is a substantial break with the concept of discourse as it deals with the "literary" images or representation of the other (Todorova 1997, 7). First, it assumes the status of "otherness" from the beginning and thus does not allow an analysis of the fact of categorization in itself. Second, it even more straightforwardly relies on the idea of an object being an organizer of knowledge and it clearly assumes that anything told with regard to a region is inherently linked to anything else. Third it presupposes an object outside the "discourse". This is very clear in the case of Todorova, who—as we will see later—in a contradictory manner explicitly says: "In the first place there is the historical and geographic concreteness of the Balkans as opposed to the intangible nature of the Orient"(Todorova 1997, 11); on the inconcreteness of the Balkans see Antohi's revealing essay about Romanian "links" to the Balkans (Antohi 2002). At this point it is worth pointing out that the idea of the represen-

tation or imagination of otherness certainly contradicts discourse analysis as understood above and can therefore distinguish "innocent" inaccuracies from politically minded pejorative speech and ideologically loaded designations.

4 See also the work of Csizmadia, who links hegemony with the formation of social groups (Csizmadia 2001, 93–133).

5 In this book individual narratives and the related methodological questions will be discussed in chapter 4. That will be the point at which I address Said's analysis of "narratives" by influential "Orientalist" authors such as Sacy, Renan, Lane, Flaubert, Nerval etc. in which the discursive elements were recombined and advanced in an original manner (Said 1978, chapter on "Orientalist Structures and Restructures", 113–200).

6 As an important comparison see the same patterns with regard to Indian history (Chakrabarty 2000, 30–37).

7 Self-colonization as a pattern is only one of the possible ways of moving onto the East–West slope. In the course of this book I will elaborate further patterns. It should also be noted that Böröcz, in an excellent piece, has found the same machinery of transforming differences into values in a letter written by Hungarian intellectuals to the French government (Böröcz 2005).

8 Concerning racist scales see also the introductory essay in: Böröcz and Kovács 2001.

9 For the recurrence of the title "old wine in new bottles" see Fisher-Galati 1992, Richards 1999.

CHAPTER 2

Exclusions "East" and "West". Population discourses and the civilizational slope

2.1. "Eastern" seaweed?

In August 2001 a bright and influential liberal politician called István Szentiványi published a small article entitled "The Right to Hate." In this piece the author passionately argued that in today's Hungary Gypsies, Jews, gays and other "minority" groups can be freely hated with no real public control. Naturally he also asked why, and answered as follows:

> Recently a Budapest correspondent of one of the global newspapers asked how I could explain that while Hungary is within an inch of European Union membership, its public life is moving further and further away from Europe and becoming less and less European. I said something, but could not give a satisfactory reply. The question still haunts me. Today it seems that the great promises and hopes of the regime change—that our country would rapidly catch up and be integrated into Europe—are evaporating before our eyes. Like a ferry, our country is still wavering between East and West. The Eastern seaweed of corruption, xenophobia and racism does not easily let us go. (Szentiványi 2001, translated by A.M.).

This passage contains all the elements of the discourse of the East–West slope. There is "East" and "West," with the "West" free of corruption, racism and xenophobia and Hungary moving between the two poles. But in addition this text relies on a characteristic "theory" of why racism is spreading in this country. According to this "theory," racism is a sign of being non-European and "Eastern," which are traits that must be left behind in order to enter the "West." Szentiványi makes this clear by quoting the "naïve" question of a foreign (presumably West European) journalist. The text links EU membership and Europeanness to racism in a negative fashion and wonders why the same link is positive in the case of Hungary. This "naïve" question is prescriptive, as the answer suggested by both the journalist and the author points toward the seemingly prevailing "non-Western" elements of Hungary.

But is this really the case? Has the European Union invented any social mechanisms against racism? Or, more precisely, is there a negative link between the process of European integration, the move from "East" to "West" and the rise of racism? On the contrary, it seems that there is a partly direct and partly indirect positive link between "Europeanization" and racism. Therefore the journalist's question was well formulated, but instead of readily orientalizing Hungary we must face the possibility that the rise of racism is directly linked to the geocultural movement of the country. In order to address the rise of racism in the era of ongoing "Westernization" it is very fruitful to turn to the field of population discourses.

2.2. The comparative study of population discourses

In the light of the tragic events of the past century and the rapidly advancing genetic revolution nowadays, it is not surprising that since the 1960s there have been serious multidisciplinary endeavors to study the political, ideological, social and intellectual background of population policy. Foucault introduced the concept of *biopolitics of population* linking different spheres of social and intellectual life in the 18th century (political economy, medicine, demography and statistics) (Foucault 1991; 1992). Demographers, sociologists and anthropologists have analyzed the *ethnography of the state* (Kligman 1998), *population politics* (Quine 1996) and the *national forms* of population debate (Teitelbaum-Winter 1998). In other words, they all moved beyond the analysis of direct population policy measures and tried to throw light on changes and special twists of public debates by underlying "structures" or "traditions." This "post-structuralist" shift is important from a heuristic point of view as it allows comparative analysis, not on the basis of formal similarities and differences (anti-natalist versus pro-natalist) or immediate political-ideological connotations (liberal, fascist, nationalist), but on the basis of cognitive structures and mechanisms generating political moves and actions. In the present chapter this approach within our interpretative framework serves to lay down a teleologically unbiased basis for the narration of both "Western" and "Eastern" histories. We need such "shared histories" of the "East" and the "West" in order to throw light on the rise of racism and the "strange" shifts in the population policy of a country such as Hungary that is imagined to be on a lower point on East–West slopes.

The first part of this chapter builds on the concept of "biopolitics of population" and the "disciplining," "normalizing" discourses of the 18th and 19th centuries described by Foucault, whose analysis establishes a straight, unavoidable connection between racism and modern political systems of domination. The chapter then focuses on the direction and the method of "stigmatizing" the demographic behavior of certain social groups as well as the role of the dominant East–West slope and dichotomies in these mechanisms. Within a "biopolitical" framework I will stress the importance of Malthus in establishing Anglo-Saxon discourses which stigmatized the lower classes on biopolitical grounds, and which is the dominant discourse in the particular local framework of the United States in the first decades of the 20th century. I will then analyze the role of the East–West slopes as some kind of transmission belt by which local discourses are globalized and universalized in the framework of demographic-transition theory. In other words, using new archival material related to one of the founders of this theory, I will demonstrate that the pre-Second World War anti-natalist stigmatization of the lower classes in America is later used in the population discourses on the "non-Western world" in the framework of global family-planning programs and different types of liberal humanitarian utopias. Within this comparison I will pay special attention to the creation of "Eastern" and "East European" otherness in the discursive structures of the modernizationist and qualitative East–West slopes as it appears in "Western" texts.

In the second part East European and mainly Hungarian population discourses will be interpreted in the light of East–West slopes. These dominant Hungarian biopolitical discourses are those appearing in the texts of pre-Second World War "populist" writers and in "socialist" population-policy documents and statements after the Second World War. Showing a non-Western method of stigmatizing the demographic behavior of the middle classes or the lower groups of the semi-bourgeoisie, the Hungarian discourses to be analyzed will serve as important examples of the operation of the East–West slope and East–West dichotomies. The chapter will end by showing how these different "Eastern" and "Western," local and global discourses come together in Hungary from the 1970s and what implications this might have for the spread of racism in the process of Westernization within the framework of East–West civilizational slopes.

It is important to note that by "Western" discourses and perspectives I mainly refer to discourses and discursive statements which place the textual perspective at the apex of civilizational progress. This can be called the "Western" "locus of enunciation" (Mignolo 2000). At the same time, by "Eastern" locus of enunciation I mean an imaginary or discursive perspective which locates the speaker and his/her society at a point other than the apex. These loci can vary historically; today some Central European texts utilize the "Western" perspective even if historically this has not been the case. These movements are of prime interest to me. By "Western" discourses I mean mainly American and British statements on the management of population development. I do not want to say that this is historically comprehensive or that those statements are the most important ones. I naturally accept that there were other "Western" perspectives on population development, which played a very important role in European history. Nonetheless, I maintain that through the idea of "Western" or "Eastern" loci of enunciation we can interpret all other population discourses not analyzed in the chapter below, including French radical pro-natalism and the population discourses of Nazi Germany or fascist Italy.

2.3. American population discourses on the "unworthy" in the first half of the 20th century

2.3.1. The origins: biopolitics and demography in the 18th century

Although the history of demography reaches back into the 17th century, the processes of mass population growth did not attract the attention of the authorities until the middle of the 18th century. This is well illustrated by the fact that the census became common in Europe from the 1740s. The growing political interest in society's demographic situation signaled the arrival of a new discourse. The new discourse not only focused on the number of men available for conscription, but also on age structure, mortality rate, life expectancy, fertility, possibilities of measurement, and issues of migration. The ideas of measurement, care, and intervention in the interest of possible "balance" all came to the fore at once. Besides the issue of epidemics, which had had earlier political implications when local revolts took place as reactions to disasters, other problems, such as the general health of the population, or the form, nature, spread, period and intensity of diseases within the population (endemics), were also put on the agenda. (Andorka 1985, Őri 1998, 1998a, 1999) This can well be demonstrated by the development of public health, for example through regular public-health reports and studies. Thus, the caring and managing, "rational" problem-solving state invaded more and more areas.

Foucault's highly revealing analysis of the period show how discourses of biopolitics and biopolitical regimes were produced in which, at both an individual and a collective level, the need for political intervention was conceptualized for the purpose of controlling individual and "mass" bodies (Foucault 1991, 1992; Stoler 1995, 55–94). At the collective level this control aimed at securing "balances" between different statistically measured mass processes (fertility, nuptiality, morbidity, mortality, economic growth) in order to secure the "survival" and stability of the society.

Dealing with life, e.g. following, supervising, and influencing the main demographic and social processes, raises the question who, or which groups, are worthy of having their lives supported, and which should be neglected, or carrying things *ad absurdum*, left to die—left to die, given that the acceptance of power over death is in rapid decline. Foucault's first response is that this choice is essentially racism: "What is racism? A tool for dividing the areas of life controlled by authorities into separate spheres: those who are worthy of life and those who are unworthy." (Foucault 1992, 51; see also Stoler 1995, 55–94) This functional idea of biopolitical racism is based on the vision that different social groups are constantly at war for the "survival" and improved quality of life of the "worthy." The demographic and social behavior of the "degenerates" represents a constant threat to the "normal" groups. The targets in this fight for "survival" can change and in theory any group can be the object of racist exclusions.

In writing about this extremely revealing linkage between biopolitical regimes and racism Foucault does not really address the different social directions and methods of this inherent selection process. However, as we will see below, the direction and the method of the identification of "strangers" and the "unworthy" vary substantially in the framework of East–West slopes.

2.3.2. Malthus on the lower classes

The texts of Malthus, the most influential Western demographic thinker, can easily be interpreted with the help of Foucault's ideas on biopolitics. Malthus is the author who, debating the arguments of the French Enlightenment philosopher Condorcet, formulated one of the fundamental hypotheses of population dynamics: the competition between population growth, global resources and the development of economic growth (Malthus 1798, 1960, 1966. especially 71–101; Simon 1998 53–57; Sen 1994). This well-known set of statements can be interpreted as a biopolitical survival theory, as it examines whether we can survive as a group without having to limit our tendency to expand. Malthus answer is a definite "no." According to him there are two types of control: positive brakes (wars and epidemics occurring in periods of overpopulation) and negative brakes based on self-restraint (late marriage, control of desire within marriage). Malthus naturally neither welcomed nor advocated positive brakes. Instead, he argued in favor of "morally correct" negative brakes, such as controlling sexual desire, delaying marriage and thereby controlling fertility. In his view this sense of responsibility developed through property ownership, property rights being the most important "positive rights" of social beings. In contrast to Adam Smith and David Ricardo, Malthus argued passionately that this brake (being necessarily present in all societies, even in the future) could not function in the propertyless classes and caused economic hardship. He thus opposed the English Poor Law, because, as he wrote, support would only increase the already high rate of population growth among the lower classes, and thus reduce the chances of attaining a balance (Malthus 1798, 1966. 71–101, 1960; Simon 1998, 53–57):

> But whatever steps may be taken on this subject, it will be allowed that with any prospect of legislating for the poor with success, it is necessary to be fully aware of the natural tendency of the labouring classes of society to increase beyond the demand for their labour or

> the means of their adequate support, and the effect of this tendency to throw the greatest difficulties in the way of permanently improving their conditions (Malthus 1960, 58).

By connecting two factors, namely the situation of global competition and the tendency of the lower classes of the population to expand, Malthus defined the basic structure of a population discourse which, as we will see, essentially defined American perspectives on population development at home and in the non-Western world. This biopolitical discourse at the apex of the East–West slope brought on a hysterical fear that the well-being or even the "lives" of those social groups already limiting their fertility depended on the reproduction tendencies of others, who do not apply any brakes. In concrete terms the high fertility of the poor or the immigrants is a threat not only to their own classes but also to the "disciplined" life of the "Western" middle or higher classes.

2.3.3. American discourses at the beginning of the 20th century

In a seminal article on the establishment of the Population Association of America Dennis Hodgson identified four groups as founders: the representatives of immigration restriction, the still quite strong eugenicists, the birth-control activists, and the scholarly statisticians interested in the issue of population development (Hodgson 1991; Greenhalgh 1996). At first glance these varied groups seem to be worlds apart and, according to Hodgson their alliance was a product of values which would not be seen as acceptable by today's population-policy makers and demographers. Nonetheless it seems that this "awkward" intellectual coalition was formed on the basis of the Malthusian biopolitical discourse described above. "Racially subordinate" groups were understood as posing a threat to "native" and "birth-controlling" middle classes and otherwise diverging groups came together over the issue of designating some lives as not having great value ("quality"). There was an "inherent" need to sever the "human continuum" (Foucault 1991, 1992): the exclusion target being "racially different" immigrants and the lower classes.

The immigration-control group was first of all afraid of the East and Southern Europeans and Asians who arrived on American shores in mass waves from the end of the 19th century. Initially, they feared that the presence of cheap labor would lead to a reduction in wages. This position was soon supplemented by fear not only of immigrants, but of their children as well, given that the immigrants were more fertile than the "natives." The argument did not stop there, but also incorporated the issue of race. The prominence of the racial question, strangely enough, did not lead to a demand for the fertility of immigrants to be limited (this would have been the logical step in a Malthusian framework), but instead resulted in the idea that the rise of immigration would reduce American fertility by taking away space from already settled peoples—an idea that legitimized immigration control. This control effort, assisted by urban unions, led to the National Quotas Act in 1924 which limited the admission of "failed races" (e.g., East Europeans, see: Hodgson 1991, 8). Only after this success did representatives of this group acknowledge the importance of the fertility of the lower classes for the "racial" composition of the future. This led them to pay attention to the "quality" aspects in population development.

This was the point shared by the eugenicists, who attempted to interpret social questions on the basis of "biology." They were clearly interested in "racial" composition (see also Hannaford 1996, 325–348; Quine 1996, 116–123). There were two kinds of eugenicism, one positive, which hoped to increase the fertility of "superiors" (i.e. the middle and upper classes) and one negative, which sought to control the fertility of "subordinates" and the "sick." In the latter case this did not exclude using legal force in the interest of achieving the desired composition. Such measures were implemented by states and courts heavily biased against the "feeble-minded," the "criminals" and the uneducated from the lower classes. (Quine 1996, 116–123) This group, which by the 1930s was on the defensive, used the issue of population growth as a last resort to discuss "quality" questions.

The coalition of the groups was even odder in the case of the birth controllers, who, in the early 20th century under the leadership of Margaret Sanger, hoped to "liberate" middle- and lower-class women from the burden of the reproductive cycle and child bearing as a whole, as well as from the accompanying domestic controls, stressing the importance of sexual pleasure and emotional satisfaction (see also McLaren 1990, 215–251). Their first enemy was legal regulation, which, from the 1870s, banned birth control devices and the distribution of "obscene" literature. This liberal-minded movement changed its political direction after the First World War. Until then it opposed the eugenic movement, after eugenicist activists had stressed the child-bearing responsibility of middle-class women towards society and the state. Sanger changed her policy and found allies among the eugenicists. To this end she attacked the above-mentioned law, claiming that it prevented the realization of the desired goal. Not only should better-informed middle-class women limit their fertility, but also the "ignorant" and "subordinate" classes should follow their example. Given this solution, the eugenicists believed that the lower classes would reduce their reproduction (as became clear in the 1930s), while the birth controllers could continue their "liberation" activities. It should be noted that the rise to prominence of questions on differential demography led Sanger to raise funds for the inaugural meeting of the Population Association and the better representation of population studies.

The link between open or hidden eugenic agendas and the birth-control movement was so strong that even during the fight against the Nazis some people tried to envisage a "Vital Revolution" to control the quantity and the quality of the population. On October 10, 1941 in an unpublished letter to Notestein, one of the founders of American demography, Guy Irving Burch (director of the Population Reference Bureau, and a founder of the Population Association of America) described the idea of the revolution of "voluntary selection" in an enthusiastic letter (emphasis in the original):

> You will see by my mimeographed manuscript that I have introduced the term "Vital Revolution." (Of course you know that this term was coined by Norman Himes. At least, that is how I understand it.) However, I think a great deal more can be done with this term that Himes had an idea of. Why can't we all get together and make the "Vital Revolution" this coming historical epoch. As a matter of fact, we are already half in it now. We have reduced the birth and death rate greatly and prolonged the length of life in a revolutionary manner. But in saving those who would have died in former times we have done little selecting, the selecting nature would have done if left to herself. Hitler says *we* can't do it as well as nature and

> then turns around and loses a great part of his "superior Nordics" in war.
>
> And why does society need a "Vital Revolution?" Well, present national and international conditions have demonstrated that the discovery and exploitation of a rich "New World" vastly expanded international trade and commerce, and the Industrial Revolution has not been able to solve the major problems of mankind. Furthermore, it seems that the scientific evidence available indicates that about the only thing that can solve the major problems of mankind, is a *revolution in mankind itself* (italics in original)—a vital revolution. A vital revolution based upon the conscious and voluntary control of the quantity and quality of population growth with due attention to *both hereditary and environmental forces* (Seeley G. Mudd Manuscript Library, Princeton Box no. FW. N. 1).

Here not only the belief in scientific progress and biopolitical intervention is evident but also a rather open flirtation with racist eugenic ideas. The only difference between Burch's ideas and Nazi-type intervention is that the American demographer puts a clear emphasis on the "conscious and voluntary" nature of selecting people on a quantitative and qualitative basis. Since he does not socially specify the locus of this consciousness he indirectly transfers the power to social mechanisms and institutions representing the consciousness of a utopian progress toward reduced population growth and the related checks on the "proliferation" of the "unworthy."

Researchers and scholars identified with pro-selection arguments only partially and on some points took to arguing with the positions of the above groups. Both hostility and caution toward the so-called "ideologues" characterize an unpublished letter written to Diego Suarez (the chairman of the Citizens Committee for Planned Parenthood) by Notestein on March 13, 1939:

> It is precisely because I believe the birth control movement a powerful agency for social betterment that I am alarmed by certain passages in this brochure. It seems to me to have too much the atmosphere of an appeal to the wealthy to save themselves from the burden of taxation. It gives too much the impression that uncontrolled prolif-

> igacy of the unworthy is the root of our current economic difficulties. ... Certainly the vast number of unemployed are much more than human waste. ...
>
> As a matter of fact I doubt the accuracy of the prediction that birth control will lower taxes....
>
> You can be sure that such material will be used against you. I have already heard a thoughtful Catholic Priest tell laboring men that the birth control group is a wealthy one desiring to escape just taxation by infringing on the working man's right to a family, that the group is attempting to avoid a sound reconstruction of the economic order, which would penalize the rich by denying human rights to the poor. To my mind his case is nonsense but this pamphlet lays itself open to being utilized as evidence of it (Seeley G. Mudd Manuscript Library, Princeton Box no.FW. N. 1).

Even in this polemical answer the proliferation of the unworthy, the unemployed, seems to be the main issue and Notestein is warning the representative of the birth-control movement not to use arguments that might allow criticism revealing some kind of a class bias in the proposed intervention.

Regardless of this caution and resentment toward a class-biased biopolitical intervention, demographers could not escape from the discursive structure dividing the human race and social communities. This is evident in the fact that Notestein later joined the sponsoring committee of Planned Parenthood (due to news of some changes in the criticized text), and also in the way that demographic-transition theory was formulated and reformulated. A product of the need to categorize the world population as "valuable" and "unworthy," the demographic transition theory, the first major contribution of American demography, was an attempt to establish a global "biopolitical" framework. After a "descriptive" phase, discursive structures forced this theory through an interventionist reversal. This turn was not merely the result of political influence and shifts in interest as argued in recent literature (Greenhalgh 1996, Szreter 1993). It reveals the working of the East–West slopes as another major discourse linked to biopolitical controls.

2.4. Looking down the East–West slope. Regional otherness in the "Western" perspective: from modernizationist to qualitative/civilizational discourses

2.4.1. The theory of demographic transition

The theory of demographic transition can rightly be considered the 20th century's most successful demographic theory. According to D. J. van de Kaa, a leading European demographer to this day, it is the most important "narrative" in demography and historical demography (van de Kaa 1996; Szreter 1993). This theory was successful not only in scientific thought, but had an appeal outside the social sciences as well, i.e. it became an organic part of wider public knowledge and political thinking (Burch 1996; Valkovics 1982; Szentgáli 1991; Dányi 2000). The same cannot be said of other demographic theories.

The reason for the theory's success is clearly its simplicity and plausibility. Nonetheless, this popularity may also be seen as a result of the fact that over time the demographic-transition theory became deeply embedded in the discursive web of liberal utopias and, by way of the East–West dichotomy, could easily be globalized. It is this discursive web and not some integral coherence which lends demographic transition theory its explanatory power.[1]

The theory dates from about 1944–45 and is attributed to Notestein, who presented it as the second part of his lecture at a United Nations food supply conference (Notestein 1945). In very simplified "modernizationist" terms the theory states that as a consequence of urbanization, industrialization, rising standards of living, education, and the spread of democracy and individualism, mortality and fertility irreversibly decline and these two processes, after a period of transition, stabilize at low levels. The theory defined the size of population as a dependent variable in relation to social processes, and interpreted these processes regionally. It defined three great regions in which development had attained different levels. The first was the "West" (mainly Northern Europe and the largely German areas of Central Europe), which had completed the transition. In the second region, which comprised Eastern and Southern Europe, the transition was at an advanced stage, but had not been completed. In the post-colonial Third World the transition had just begun, and at most the beginning of a decline in the death rate could be observed. The key element in the theory is linear modernization and its regional representation and distribution.

Although the theory of modernization definitely did not argue on the basis of unchanging, "inborn" traits of different social groups or societies it did allow itself to be transcribed into racist discourses as understood by Foucault. The first point in this respect is that the theory had existed previously, as Szreter, Hodgson and Greenhalgh have shown. The Frenchman Adolphe Laundry and the American Warren F. Thompson outlined the basic elements of the theory and published them as early as 1929 (Hodgson 1983; Thompson 1929; Szreter 1993; Greenhalgh 1996). This was precisely the time when the above-mentioned discourses on the "quality of the population" was dominant. Thus the demographic-transition theory came under the shadow of the discourses of the day, or, to be more precise, adapted elements from those discourses.

The second point is that the theory seems to have been tied to the immigration controllers, since precisely those areas were described as "lagging behind" the "West" in the transition which at the beginning of the century had been seen as threatening the "northern" races with a massive outflow of migrants to the US: mainly Eastern, Central and Southern Europe, or some Asian areas.

An interventionist or racist turn can also be seen in the fact that the main problem of the theory is the rising reproduction rate of underdeveloped regions in contrast with the decreasing, and already fairly low, rate of developed regions. To simplify, we can argue that while in American domestic debates the desired target state was that of the middle class, in the demographic-transition theory this role is given to the "West" (demarcated by a letter "A" in Thompson's scheme).[2] In other words the theory of demographic transition, with certain changes, was able to utilize the former elements of the domestic debates on a global scale, replacing the concern about the reproduction rate of the "racially different" lower classes (where it was already visibly decreasing) with that of the "non-Western" world.

This teleological perspective and the "interventionist" tensions within the "transition" discourses are clearly revealed in the unpublished minutes of the forty-third meeting of the Territorial Group Council on Foreign Relations attended by Notestein (January 18, 1944). The meeting was one of a series preparing the post- World War scenario and the very active role of the United States. The debate over the issue of overpopulation with regard to territorially separate "colonial" or "non-European" people went like this:

> Improvement in this situation is slow to develop, because it has so happened that the advanced nations have tended to transfer to dependent peoples that part of their culture which reduces mortality, but they have not disseminated the complementary cultural developments, which tend to bring about a rational control of fertility. …
>
> The dissemination of birth-control information, while of undoubted use in reducing population growth, would not meet the needs of these colonial populations. Therefore, the only lasting solution is one which would bring about a reduction of growth potential.
>
> Continuing, Mr. Notestein pointed out that in all probability a reduction of growth potential can only be brought about by education, urbanization, and a gradual increase in the standard of living (Seeley G. Mudd Manuscript Library, Princeton Box no. FW.1).

The above text considers how the "West" in the form of liberal utopias should help these regions in terms of culture and in what other ways it should intervene in the lives of "dependent peoples" to establish control over "population growth." Notestein's remarks clearly show the uneasy marriage between a clear-cut modernizationist discourse (stressing behavioral changes as a result of social and economic progress) and an overtly interventionist framework for reducing the "growth potential" by disseminating birth control information. It seems, then, that despite the idea of social progress as an independent variable in demographic changes, the original demographic-transition theory had to be substantially altered in order to accommodate direct anti-natalist intervention instead of social progress. Due to the discursive pressure of biopolitics and the modernizationist or cold-war variant of the East–West dichotomy it would not be long before the role of progress lessened.

2.4.2. Demographic-transition theory rewritten

At the end of the 1940s, after returning from a trip to the Far East, Notestein radically changed his position on the fundamental relationships contained within the theory of demographic transition. He repositioned fertility as an independent variable, arguing that it was not reasonable to wait for social progress alone in order to decrease fertility in the "East" since that region did not have an "efficient" system of population replacement: "The East, unlike the West, cannot afford to await the automatic processes of social change, incident of urbanization and industrialization, in order to complete its transition to an efficient system of population replacement..."(cited by Szreter 1993, 674).

In 1949, in an unpublished lecture revealingly entitled "Demographic Sources of Power," Notestein goes even further, hinting that beyond the time factor the relationship between demographic and social processes is substantially different in the "East." Due to this alternative development there is a need for immediate intervention.

> I think one can only come to the conclusion that ... [fertility decline] will not come about. [in the case of China and India because of the size of the population] by the normal automatic processes of urbanization, industrialization, education and so on which have been rather effective in the case of Japan; that if this area is to get out, some means, as yet unknown, must be found for speeding up the process, and by speeding the process I mean dropping the fertility of the rural population in the hinterlands. (Notestein 1949, 17).

As Szreter has shown, the political environment is significant here. At the time of the statement the construction of the Soviet atomic bomb had just been revealed and Mao had taken the Chinese communists to victory, establishing a communist political order (Szreter 1993). This set of circumstances was interpreted by the leading American demographers of the time, and the Rockefeller Foundation which funded them, as a threat to the "West." In their view "overpopulation" could easily lead to social discontent, which could prepare the ground for a communist takeover. In this way not only did the global biopolitical push for decrease in fertility receive ideological support, but as the texts cited above show, the population-growth debate was formulated in an East–West framework.

But this neo-Malthusian, biopolitical turn was more than merely Cold War politics. There was also a logical withdrawal into the shells of the pre-war discourses, retaining some of the previously despised elements. On demography and power Notestein aims, in a Foucaldian and colonial manner, at penetrating into the deeper reality of those societies "inherited" for control from their previous colonizers. Instead of mere mortality he is seeking control over fertility, or as he puts it, the "intimate details" of social life:[3]

> We have given these societies elements of complexity… (Notestein 1949, 21).

and

> We have touched these societies at their exterior, but the intimate details of their existence remain pretty unchanged (Notestein 1949, 22).

This discursive victory over the elements of an anti-interventionist social progress created the social and financial basis for what Paul Demény has called the "family-planning industry" institutionalizing the pre-war discourses on a global, West-Third World scale (Demény 1988). The successful reconnection to the previous discourse elements provided new opportunities for population activists and some business groups to initiate a new campaign. This network was extremely influential in American-led global-population policy and was not seriously challenged until the early 1980s. Before then the "family-planning" discourse was able to weather the liberal-conservative turns in domestic American population policy (Demény 1988; Teitelbaum and Winter 1998, Chapter. 7, Greenhalgh 1996).

2.4.3."The golden age of the family-planning industry" up to the early 1980s. The control of non-Western population growth

The discourse of global-population policy which had been based on the mixture of modernizationist and racist-interventionist discourses described above, unambiguously presented fertility decrease as a virtue in itself. On the one hand, the possibility of the exhaustion of global resources as a result of "overpopulation" was formulated, while on the other hand prejudice toward the lower classes was repeatedly directed at the Third World. This is well illustrated by a sentence in Notestein's introduction to the 1960 new edition of Malthus's work: "These populations [of technologically underdeveloped nations] have grown rather slowly since the beginning of the nineteenth century, and often present a picture of disease, illiteracy and poverty for the masses with which Malthus was wholly familiar" (Notestein in: Malthus 1960, vii).

The same pattern appears in the same book in an essay written by Frederick Osborn, who harbored eugenic views in the 1930s and was a founding member of the Population Association of America. The essay maps the world, with its regions, religions and cultures, on the basis of their propensity toward the control of fertility and the reduction of large families which are unable to improve "the quality of family life." In addition it provides elaborate instructions for intervention: who should be considered a local leader, how to take into account the nationalistic spirit or how to overcome "cultural and political barriers" (Osborn 1960). The central claim is that the high fertility of the social groups in question is the main cause of the "qualitative" problems. From this it follows that the "extra" children of these groups should not be born. "But as a general rule it must be recognized that for most people in areas where birth rates are high and incomes are low, large families make it difficult to improve the care and education of children, and handicap all efforts to improve the quality of family life" (Osborn in: Malthus 1960, 93).

Despite the universal anti-natalist argument it is to be noted that the author allows for indirect improvement by way of social conditions where members of an "us" group are concerned.

> In advanced countries:
>
> Excessive fertility by families with meager resources must be recognized as one of the potent forces in the perpetuation of slums, ill health, inadequate education, and even delinquency. A greater acceptance of the idea that parents should be responsible not to have more children than they can care for should go a long way toward improving the situation... More attention should, therefore, be given to the economic and social conditions which influence reproductive trends in human life in its qualitative aspects (Osborn in: Malthus 1960, 94).

This intervention on the social side was secured only for the American lower class, while in other territories (Latin America, Asia, Arab states etc.) high fertility was considered to be a prime cause of social ills. There is no elaborate discussion of the possibilities of economic progress in the Third World.

> The rate of population growth in many underdeveloped areas is now much greater than was ever experienced in European countries. In most of the others it will be so in the foreseeable future. And the population base is far larger than it ever was in Europe. Unless an effort equal to that made for the control of death is made for the control of fertility, and unless a reduction of births is achieved within a few decades, the hopes of great but underdeveloped nations for better conditions of life may prove futile, while the present standard of economically advanced nations will decline (Osborn 1960, 95).

It is important to note that this neo-Malthusian or interventionist move was coupled with, and legitimized by, forms of cultural essentialism. European social and cultural structures are seen as lowering fertility and promoting "responsible" parenthood, while in the case of other regions, mainly in some Latin American and Asian countries, procreation is "prescribed" socially (Osborn 1960, 115–138). Interestingly, despite being discussed in complete isolation from the region called Europe, the Soviet Union (no mention of Eastern or Central Europe) is counted as a modern industrial area, which together with the United States has a special responsibility in handling its own population growth. As Osborn argues their population problem is important not only to their own people, but also to the well-being and even to the peace of the world as a whole (Osborn 1960, 127).

To make the fertility-control campaign efficient the neo-Malthusian global-population policy discourse adopted a war vocabulary (Bandarage 1998, 65). To achieve the precisely-stated goals of various programs there was to be a "war" on "dangerous" elements using a new "arsenal" of scientific results. Texts often described a "catastrophic situation" in the non-Western world in need of constant crisis management. The possibility of the exhaustion of resources was raised, as was the scare of significant famines, and these provided background for the formulation of a negative picture of population growth.

Thus this period was clearly in favor of "overriding" (Sen's term, Sen 1994) and "intervention," and American governmental organizations and their related population-policy organizations and foundations tried to sell these intervention programs to the governments of the countries of the Third World. Intervention occurred at the level of international politics, but these organizations also prepared to countenance the violation of human rights. They presented birth-control and sterilization programs as economic-aid programs (e.g., 25 dollars for a complete sterilization), and in a covert manner they supported the direct use of violence (Bandarage 1998, 70–78; Sen 1994; Andorka 1990, 133–41).

Such intervention programs are well-documented policies followed in India and Bangladesh. In India a population "emergency" was declared in 1975 and the government assisted the carrying out of 8 million abortions. This program did not shrink from using violence, and such cases contributed to the collapse of the first Indira Gandhi government (Andorka 1990, 136; Bandarage 1998, 72–78). Steps similar to those taken in India were suggested by foreign organizations in Bangladesh as part of the five-year plan from 1973 to 1978.

Although not a direct result of international pressure, Chinese population-growth intervention may also be listed among those programs which wished to limit population growth by violent means (Andorka 1990, 135–36; Bandarage 1998, 78–80). China introduced its fertility-control program, which contained eugenic elements, in 1979, and within this framework granted or withheld social aid to promote "one-child" families. But beyond the social system there were instances of coerced abortions and sterilization, and the population itself was pushed to execute these acts of violence (e.g., the "disappearance" of undesired, usually female, babies). The "one-child" program was Chinese, but this does not mean that it did not receive international aid and support. To this day in debates on population it is brought up as a "successful" example of intervention. In the golden age of the "family-planning industry" and population growth control in the name of development, there was hardly any counterbalance to such efforts. At the international level the countries of the Third World depended on material aid and, being enframed in the discourse, subjected themselves to the attempts and programs in question.

As we will see later, only the cold-war antagonism limited the spread and effective execution of such programs. For example, at the 1974 Population World Conference in Bucharest, the "Eastern" block, in concert with the countries of the Third World, stressed the importance of social progress and planning. This was a modernizationist rhetoric, stressing "development." Characteristically, as we will see later it also covered up the pro-natalist intervention attempts of East European governments in particular that of the host country Romania (Kligman 1998, 90–92).

2.4.4. Global population discourses from the 1980s

From the late 1970s the combined pro-intervention and modernization approach within a directly or functionally racist discursive framework has been attacked in several respects, coming under serious criticism from Third-World activists and American feminist writers. The UN, through special conferences and publications, studied human-rights problems (e.g., Population and Human Rights, 1990) and wrote recommendations for the program planners. Critics also drew attention to reproduction in its entirety and the position of women, along with the view that discrimination against women should be eliminated. This view formed the basis of the belated international rejection of Chinese population policy. On the other hand, American pro-life activists put tremendous pressure on the US government to withdraw from programs that actively promoted abortion (Teitelbaum and Winter 1998; Greenhalgh 1996; Bandarage 1998).

Furthermore, an unambiguous change occurred in the integration of population growth and questions of development strategy. The inseparability of the two areas was declared counter to the general position that environmental degradation is merely a Third-World and population-growth problem.

But apart from political challenges there were also changes at the discursive level. On the one hand the modernization approach, with its stress on measurable progress, was replaced by discourses focusing on "qualitative" "civilization" issues. After modernization discourse and its combination with partly hidden "qualitative" concerns, a new phase emerged in which the belief in large-scale quantitative progress disappeared. Instead of stressing numerical targets (e.g. in fertility decline) emphasis was increasingly placed on issues such as gender inequality. The danger of quantitative overpopulation evaporated and long-term ecological considerations promoted an "image of imbalance." The simplified and generalized idea of population as a dependent or independent variable (with intervention simply speeding up the work of progress) disappeared and the stress was laid instead on the interrelationship of cultural, social, technological and demographic processes. This also meant the articulation of different regions, a process in which Eastern Europe, as a region was included. Thus it seems that after rewriting the demographic-transition theory and forming a global biopolitical framework the pre-Second World War patterns focusing on "qualitative" differences reappeared rather vividly in a "politically correct manner." These changes clearly appear in the documents of global foundations (which will be analyzed in chapter III) and also in the theory of the so-called second demographic transition. But before analyzing this later theory it is worth examining the shift in discourses in historical demography and particularly those of family history, which were among the first fields of study to establish the ideas of qualitatively different regions within Europe being our prime concern.

2.4.5. Eastern Europe as the other: the Hajnal line

Eastern Europe and Southern Europe have never been fully integrated into the first modernizationist "transition" discourse. These regions have been relegated to an intermediate category of "almost developed"—a separate world which caused no serious alarm regarding population growth. In terms of Anglo-Saxon discourses, Eastern Europe first received considerable attention in historical demography, mainly in Britain. It was John Hajnal, a statistician of Hungarian origin, and the researchers of the Cambridge Group for the History of Population and Social Structure who first attempted to overcome the "fallacies" of modernization theory in the area of population and family history. Their main aim was to demonstrate that (in the "West" at least) there was no development from "large families" or complex households to the "modern nuclear family." Other regions of Europe were shown to belong to a different household and family system (see among others: Hajnal 1965, 1983; Wrigley–Schoefield 1981; Laslett and Wall 1972, Wall 1983; Saito 1996; Laslett and Melegh 2001; Faragó 1997; Todorova 1993; Schneider-Schneider 1996; Macfarlane 1978, 1986, 1987).

In 1965 Hajnal divided turn-of-the-century Europe into two halves along a line from St. Petersburg to Trieste. The division was based on age at first marriage and the proportion of people who never married, that is, on the indicators of "moral" self-restraint promoted by Malthus. In contrast to the "West" (according to Hajnal) Eastern Europe could be characterized by a relatively early age at marriage (for women under 20, for men under 24) and an almost complete absence of never-married singles. Later this model was further developed as a system of household formation, and the region of Eastern Europe was linked to India, that is, the Third World (Hajnal 1965, 1983).

The Hajnal pattern based on statistical averages was interpreted by the members and collaborators of the Cambridge Group as the cornerstone of a general model of household structure (Laslett and Wall 1972; Wall 1983; Macfarlane 1978, 1986). In later social-historical and demographic literature, this model assumed a primary role. Counter to Hajnal's original statement it was relegated further into the past, beyond the point of the "great transformation" from a "peasant economy" to capitalism (Macfarlane 1978; Smith 1984) and presented as a significant factor in the "unique" development of Europe (Jones 1981; Laslett 2001). In this way the Malthusian discursive system acquired additional historical "evidence" which could be applied and repeated within Europe, creating qualitatively different regions.

This Malthusian reformulation did not only appear in historical analyses of marriage patterns and household formation but was integrated into the historical analysis of European population processes prior to the 20th century, that is to say, prior to the demographic transition. This is evident in the highly influential work of Wrigley and Schoefield on the population history of England, based on the data of a large number of English parishes and the method of retrospective population projection (Wrigley–Schofield 1981). The authors openly relied on the Malthusian idea of a relationship between population and economic growth, or more concretely, the relationship between the development of prices and marriage formation, fertility and mortality. Between the 16th and 19th centuries, mortality figures (average life expectancy at birth) and prices were seen to correlate, while a relationship could be found between price waves and the change in age at first marriage. Not marrying in times of economic hardship was understood as the basis of the "low-pressure" Malthusian system in contrast with "high-pressure" ones. These "civilizational" findings then further extended the neo-Malthusian revision of the population history of England and together with the Hajnal line served as a basis for setting up separate regions in Europe, whose regional identities have been used as explanations of the differential well-being of various countries and the hierarchies among them. In other words, the demarcation line used by Malthus against the lower classes gave birth once again to the hierarchization of different societies in the world and now, within this system, to the category of "Eastern" and "Central Europe."

2.4.6. The second demographic transition [4]

The anti-modernizationist criticism of the historical sociologists and historical demographers provided a strong impulse for the further revision of the demographic-transition theory begun in the late 1940s. In the mid—1980s a new attempt was made to revitalize the idea of transition by creating a "second demographic-transition theory." This new theory was cherished by European demographers (van de Kaa 1987, 1988, 1996, 1999, 1999a; Lesthaeghe 1991; Cliquet 1991; Hablicsek 1995; Dányi 2000; Kamarás 2001).

The theory consciously refers back to its predecessor but agrees with it only about the idea of the "West" as the pioneer and apex of historical development. In all other respects the differences are so great that it is dubious to use the same term for both. It even seems that the second demographic-transition theory has more in common with the rewriting of the first theory on qualitative, civilizational grounds than with the original idea that social progress everywhere leads to certain changes in demographic behavior. Let us now turn to these differences and the way the biopolitical and linked East–West discourses appear in the "theory" of the second demographic transition.

The first great difference between the theories is that in the 1940s the so-called first transition theory was written as a glorious narrative of progress in which the modernization of society solves the long-term problems of an imbalance between resources and population. The second transition theory is certainly much less "victorious" and much more "defensive." Counter to the originally assumed stagnation after the completion of the transition (predicted by Notestein, but not by earlier theorists such as Thompson), by the 1980s there was extremely low fertility in many countries of Western Europe which in the current demographic structure was not sufficient to reproduce the population. Divorce rates reached extreme highs, and new generations were no longer willing to get married, preferring cohabitation to legally binding arrangements. Thus there is a clear sense of crisis, recalling the pre-war ideas of a civilizational catastrophe due to the decline of fertility among more civilized groups. As in the case of family-planning programs, in the idea of the second demographic transition, the danger of "flooding" is not related to the lower classes but to other regions of the world. One of the most prominent theoreticians of this transition, van de Kaa, speaks about the "management of decline" and is clearly worried about the fate of European civilization from a demographic point of view:

> Interpreting Europe's current demographic condition in terms of a process stretching over several centuries evidently casts new light on the way the relative, and soon probably absolute decline in numbers, should be managed. Samuel Huntington's view of the future, for example, is one in which civilizations will clash. These views are not universally applauded. Even so, the thought that future armed conflicts will be fought not between nation states, but between groups of kindred nations is, from a European perspective, quite compelling. Should such considerations influence the thinking about European population issues? Yes. To some extent they probably should. However, in my view, it is a matter of degree rather than fundamentals (van de Kaa 1999, 39).

This sense of gloom over the fate of European "kindred" nations is a very clear reference to the idea of defending a previously achieved superiority based on the concept of civilization and, most probably, race. Such reasoning with regard to population development is obviously linked to the issue of immigration. The theoreticians argue that due to all time low fertility rates the population growth of Western Europe can only come from migration. Here the prime consideration is once again not the number of people but their "quality." A little later in his text van de Kaa writes, in line with pre-war ideas about the quality of immigrants and the fate of European civilization:

> Long-term considerations lead to the conclusion that the quality of immigrants and their willingness and ability to integrate are important for the viability and continuity of European civilization. This

suggests that a policy aimed at accepting only those who cannot reasonably refused entry, is not optimal (van de Kaa 1999, 40).

The clear promotion of active selection on the basis of quality and "viability" certainly reminds us of pre-Second World War American biopolitical cognitive structures. Here it seems that, instead of disciplining highly fertile immigrant and "racially different" lower-class groups, the main idea is the filtering of immigrants and selection of those who would contribute to the success of West European countries through their "quality". It should be noted that in the 1990s fear is not only directed toward people coming from previous colonies, but also toward migrants from East Europe and especially Russia and the Ukraine (Okólski 1999).

This defensive spirit also casts a shadow on other aspects of the theory. Compared to the numbers and progress indexes of the "first transition," in the new theory there is considerable emphasis on the interaction of values and efficient contraceptive techniques. According to its proponents the idea of self-fulfillment replaces the idea of serving the family, while marriage is postponed or totally rejected (Baumann 1996, Lesthaege 1991). Some authors welcome this "liberation" as a new achievement of European individualism or "bourgeois postmodernity", while others despise it as "selfishness" or at least regard it as problematic (Lesthaege 1991 versus van de Kaa 1987; Pongrácz, 1998).

Consciously utilizing the results of the historical demographic maps analyzed above, values and related marriage patterns are used to divide Europe into regions (Macura et al. 1998). The important thing to note is that in contrast with the first theory, where the Third World was placed at the other end of the developmental scale, here, as in the case of historical demography, the constitutive Other of Western Europe is Eastern Europe. In 1988 van de Kaa praises the new theory as being able to give a very good overview of the differences between East European countries and other parts of Europe" (van de Kaa 1988, 19).

Differences discovered between regions are seen as partly temporal ones: Eastern Europe has only just begun to move toward the new demographic patterns. These characteristics are stressed for instance by David Coleman, who argues that after 50 years of "aberration" (sic) Eastern and Central Europe are "able to resume the modernizing trajectories":

> While the collapse of the iron curtain has removed a major obstacle to convergence between East and West, it has also provoked severe but (it is assumed) short-time crisis responses in sharply lowered birth rates, sharply raised death rates and heightened internal and external migration. These are likely to take several years to iron out, although vital rates in some countries (Poland, Czech Republic) are already showing signs of returning to a more "normal" level or at least a Western European level. What "normal" levels actually are in an Eastern Europe which is modern, prosperous and free, remains to be seen. Populations of that region have not previously enjoyed such a combination of circumstances. If their future could be predicted as a return to some "normal" trajectory or logical continuation of earlier interrupted trends, then our work would be mostly done (Coleman 1997, 27).

But in addition to the arrogant use of "Western" norms and the total exclusion of some European regions from "normal" European history Coleman hints that historical patterns might win over convergence and temporal leveling: "Whether Hajnal's line will continue to divide Europe in any important ways remains to be seen, although some of the differences in marriage formation and in the timing of births have been remarkably resilient to change up to 1995" (Coleman 1997, 27–28).

Van de Kaa, the father of this new transition theory, goes even further and actually starts speaking about the relevance of "Europa major" (including the non-Muslim Soviet territories), "Europa minor" (including the European Union plus Central European states) and "Europa Unita" (European Union plus Central European states soon to be member states) According to him the historical differences between these categories of Europe might explain the long-term population trends. Thus in his view we cannot assume the rapid disappearance of Cold War (East–West) divisions: "The current differences between the two sides of the Iron Curtain are easily understandable in this perspective. They should in due course diminish, but to the extent that the Iron Curtain coincided with earlier fault lines, they are unlikely to disappear entirely" (van de Kaa 1999, 32).

It is apparent that historically understood essentialist East–West "fault lines" capture the minds of the theorists of the second demographic transition in drawing up civilizational maps. With this mental cartography theorists eliminate, to a large extent, the rule of general progress promoted by the first transition theory. The "West" here is not only a goal to be achieved but a qualitatively different model which can be followed only by some kind of "integration" or "civilizational" process. In other words, we find the "essentialization" of regional-cultural categories, those qualitative aspects of demographic change which remind the reader of the pre-Second World War Orientalist maps, and the language used in the "awkward" population discourses of the early 20th century. This link becomes rather obvious when van de Kaa formulates his vision of the long-term development of Europe and its population in the following comments, promoting a "new Europeanness" instead of multicultural heterogeneity:

> Will Europe again become a melting pot of different peoples from which a new "Europeanness" will emerge, or will we witness the emergence of a multiplicity of "adjective" Europeans? I'm happy to conclude by stating that I do not have the answer. However, I prefer the first outcome to the second, even though it implies that the classical discussion in literature about the positive selection for tall, blond and blue-eyed people amongst those following the retreating glaciers north to Scandinavia (completed 6500 BC), will ultimately only meet dark eyes full of incomprehension (van de Kaa 1999, 43).

With this statement van de Kaa clearly pleads for the openness of Europe in terms of immigration and creating a new integrative "European" identity instead of a multiplicity of identities. Thus he is trying to revitalize a new sense of common European identity on non-racist grounds, but his intention is formulated in a language which offers a great deal of ammunition for those trying to close the borders or to "purify" Europe. We might say, looking at the development of Western population discourses in the 20th century that such "progressive" intentions have not been able to rewrite the basic discourse and it even seems that the "original" biopolitical, civilizational discourses and the related power structures of the modern colonial period have been reproduced. And in this recent "Western" discursive seaweed the East–West civilizational differences have become of crucial importance once again. But for a better understanding of discursive mechanisms we should move beyond the established East–West walls and lines, that is to say to "Eastern" areas, where the speakers imagine themselves neither in the "West" nor at the bottom of the civilizational or modernizationist slopes.

2.5. Being on the Slope: Hungarian and East European population discourses in the 20th century

2.5.1. Hungarian populist writers in the 1930s. The biopolitics of pro-natalism

In the late 1920s and early 1930s Hungary's agrarian sector was in deep crisis. It suffered great difficulties due to lack of proper machinery, low agrarian wages and the product structure of small-scale units as result of the development of world capitalism. Owing to the combined effect of such imbalances and an unfavorable ownership structure the sector relied either on big estates exploiting extremely cheap labor or on inward looking, non-market oriented peasant economies. This made the fate of the peasantry a central issue for certain young radical writers and social scientists, who were appalled by the "underclass" status of the peasantry and who in line with other, agrarian-populist types of criticism throughout Eastern Europe (the Romanian village-monograph movement, the narodniks) revealed characteristic perspectives with regard to population discourses and positioning on the East–West civilizational slope. Apart from world-famous Russian and Romanian intellectuals (among others, Gusti, Stahl, Chayanov) the most significant Hungarian populists were Imre Kovács (Kovács 1989), Lajos Fülep (Fülep 1984), János Kodolányi (Kodolányi 1963), Ferenc Erdei, László Németh, Péter Veres (for analysis see: Andorka 1969, 1975; Monigl 1990, 20–45; Melegh 1999c; Némedi 1985; Kovács and Melegh 1997).

In the eyes of these radical intellectuals the most relevant symptom of the agrarian crisis was the falling fertility rate of the peasants, especially in the "cursed," "single-child" areas. The "sociographers" aimed to expose certain practices in certain regions of the country where peasant women used crude birth-control devices in order to control the number of children and to have (ideally) only one child. This "lack of vitality" was understood as a sign of social crisis and the "self-destructive" behavior of these groups morally rejected (see Fülep 1984) the phenomenon being seen as collective "suicide" or "silent revolution" against the "aristocratic," "lordly" Hungarian agrarian system (Kovács 1989). Kovács saw the negative consequences of "abortion" in the following way: "Abortion, the biological implementation of fertility control ... leads to the spiritual, intellectual and moral defeatism of the society" (Kovács 1989, 91, translated by A. M.).

Writing about peasant society Erdei established the same negative links between fertility control and social development in Hungary. Like Kovács he saw "abnormal" East European social arrangements behind fertility control:

> The single child system is only one indication of a peasant society forced to strike. It is accompanied by a distortion of life in its entirety.... In contrast [to normal peasant life] the life of peasants with one child is totally decadent, exhausted and alienated. Here not the man but the woman is the leader, being young is of no value and youth is not respected, it is ruled by the cynical generation of the elderly; here there is no vitality, there is no fight for the girl: the lads, the young husband does not kill the mother-in-law, does not even bang the table if he is not allowed access to his wife for the night (Erdei 1942, 67–68, translated by A. M.).

At the root of this populist (plebeian) anxiety was a biopolitics focusing on the loss of "national character" as a result of low fertility rates in rural social groups. The reproduction of the middle classes was seen as threatening, and populist writers always stressed the non-Hungarian (Jewish, German) character of the urban and rural middle classes which "exploited" the lower classes. Due to the "true Hungarianness" of the peasants they put a value on peasant children while rejecting the social and demographic behavior of the ethnically different middle classes. This rejection emphasized the lack of middle-class solidarity with and the exploitation of, lower rural groups, the spread of urban patterns and also the proliferation of "alien" elements in rural society. Worry about the increase of ethnically different groups (mainly Swabian Germans) is evident in Imre Kovács's remarks on the development of "sunk" (i.e. depopulated) villages:

> The life and death struggle of the Transdanubian region was first recognized three years ago when in Hidas [a Hungarian village in South Hungary] the Hungarian church was transferred officially to the Germans. The Hungarians have been dispersed in the storms of the centuries and they have been replaced by the Germans. The statisticians have not ignored the problem and have shown that the Hungarians of Hidas exist: in the cemetery, in neighboring villages and in America (Kovács 1989, 97, translated by A. M.).

This type of biopolitical discourse differed widely from the American debates of the 1930s. The differences lay in (i) historical discourses on progress, (ii) methods for defining the "alien" and the "unworthy," (iii) modes of connecting "stylistic" elements in the discourse. These differences can be understood as the dominant discourse of modern world capitalism in the context of the East–West slope, on which Hungarian society is imagined at a lower point.

The most important difference lay in the interpretation of modern development. In the "Western" context the main focus was upon a general civilizational progress led by the "West" and its middle classes, which among other things initiated the decline of fertility as described by the theory of demographic transition. Appearing in the writings of the Hungarian populists, this discourse articulated the opposite with an odd twist, arguing that Hungary or certain Hungarian social groups had been part of an unbalanced progress of civilization and it was this that forced low fertility upon the peasants. Here progress was not a "liberating" or "glorious" process, but an ambiguous social advancement that removed certain traditional values without providing viable new alternatives. In contrast to the "Western" discourses Hungarian variants treated "civilization" and its consequences with suspicion. It should be noted that, just as in the case of the demographic transition theory, population development was not seen as an independent variable but as an aspect of social structure and power, which only affected demographic processes in an indirect way (Erdei 1942; Kovács 1989).

Moving to the second most significant difference between "Eastern" and "Western" discourses, a contrast can be located in definitions of "aliens" and the "unworthy." Both sets of discourses were based on a biopolitical separation between high- and low-quality groups. While "Western" discourses on population development tended to identify the lower classes and "racially different" migrants of lower value as biopolitical threats, excluding them on a racial or class basis, Hungarian populists in the 1930s used an ethno-status system to identify a "status-oriented" conservative Hungarian and Jewish-German urban *middle* class as "aliens" endangering the social space of "Magyar" peasants. This enemy category included the better-off German (Swabian) peasantry and the German-Jewish urban middle classes. In Erdei's words, Hungarian peasants were subject not only to the traditional, conservative middle classes in the form of a lord-serf relationship but also the new urban bourgeoisie:

> The real bourgeois society satisfying the criteria of capitalism was not only a form without history, but also an isolated separate structure appended to the historical status system of the "natives". ...Thus it became a colonial formation and a "foreign body" within the general social system (Erdei 1976, 23, translated by A. M.).

Finally, significant differences are also to be found in the linguistic approaches. In "Western" discourses critical elements operated in the interest of already existing power constellations. In Hungarian discourses general criticism formed part of a program of radical and comprehensive social and political change.

The "strategic field of opportunities" of the two discourses is largely similar.[6] In "Western" discourses social development could be forgotten in order to exercise direct control over demographic processes (as we saw when analyzing the theory of demographic transition). Similarly, the Hungarian "populist" discourse could also ignore programs of social improvement and looked to exclude bourgeois Jews or Germans directly. During the Second World War this racist/interventionist attitude could be seen in the lack of solidarity with, or open hostility against, "alien" groups of Jews, in promoting a complete "change of guard" to replace the ethnically "alien" social and economic elite of the early 1940s, and later in open support for the total exclusion and subsequent Holocaust of the Hungarian Jews on the part of some populist intellectuals studying and glorifying village life (Lengyel 1990). Thus Hungarian biopolitical discourses can be regarded as fertile ground for the Nazi policies representing another perspective on the East–West slope. Furthermore, after the war, with a certain political twist, this discourse created a basis for the forced expulsion of several thousand ethnic Swabians in reprisal for their alleged collective collaboration with the Nazis and their lack of "loyalty" to the Hungarian nation (Kovács in the newspaper Szabad Szó, 04/22/1945).

As can be seen from the above, discourses concerning Hungarian population development cannot be interpreted without the East–West dichotomy and the East–West slope, which explains the "odd twists" noted earlier. The discourse of "Western" superiority and its civilizational achievements sometimes appeared in Hungarian discourses but was seen from a different perspective. The use of the "Western mirror" as a means of qualifying Hungarian developments and the existence of different perspectives on the East–West slope make discourses meaningful (Melegh 1992, 1994; Böröcz 2003, 76–89). Being on the slope means that the experience of civilizational progress was seen as simply following somebody else's achievement, and therefore as not entirely authentic. At times it was even seen as some kind of aberration. In the texts of populist writers, imitated social development differed from the "real Western" one and displayed some elements of being an inferior type. In the field of population development this perspective included frustration at not being at the top point of the slope, with the result that the decrease in fertility was seen as a further decline in the "global" position of the country.

This perspective was quite clear in the case of Erdei who, in a longer essay on the social structure of Hungary, used a "Western" mirror to understand inferior types of "East European" social development, leading to the social and demographic crisis described earlier. "In the original capitalist society the technology of production, capitalist social relations and the bourgeois structure of class society developed jointly on the basis of a structure created by medieval formations... By contrast, modern development did not proceed in the same manner in East-European societies" (Erdei 1976, 23, translated by A. M.).

In this "mirror" Hungarian modernity appeared unfinished, distorted, inauthentic and even unreal. This creation of an "Eastern" modernity led to a clear inferiority complex without an awareness of which Hungarian discourses on population cannot be understood. Fertility decline became a sign not of modernity, but of the total corruption of the whole community.

> Villages practicing the single child system are the best demonstrations of the distorted development of the peasantry, for the single child system is not the same phenomenon as fertility control in bourgeois society. Bourgeois fertility control—as all the phenomena of this society—is not a structure crystallized into frozen and objectified forms, but an intermediate phenomenon of life channeled by interests which immediately changes and transforms if interests change. ... By contrast the single child system of peasants is not so directly consequential. This control of fertility is the alleviation of an unmanageable situation through the production of social forms (Erdei 1942, 86, translated by A. M.).

With a clear nationalist overtone and a direct reference to the loss of Hungarian territories after the First World War, Kovács even prophesied the "disappearance" of the Hungarian nation: "We are a disappearing nation. ...The cool laws of sociology indicate a devastated and cruel future: after the aging truncated country comes the weakened and depopulated truncated country" (Kovács 1989, 137–138, translated by A. M.).

Social forms originating from distorted, "non-Western," development corrupt the behavior of the peasants. From this position comes the specification of the "unworthy" (the "corrupt" conservative Hungarian ruling class plus the "alien" bourgeoisie) and the emergence of pro-natalist ideas. By designating this region as "semi-developed," the discourses of the Hungarian populists reveal an East–West perspective which explains the differences in the way aliens are identified and population policy articulated. In the "West" the alien group was the one which did not follow the model of "self-restraint" represented by the middle classes and thus endangered the biopolitical balances, while here in a region "following the West in a distorted manner," the anxiety was directed at the middle classes, which corrupted the social and demographic behavior of the lower classes. This type of discursive positioning, which may explain much of the tragedy of the Second

World War throughout "half-Western" Europe, was also what guided the statements of the communists who overtly fought against the "West" in terms of a modernizationist/ideological competition.

2.5.2. Pro-natalism and Eastern and Central Europe in the 20th century. From modernization to civilizational discourses

Eastern and Central Europeans have never been good students of Malthus. It can even be said that there was overt hostility to Malthusian ideas, especially after the Second World War (Petersen, 1988). Communist ideologues openly rejected the idea of "overpopulation," referring to a few statements made by Marx to the effect that there is no eternal law of population development but only specific laws linked to different social systems. As part of an ideological war in the United Nations Population Commission, the Ukrainian and Yugoslavian delegate described the Malthusian system as "barbaric": "I would consider it barbaric for the Commission to contemplate a limitation of marriages or of legitimate births, and this for any country whatsoever, at any period whatsoever. With an adequate social organization it is possible to face any increase in population" (cited by Petersen 1988, 93). "Cruelly, you [Western demographers] intend to adjust the population to the economy, while we Communists want to adjust the economy to the population" (cited by Petersen, 1988, 93).

But behind this sharp reaction there was more than just the willingness to show loyalty to Marx's ideas. We have already seen how Eastern and Central European discourses were formulated in the same pro-natalist and non-Malthusian manner, even without communist influence. The link between "populist" and "communist" discourses is the East–West slope which lends both populism and communism a similar perspective. The development of "communist" post-war discourses on population provides additional insight into this positioning mechanism and the interaction of "East" and "West" within the dominant biopolitical discursive framework linked to East–West discourses.

2.5.3. Overtaking the "West." Rapid modernization and pro-natalism in state-socialist Hungary

Most analysts writing on the population policy of Eastern European socialist countries invoke ideological radicalism and even totalitarian warfare against the population (Kligman 1998; Petersen 1988; Teitelbaum and Winter 1998). The development of Hungarian socialist population policy only partially corresponds to these images. A gradual movement can be seen from intolerant pro-natalism toward a tolerant version incorporating some elements of neo-Malthusian family planning, preparing the ground for a mixed population policy of direct pro-natalism and indirect anti-natalism with regard to certain groups in the 1990s. In other words, there was a movement from an active anti-Western position into a discursive space in which the anti-natalism of the "West" was combined with a "frustrated" "Eastern" pro-natalism. This change, related to the East–West positioning of countries, explains much of the emerging racism in Hungary.

After the communist takeover in 1948 the radical party ideologues immediately instituted a program of rapid "progress" at all levels of social life, including mortality (especially child mortality), fertility, medical care and the incorporation of women in the planned economy. The basic discourse was that of a modernizationist and ideological competition with the "capitalist" countries reassured against the past of the country. Most party reports started with "inferiority – superiority" comparisons in terms of quantifiable indicators of social and demographic life. The following party document in 1953 stressed the issue of infant mortality: "Although infant mortality decreased from 13,1% of 1938 to 7.4% in 1952, it is still high as compared to certain developed capitalist countries" (Monigl 1992, 39, translated by A. M.).

In the main they concluded with proposals for propaganda activity and intensification of the ideological competition. In the same year the central agitation and propaganda department of the Hungarian Workers' Party, for instance, made the following suggestions for ways to increase fertility:

> Propaganda should be organized around the following main questions:
>
> ...
>
> 2. The superiority of the communist morale as compared to the bourgeois one with regard to family life and gender relationships.
> 3. To show the protection of pregnant women, mothers and children by the state. The prestige of the working mothers contrasted this with the situation in the capitalist countries and the propaganda against propagation (Monigl 1992, 63, translated by A. M.).

The above idea of ideological superiority could not be demonstrated at the actual level of the number of marriages and live births, which showed no improvement of any kind or even a decline. This failure in concrete numbers was tackled in two ways. Firstly, with a kind of "positive" utopia of social progress, according to which the planned economy "must" provide all necessary social and household facilities (24-hour kindergarten, delivery of ready meals etc.) for women performing their "national duty". Secondly, failure was tackled using a "negative" approach, which penalized those who did not behave according to the expectations of the state. Childless couples were obliged to pay a special tax as they did not take their share in the "collective efforts" to build a socialist society (in which the rise of fertility is a sign of progress). In 1953 abortion was banned and those asking for or performing illegal abortions faced criminal proceedings. This one year was frighteningly similar to the late period of Ceauşescu's rule in Romania (Kligman 1998).

The stigmatization of social groups followed a special "Eastern" logic: any social group that reduced its fertility was accused of not doing its "national duty." In this respect peasants in particular were publicly ridiculed. In communist propaganda they were not only shown to be against socialism, and collectivization (a basis for deportation), but also to be refusing to take part in "producing" enough workers for the growing socialist industry despite "rising" living standards.

Recalling the pre-war discourses, the communist radicals thus adopted the familiar line of harping on the excessively low fertility of the peasantry, denying the need for its social empowerment and even looking for its abolition in the longer run. They stigmatized not only the middle classes but also the "heretical" working classes, who should have increased their fertility. Counter to the populist categorization this type of biopolitical discourse relied exclusively on *social* composition and totally ignored *ethnic* composition. Characteristically, the idea that social progress would lead to higher fertility also reappeared, based on the assumption that "pioneering" workers were more fertile and that the state, "taking care" of pregnant women, children and mothers, would eventually provide enough facilities for large families.

After 1953, owing to heavy internal criticism of "interventionist" pronatalism, Hungarian communist leaders placed greater and greater emphasis on the social empowerment of families and the need to avoid any kind of direct control over their fertility. Any ban on abortion for pro-natalist purposes was immediately ruled out or new regulations implemented. This anti-interventionism increased after the legalization of abortion in other communist countries and after 1956, when the Hungarian revolution revealed the weakness of repressive rule. While there was a growing consensus over non-intervention by governments and their advisors, the political elite became increasingly troubled by the idea that social progress, rather than increasing fertility, led to a decrease. By the early 1960s complete chaos surrounded this question. In March 1960 the Ministry of Health gave the following account of population development:

> Strangely, the rise of the living standard had a negative impact on the number of births. This is proved by the fact that since the counter-revolution [the then official term for the 1956 revolution] the number of births has declined, although since the counter-revolution the standard of living, the working conditions and the housing of the people has improved. According to the views of doctors and the abortion committees this is due to the fact that families do not undertake having children since they are seen as an obstacle to the raising of individual living standards (e.g. furniture, a television, a motorcycle) (Monigl 1992a, 34, translated by A. M.).

The overall answer to this strange relationship was to create a public atmosphere in which parenthood received "prestige and honor." Besides regular campaign measures, aimed at the "simple reproduction" of the population and the "ironing out" of the irregularities in Hungarian age-structures, the state-socialist population policy tried to compensate for the costs of having children. This overall aim has proved stable in the longer run. Even today, the main discourse on population development follows this line. But compared to the 1960s, since the establishment in the early 1970s of a universal family support system, universal solidarity with large families has been gradually abandoned and a selective policy has appeared instead. The direction of stigmatization and the methods involved have become much more complex as a result of the mixture of pro-natalism and indirect anti-natalism. More and more party ideologues gave up their combative approach to the "West" in terms of an anti-Malthusian revolution and more and more withdrew into the shell of a "silent" modernization of the country.

2.5.4. Back onto the East–West slope. The appearance of anti-natalist elements

The idea of family planning first appeared in relation to the high abortion figures. In the 1960s these rose above the number of live births. Among other discussions this fact provoked an internal note within the Planning Office in charge of the complex 5-year plans. A head of department wrote: "Fertility control should be based on contraception and not on the termination of pregnancy" (Monigl 1992a, 8, translated by A. M.).

The note directly refers to a publication of the Milbank Memorial Fund Quarterly on family planning in Japan: "It is to be noted that in certain states modern and efficient attempts are made for the organized campaign of contraceptives" (Monigl 1992a, 86, translated by A. M.).

This anxiety over the consequences of abortion was only partly due to concerns over the reproductive health of women. The main problem was that abortion increased the number of mentally retarded children. This "quality" problem in the smaller and smaller group of new births provided the focus of discussions in the early 1970s and particularly the late 1980s.

But from the 1960s other ideas of selecting higher "quality" also appeared in the documents, most notably concerning the declining progressivity of child allowances after the third child in a family. In 1971, a report to the Economic Policy Committee argued that the ideal number of children was three and social groups with higher fertility should not be supported. Their fertility was to be reduced, especially in the case of those who, for "subjective reasons," could not provide "average levels" of care for their children: "…in some families with a large number of children child care is below the average social level due to objective (housing) and subjective reasons" (Monigl 1990, 92,. translated by A. M.).

This is the first time that, in a public document, the high fertility of a lower social group (the "Gypsies", the "lumpen") is directly stigmatized on the basis of "quality." This selection discourse emerging during the 1970s received the support of human genetic arguments. Endre Ceizel, an extremely popular TV star geneticist in the 1970s, carried out several research programs on certain "deformities" and one set of findings related to marriage between cousins. According to a report: "The rate of cousin marriage in the Gypsy population is 6–8% as compared to the national figure of 0.3%. This partly explains the higher frequency of Gypsies in certain deformation types" (MTA Demográfiai Bizottság 1982, 48, translated by A. M.).

This ethnically based genetic research and the understanding of "Gypsy problems" as deviance shows in full a selection discourse with regard to lower status groups in state-socialist Hungary (see also: Ceizel 1972, 1976).

The increasing importance of severing the social and human continuum is also reflected in the "pro-natalist" innovations of the 1980s (Adamik 2000). At that time, due to the "worsening" demographic situation, the government, the Demographic Committee of the Hungarian Academy of Sciences and the Central Statistical Office made repeated efforts to find a way out of the population crisis. Besides the actual demographic situation, there were also ideological reasons for handling population issues. According to the party officials "populist" and "new-left" opposition groups increasingly monopolized the "population issue" in public discussions. The conclusion of the analysis was that there was a need for increasing support for those families which undertook having children (Monigl 1990a, 72). Two alternative policies were formulated: one would have raised the flat-rate child support (GYES) of the first three years and the other would have introduced a sick-pay type support (a percentage of the salary, called GYED). The document acknowledged that the first type of assistance was more helpful to the "less educated," while the other assisted the better-educated and better-paid. The latter version was chosen for its "better impact on population development." Thus by the mid 1980s anti-natalist discourses had become indirectly institutionalized, although solidarity with families with large numbers of children continued to be maintained.

2.5.5. A "ferry country" between "East" and "West." Qualitative discourses in the 1990s.

In the 1990s Hungarian discourses experienced dramatic changes. On the one hand, there appeared some anti-nationalist and liberal ideas about fertility and reproduction which consciously referred to the "liberating" elements of "Western" discourses and the need to follow the "developed West." These statements on the reproductive rights of women have become part of a local, domestic, so-called "urban" and "liberal" discourse, which is intellectually opposed to pro-natalist intervention (Melegh 1999c). The second serious change is the "welfare exclusion" which is directed against the lower classes on the basis of ethnicity or race and which, in the sphere of fertility, adopts some downright anti-natalist elements.

These later attempts are quite visible in the debate on the "quality" of the population in answers given to the general questionnaire issued to intellectuals by the Demographic Research Institute in 1998 (Melegh 1999d, 206–07, 256, 288). Arguments were made for controlling the birth of so called "strategic" children—allegedly conceived for the additional family support they would bring and possessing poorer "quality." Even the fear of being "flooded" appears, illustrating the change in the direction of stigmatization and the invention of a too fertile lower class just as in the "Western" perspective analyzed above. In pre-war and in early state-socialist Hungary the "danger" was not the flood of the poor-quality lower class, but "colonization" from above or the heresy of not performing one's "national duty." After the interim period of late state socialism the idea of general pro-natalism was transformed into a selective pro-natalism:

> [If the trend] continues then in half a century the ethnic structure of the Carpathian basin will undergo the most thorough transformation ever observed in the last 1100 years, and in the Carpathian Basin the Magyar population will be replaced by a frugal but life-adoring and fertile Gypsy population that today is living in the greatest misery (Melegh 1999d, 206, translated by A. M.).

But these anti-lower class, anti-Roma feelings are apparent not only in intellectual discourses. They are also visible in changes to the family-support system. For some years now the real value of the universally available family allowance has decreased, while the middle classes producing "quality" children have received relatively great tax exemptions for raising children. The related public discourse is more and more about supporting those who "work in an orderly manner." Or, as the president of the then ruling party FIDESZ declared in early 2001:

> The greatest problem is that children are mainly born not where the conditions for bringing them up in a decent material, moral, cultural or intellectual manner are given or can be guaranteed with some help from the state, but in such families where these conditions are missing and cannot even be established due to the state of the family. Thus childbearing should be promoted in those families where the upbringing of healthy personalities can be expected, who, twenty years on, will be able to carry burdens of the country (cited in Zoltán Kovács, Élet és Irodalom, 2001 no. 6. translated by A. M.).

At the same time support for the Roma population (sharply distinguished from the "Hungarian" group) was questioned and concrete measures were taken to link the support to "schooling" and other "integrative" steps. These policies, in the context of heavily "xenophobic" attitudes in the Hungarian population, are clearly directed against the lower classes on an ethnic basis and aim at regulating such groups while supporting "quality" reproduction (Fábián 1998).

Hungary is thus witnessing the emergence of a new type of discourse, or a mixture of "Eastern" and "Western" discourses on a "quality" basis (Krémer 2001). This new "double" or "border" discourse, which distinguishes social groups in the name of "quality population growth," combines anti- and pro-natalist elements and as a result different biopolitical selections and controls.

Such a combination of discourses—one based on the idea of inferiority to the "West" and the need to support "quality" reproduction in order to achieve a better position in the global world, and the other aiming at the reduction of the size of "problematic" groups—is not only rigid and harsh but also shows a new positioning on the East–West slope. This perspective combines a need to move upwards and a downward gaze on the civilizational slope, finding "Eastern" elements inside and outside the country which are to be excluded or controlled "from above." It seems that this new positioning is an answer to the paradox of racism raised at the beginning of this chapter. To show the internal mechanism of this new positioning let us now turn to a recent scandal concerning some Roma families which perfectly shows the discursive East–West game in Hungary as it undergoes a thorough "Westernization."

2.6. The seaweed[7]

A few years ago some Roma families were forced out of their own houses by the local government, based on the allegations that the houses could collapse. The families moved into a community house in a settlement called Zámoly, one of the booming areas of the country in terms of foreign investment. A year later they had to leave under pressure from the local mayor and they asked for direct assistance to build proper homes. There was no satisfactory solution and the residence became a source of local and later national outrage, which led to physical violence, including the murder of a young man who had threatened the Roma families. In July 2000, under the supervision of a Roma activist called Krasznai, some of the Roma families left for France to ask for political asylum on the basis of persecution and lack of protection by the Hungarian authorities. Krasznai was determined "to draw the attention of Europe to what is happening in Hungary" (Krasznai 2000, 6).

Soon after the decision of the French Office for the Protection of Refugees and Stateless people (OFPRA, March 8, 2001) on February 23, 2001, the well-known British security journal *Jane's Intelligence Digest* published an article on "The New Russian Offensive," claiming that Russians under the presidency of Vladimir Putin had tried to interfere in the affairs of soon-to-be EU members. Among other accusations the periodical declared:

> And if surreptitious acquisition of industrial influence or illicit deployment of surveillance hardware were not enough, we have it on good intelligence community authority that recent events surrounding the Hague and the Zámoly Roma of Hungary has also been to a large extent engineered by Russian operatives. Members of the gypsy community of Zámoly appear to have been encouraged to plead persecution and violation of human rights before EU bodies

> and even to request political asylum so as to make Hungary look much worse than it is during the crucial EU accession negotiations which are currently taking place. This perhaps is one of the most damaging methods employed by Moscow of late, one that was tried in the aspirant Czech Republic first and subsequently transplanted to Hungary (*www.janes.com/security/regional_security/news/jid/jid010226_1_n.shtml* – 37k, accessed August 30, 2001, The new Russian offensive).

The reasons behind this text are of course hidden, but certain circumstances are rather clear. As we learn from the deputy prime minister of the Czech Republic, Pavel Rychetsky, in 2000 the British Home Secretary, Jack Straw, asked the Czech authorities to investigate the "forces behind the exodus" (reported by the Hungarian daily *Népszabadság*, Ki szervezi a romák kitelepülését? A prágai kormány egy müncheni központot sejt a háttérben, 08/14/2001 [Who is organizing the dislocation of the Romas? The Government of Prague is suspecting a Munich Center in the background]). Thus on behalf of the British government and presumably its secret services, there was a deliberate attempt to find those taking impoverished Czech Roma families into Britain. In all probability then this investigation was extended to Hungary when the above group of people left for France. The timing of the publication could be accidental or it is possible that that amount of time was needed to complete the investigation. But there may be an alternative reading of the facts, according to which the article was a warning to the relevant French authorities not to grant political asylum to people being manipulated by the Russian secret services. This was later clearly claimed in a follow-up article, which presented the case in the interpretative framework of a Russian-Israeli-French communist plot:

> What is interesting, however, is that the political patron of the Zámoly group in Paris and Strasbourg, is the French Communist Party, which according to credible military intelligence authorities is known to have had strong associations with the KGB in the past. Add to this the information that the Zámoly group appears to have been financed by sources from Israel, which with the recent influx of Russian émigrés is known to be highly penetrated by foreign intelligence, and the story takes on a new dimension (*www.janes.com/secu-*

rity/regional_security/news/jid/jid010309_1_n.shtml. accessed August 30, 2001, Questions in Budapest – Jane's Security News).

This article was later published, with additional comments, in a Hungarian newspaper close to the current government (*Magyar Nemzet*, March 3, 2001). It was commented on by Ervin Demeter, the minister for security affairs, in a public TV news program the next day. In this he indirectly supported the claims of JID, a fact that was later widely commented on in the Hungarian and some international press organs. One week later JID seemed surprised by the interest it had aroused:

> Since we began publishing in 1938, it has been Intelligence Digest's mission to investigate and bring to light important issues in security and intelligence. Many of our articles have attracted attention from the international media and from governments. Rarely, however, has one issue provoked national interest on the scale we have witnessed in Hungary this week (*www.janes.com/security/regional_security/news/jid/jid010309_1_n.shtml.* accessed August 30, 2001, Questions in Budapest – Jane's Security News.)

This story perfectly illustrates how racism is linked to different positionings on the East–West slope, lending valuable insights into the mechanisms of population discourses embedded in current East–West discourses. Let us first examine the active role of the "Western side" in the press scandal.

From a "Western" perspective, the most probable meaning of the whole event is that JID, a British intelligence periodical, tried to manipulate the relevant French authorities by implicitly arguing that the case of the Hungarian Roma families was not a refugee issue, but a foreign-service operation involving French communists. The reason for this warning could be that in the late 1990s Roma families from Central European countries asked for asylum—for instance in Britain—in greater numbers and the British authorities were afraid of a precedent in the granting of refugee status, which might then be used against the British state's control of asylum seekers. This further raised the general issue of how persecuted people coming from politically safe countries are treated, having free entry for a limited period into EU countries such as France or the United Kingdom.

The fear of Roma groups reveals an anxiety regarding poor, uneducated refugees within the EU. As we have seen above, the fact that the European Union is losing its relative position in terms of population figures has been understood as an incentive for immigration. The case described above is in line with the biopolitical considerations discussed earlier, since the quality of the immigrants is the main problem. Roma families are feared to be less "able" to integrate and thus immigration authorities do their best to stop them before entering the country in question.

This anxiety also appeared in the acts of the British immigration officers who were transferred to Prague airport to check people flying to London. The main criterion here was skin color; a Roma journalist, claiming the same purpose of travel and the same financial background as her colleague, was not allowed to board the plane, while the "white" journalist was given a green light (reported by the Hungarian daily *Népszabadság*, Nem engedték utazni a roma újságírót. July 27, 2001). It may be supposed then, in the case of JID, that the British authorities were truly afraid that a positive response to asylum seekers' requests might start a new wave of "unwelcome" political refugees.

Besides the immediate concern of "low quality" immigrants, the investigation fits very well into an Orientalist mythological discursive framework in which "Eastern" elements conspire against the "West" or Central European countries. The interesting point is that all the elements mentioned can be decoded as being "Oriental": the Russians, Jews (in the Middle East), Roma. The alleged Israeli connection is a perfect example of 19th century Orientalism, which treated Middle-Eastern Jews in the same manner as Arabs, considering them also Semites (Said 1978, 140–48, 232–35). At the same time this can also been seen as a reminder of a Nazi image of enemies, namely Jews, (Russian) Communists and the Roma.

The French connection is also revealing. The claim that the whole operation was aimed against the EU membership of Hungary could be partly true. But in all probability the actors were not employed by the Russian secret service, but came from the French left. Fear of cheap labor and of a country promoting wild and extreme liberal capitalism makes most of the left-wing parties within the EU extremely suspicious of "Eastern" barbarians who might be used as a Trojan horse of the European right wing.

The Hungarian reaction also illuminates some important discursive mechanisms of the East–West slope (Bíró 2001). First of all the overtly anti-Roma propaganda in the right-wing Hungarian press has been effective because the Roma families were seen to have crossed a border closed to them. They went to a region, the "West," where the whole country desired to go on a civilizational basis, and this "careless" move and the consequent blame on Hungary have brought racist attitudes to the surface. The Roma are seen as endangering Europeanization and as probably being too "Eastern" to participate in that process. This is emblematically shown by a current joke about the Zámoly Roma families: "The Gypsies have come home. Why? Because they got work permits." The joke reveals a normative image of the "West" as a region where everybody has to work. Since the Roma are not capable of this and seek only money, they have to come home so as not to take the place of "white" Hungarians.

A normative image of the "West" also emerges from the reaction of the Roma, who think that the "West" offers them a much-denied dignity. This view is shared by the Hungarian liberal intelligentsia, who first blamed the Hungarian government for the whole affair, claiming that Ervin Demeter, the minister for security affairs had arranged for the article to be written during a visit to Britain. They argue that such stupid accusations could not possibly come from the "normal" West. In addition some 30 representative intellectuals wrote a letter thanking the French government (not the OFPRA) for applying the principles of human rights and accusing the Hungarian government of risking the EU membership of the country by not doing enough for the Roma minority. This idealization of the "West" was so obvious that one of the intellectuals withdrew his support and later published an excellent analysis of the whole affair (Tamás 2001). It is worth mentioning that the nationalist government also saw domestic political forces at work behind the events and accused the socialists and liberals of bribing the Roma families to return.

While the above reactions reveal the "West" as a clear norm to be followed in the "East," the reaction of the then Hungarian government and the blithe repetition of the accusations of JID show a positioning at a lower point of the slope. First of all there is the feeling of inferiority, which seeks scapegoats in the stressful process of joining the "West" and its institutions. Hungary is becoming deeply "European" or, to put it better, a "kidnapped West" and can therefore be pushed out of its proper place only by "alien" elements. (Kundera 1984). Secret services, communists and Jews once again are playing games with a small "European" nation. Such a voice speaks from an inferior position, trying to rely on European white racism which, paradoxically, can later be used against countries trying to make their way into the European Union.

This nationalist positioning on the slope is opposed to the perspective of "Westerner" East European liberals, who, as in the argument of the Hungarian liberal politician cited at the beginning of this chapter, would like to get rid of the "Eastern" seaweed of local racism. Altogether, the above story reveals several East–West exclusions: the Hungarian exclusion of Roma citizens; the Hungarian government's exclusion of liberals, Russians and Jews; the British secret service and immigration officers' exclusion of Eastern European Roma, Eastern Europeans in general, communists and Orientals; the French left's exclusion of East Europeans. And these pieces of seaweed add up to a meaningful story only in the form of a discursive web of the East–West slope. This discursive framework helps to bring biopolitical racism to life again and again and thus cannot be separated from the issue of Eastern European difference. This is a complex web, a kind of an epistemological mud, which sucks everything and everybody into itself. It reveals the working of the power arrangements of the "Eastern enlargement," or "Westernization," which *per se* leads to the rise of "Eastern" racism. In this French farce all the roles are interchanged and the real sins are hidden by a circle of false accusations. The Roma leave one prejudiced country for another in order to draw attention to their problem, "Western" racists are not seen as such by "Eastern" anti-racists, who write a supporting letter to the representatives of "Europe" as the area of human rights. "Western" racism is offered to "Eastern" nationalists, who, as a result of humiliation and their own "instincts", happily grasp the opportunity, only to be punished later for these crimes. Nothing is definite and everything is hidden. Only the faces of the victims are clear.

NOTES

1 Although this study does not deal with professional questions pertinent to the theory of demographic transition, it does not mean to argue against the "professional" strength of the theory, which has been demonstrated on occasion (Hablicsek 1996, 375–80). On the other hand it is important to draw attention to the significant professional and historical demographic critique of the theory (Szreter 1993; van de Kaa, 1996) and to the fact that over the past fifty years the theory has functioned as more than mere "familiarization" and we should not exclude "self-fulfilling" elements.

2 On the issue of Western perspectives see also Greenhalgh 1996, 36–39. The linkage between the lower classes and the Third World can also be found in the texts of Malthus himself, as Caldwell points out referring to the historian S. Ambirajan (Caldwell 1998, 680–81, 683).

3 It is important to note the overtly sexual connotations. For the link between sexuality, racism and colonization see the following works: Williams-Chrisman 1994, 1; Stoler, 1995, 2000.

4 This analysis is partly based on a study written jointly with a colleague (Melegh and Őri 2003).

5 The use of the term "populist" is rather controversial in the case of "népi" writers and intellectuals. It is misleading as it evokes demagogy and short-term political interests. Here it is used for a movement which wanted to "discover" the Hungarian countryside and mobilize the population for the cause of the "peasants" and those in the lower groups of the nation. They share some characteristics with the Russian "narodnik" movement. No exact term can be found in English.

6 For the term of strategic field of opportunity see: Foucault 1972, 64–70.

7 The Hungarian analysis of this case first appeared in the daily *Népszabadság* and in the Hungarian journal Replika (Melegh 2001, 2001c). Since then József Böröcz has also published a profound analysis of the letter written by Hungarian intellectuals to the French government (Böröcz 2005).

CHAPTER 3

Floating East. Eastern and Central Europe on the map of global institutional actors

3.1. Globalization and the East–West dichotomy[1]

In previous chapters we have seen how, during the late 1970s and early 1980s, discourses on Eastern Europe changed radically. From a discourse on competing modernizations and a global modernization scale we have arrived at an era in which quantitative progress reports have been replaced by a stress on qualitative, regional differences. As the previous chapters showed, after a break of 40 years Eastern and other non-Western Europes (Central etc.) have been "reinvented" in terms of a non-ideological civilizational difference in public and scholarly discourses. The question remains to what extent this "reinvention" has been based on the discursive structures of the pre-war modern-colonial period, to what extent these regional maps still carry traces of the cold-war period and to what extent they have been reconfigured in the era of globalization. More precisely, how has the East–West dichotomy or the East–West civilizational slope which emerged in the 18th century been (re)configured in the era of globalization: how have "Western" and "Eastern" actors woven themselves onto it? This is not just an analysis of geo-cultural mapping but also an attempt to define the discursive order of the East–West slope and to understand its "paradoxical" consequences.

After investigating the functioning of the slope in the framework of biopolitics, population discourses and racism, in this chapter I will analyze the cultural and spatial understanding of corporate and non-corporate global actors as these visions appear on the websites of transnational corporations, global foundations or in the texts of major newspapers such as the Financial Times or the New York Times. Specifically, I will investigate the generation of spatial, geocultural categories with regard to Eastern Europe, the position of Eastern Europe within the presented global order and the inner divisions within this region. I will analyze texts, tables, logos and images presented in printed hypertext form along with some analysis of the related (materialized) institutional arrangements. At the end of the chapter I will briefly consider the "Western" and "Eastern" perspectives on the new/old global civilizational slope with regard to Hungarian public debates on the support of Hungarian minorities. I will also consider the East European campaigns for the "Eastern" enlargement of the European Union. This will further crystallize our understanding of discursive structures and the East European perspectives developed in this framework.

3.2. Homogeneity and heterogeneity

The concept of globalization suggests that the world is becoming unified and previously existing large geocultural categories and exclusions are losing their legitimacy. Nonetheless, the scholarly literature on globalization is divided about the geocultural consequences of globalization. The main dividing line is not the homogenization-versus-multiculturalism dispute, since the authors concerned all speak about a fragmentation of earlier "traditional identities" or "imagined communities." According to the adherents of "homogenization", globalization involves the gradual elimination of national and regional-cultural differences and entities and the rise of uniform global cultural spheres (Berger 1997, Sklair 1999, Karnoouh 1993).[2] In contrast with the homogenization argument there are claims that globalization leads to a multiplication of differences and that we are increasingly caught up in a very complex web of transnational cultural-identity projects and borderlines, in which territorial location is becoming increasingly irrelevant (Appadurai 1996, Beck 2000, Lepenies 1996, Bauman 1996). But, revealingly, some argue that the seemingly different consequences of postmodernity and globalization are linked to each other either in terms of total emptiness or that "difference" simply does not matter and therefore can flourish (Karnoouh 1993). According to others, the conflicting homogenization projects themselves lead to hybridization and the confusion of previous cultural divisions (Kovács J. M. 1999, 1999a, 2002; Sklair 1999). Sklair openly argues that due to hybridization even the East–West dichotomy is fading away:

> Ethnic and cultural fragmentation and modernist homogenization are not two arguments, two opposing views of what is happening in the world today, but two constitutive trends of global reality. The dualist centralized world of the double East–West hegemony is fragmenting, politically, and culturally, but the homogeneity of capitalism remains as intact and as systematic as ever. While not all would agree either that capitalism remains intact and systematic or that it is, in fact, the framework of globalization, the fragmentation of "the double East–West hegemony" is beyond doubt. Ideas such as hybridization and realization have been proposed in the effort to try to conceptualize what happens when people and items from different (sometimes, but not always, dominant and subordinate) cultures interact (Sklair 1999, 148).

The real opposition to the above groups comes from those who argue that globalization leads to the re-emergence of "ancient" general dividing lines. These "fundamentalist" authors claim that cultural homogenization merely hides the "inherent" differences or even the dynamic of globalization, often understood mainly as Westernization. This leads to the emergence of anti-Western ideologies and/or the revitalization of civilizational character—Samuel Huntington being a prime representative of such "essentialism" (Huntington 1996, 56–78):

> The argument now that the spread of pop culture and consumer goods around the world represents the triumph of Western civilization trivializes Western culture. The essence of Western civilization is the Magna Carta not the Magna Mac. The fact that non-Westerners may bite into the latter has no implication for their accepting the former. It also has no implication for their attitudes toward the West. Somewhere in the Middle East a half-dozen young men could well be dressed in jeans, drinking Coke, listening to rap, and, between their bows to Mecca, putting together a bomb to blow up an American airliner (Huntington 1996, 58).

It is important to note that the these types of Orientalist, essentialist claims show an amazing similarity to the debate on the re-emergence of concepts such as Central Europe, analyzed in chapter I. The main argument of the debate on Central Europe was that due to historical changes "Europe ... is regaining its own real face" (Brezinski 1989, 83), or that, in the words of Milan Kundera, Central Europe as a "kidnapped West" (compared to the "real East") is returning to its natural sphere (Kundera 1984). It is therefore no surprise that in the view of people such as Václav Havel global civilization is only a "thin veneer" which covers the "immense variety of cultures" (cited in Huntington 1996, 57).

Thus it seems that scholarly discourses on the geocultural impact of globalization are ambiguous and the break-up of large "traditional" categories is as much predicted as the re-emergence of "fundamental" differences. The idea of globalization invokes the idea of border crossing as well as the idea of erecting and defending walls. But let us now turn to non-scholarly discourses of the globalization era in order to see how, if at all, this ambiguity appears there and how it is related to the functioning of the East–West slope as a major cognitive structure.

3.3. Maps of global actors

3.3.1. Methodological remarks

Three types of global actors will be analyzed below with special regard to the mapping of Eastern Europe: seventeen transnational corporations at the top of the *Fortune 500* list in 2000 and investing heavily in Eastern Europe,[3] eight global foundations and development banks[4] and two international newspapers, The *New York Times* (Melegh 1999) and the *Financial Times.* These are important not only in the sense of being powerful agents, but, as we will see below, also in their capacity to delineate the "borders" of different regions in the different discourses. They not only utilize different cognitive patterns but in the discourses analyzed they also appear as "signifiers" or "boundary markers" of geocultural categories. If one company appears in one area it might mean its "Westernization"; conversely the project of a development bank or charity organization in a certain country might mean the "Easternness" of the area (Melegh 1999).

Rules of the spatial understanding of different organizations can be detected directly from the spatial categories of these websites, and from shorter texts and narratives produced on the different regions. In both cases the interrelationship (hierarchies) between the categories and the texts (headlines, themes and project items, mission statements) are the most important, since the meaning of these units of texts on different regions is interpreted with regard to each other. It is in this way that we establish mental maps and ideas of the international order. In turn, the various orders reveal different discourses producing specific structures of statements. This is always an interactive game; to grasp the meaning of the different categories we need to have ideas about the order of categories, and orders can only be revealed through statements. This ambiguous game of tennis, much criticized by linguists, is the only way to perform a discourse analysis, in which both the statement as a unit of analysis and the discursive rules are functional to, or dependent on, each other (Foucault 1972, 21–134). The ambiguity is increased by the fact that several different discourses may appear on the websites or in the textual world of individual institutions.

3.3.2. Non-territorial versus territorial understanding

As we could see above, deterritorialization, the elimination of regional categories, is supposed to be one of the characteristics of our age. The tendency toward deterritorialization appears in different ways in the mental worlds of global actors and seems to be linked to different discourses.

First of all, in the "international" sections of their websites, global actors generally identify themselves as having no real location in the world. In most cases they operate with the image or the logo of the globe, which may rotate. If the globe does not move, it is generally spread out with the Americas on the left and the other continents on the right (e.g. Philip Morris-KFI, Procter & Gamble, Ford Foundation, CIPE). This image is often coupled with the pictures of people of different colors or different flags, which appear side by side, or somehow connected. Connection or interdependence can be suggested by outstretched hands (Johnson & Johnson), telephones (SBC) or reflected images of bank notes (Citibank).

This image of being spread throughout the world and "connecting" the world is also often suggested not only by the image of a borderless globe, but also through the idea of universal products. In this rather distinct type of website maps, globes or other nation-state territorial representations are generally avoided, and unification is accomplished by the product or groups of products (GE, GTE, Coca-Cola, Johnson & Johnson, Xerox). Xerox, for instance, puts this idea of crossing the spatial boundaries by the products and services of the company as follows: "So whether you are in Taepei or Toronto Xerox quality products and services are available from a sales office near you."

This idea of global reach is supported by the organization of some websites which guide the viewer according to branches of industry, or different types of products. General Electric, for instance, offers an e-business service which provides assistance in finding the nearest subnational location where the product can be bought, illustrating the cherished binary opposition of global versus local. Global foundations may also have universal products uniting the world. The best example is the Rockefeller Foundation with its slogan of "The Well-being of Mankind Throughout the World." A program structure such as "Creativity and Culture," "Food Security," "Health Equity," "Global Inclusion" etc. only vaguely refers to regional offices, which are presented as local offices without any qualitative organizatory function in terms of projects (products). The Ford Foundation may be an intermediary type; its project structure and global offices with separate missions and projects reveal no spatial structure.

In the case of corporations this idea of a universal market organized by the institutional actor and its products is compatible with an understanding of the world as group of nation states not organized into regional units. This opposition of global versus nation state, which is one of the main tenets of globalization literature, is most clearly demonstrated by the websites of General Electric, Coca Cola, Xerox and by the *Financial Times,* which regularly conducts business surveys by nation states. The websites of these corporations show the dichotomy of company versus nation state, with the company as a homogenizer or as an organization that defines or contains the nation state. The Coca-Cola company actually names countries with its product: "Coca-Cola Argentina," "Coca-Cola Belgium," "Coca-Cola Denmark" etc.

The same hierarchy can be observed in a commercial of General Electric. In the early 1990s this was made to publicize (mainly to the shareholders) the acquisition of Tungsram, a Hungarian company known worldwide. In this commercial GE was the active agent, presented as bringing "freedom" and "light" into a country looking for new hope.[5] In addition to the website and the commercial, this overriding logic was further bolstered in a talk given by Jack Welch, the previous chairman of the General Electric, who gave a talk at a business breakfast in Budapest in July, 1999. In his talk he welcomed not only Tungsram (the Hungarian competitor bought by GE as early as 1990) but Hungary itself to the "GE family":

> So we are in fact trying to expand more. We have built an infrastructure of talent that needs more business so that they can grow and flourish. And that is frankly our objective here, to make Hungary a more significant part of the GE family (transcript, by courtesy of the American-Hungarian Chamber of Commerce and Eric Kaldor).

In the same lecture he went even further, assuming a cultural mission for General Electric with regard to nation states and countries. He even assumed a role of providing "voice and dignity"—a perfect colonial-type example of cultural and political activity in "passive" lands: "People say to us, "How can you bring the GE culture to China, to India, to Hungary, anywhere?" All the GE culture is giving voice and dignity to everyone. That works in any country. Who doesn't want voice and dignity?" (transcript, by courtesy of the American-Hungarian Chamber of Commerce and Eric Kaldor).

In the global image based on the idea of universal products and companies we can find an idea of domination through cultural mission. This sense of domination increases the likelihood that the logic of expansion inherent in the idea of a world without borders links the above statements to colonial and postcolonial discourses.

This linkage is even more obvious in the self-presentation of AES, "the Global Power Company." In this case straightforward Orientalism is mixed with a kind of global jugglery criss-crossing regional categories. Here we see the setting up of subsidiary companies linking and crosscutting countries and places in an arbitrary fashion. A clear Orientalist reference structure appears in the naming of sub-companies with Oriental and—from the point of view of energy production irrelevant—"exotic" names ("silk road," "sirocco," "oasis" etc.), and in the dichotomy of economic rationality versus Oriental luxury and exoticism as a basic tenet of Orientalist structures. In contrast to those in the "weird" areas of Kazakhstan, Georgia, Hungary, Turkey and Egypt, the subsidiaries based in the U.S. and Western Europe are named "Electric," "Enterprise," "Endeavor," that is, the titles are linked to rational business and progress. The names' field of reference thus collects crucial elements of cognitive structures understood as Orientalist or postcolonial, providing further proof that border crossing is linked to a modern/colonial understanding of the world.

3.3.3. Regional Categories

Most of the global actors use regional or supra-national categories in the description of their activity or institution. In Mignolo's words, the "denotative and territorial epistemology" is especially dominant in the case of global foundations which not only live in this epistemé, but also actively construct the world in this mode (Mignolo 2000, 26). These qualitative regional classifications also reveal distinct discursive patterns with regard to spatial understanding and Eastern Europe.

In the established categorizations the main difference is that between geographical and geo-cultural classifications. In the former, names of continents, such as North America, South America and Europe, are used without any cultural-political dividing lines like Latin America, Eastern Europe. In the latter such borders are drawn. The latter, geo-cultural, type can further be divided into two types according to the appearance of Eastern Europe as a separate category.

3.3.4. "Expansion" or geographic categories

The use of geographical terms seems to be the most neutral (least qualitative, least cultural) method of presenting the world order. But, as Said has shown, geography is certainly a "carrier" of Orientalist, postcolonial patterns (Said 1978, 216–220). It is then hardly a coincidence that the idea of home versus expansion appears on websites relying on geographical terms. Exxon sets signs specifying the headquarters, regional centers, technological sites and major manufacturing plants, which guide the viewer to where the company is at "home." This localization is strengthened by showing certain technological areas in a different color, that is to say, as an area under Exxon influence ("Tunisia," "Central Asia," "Greenland" etc.). The same expansionism appears in the case of the communication company SBC, which uses as a slogan for international activity (SBC International Operations) the following expressions: "expansion, global reach, investments" (SBC). In addition to these evocative terms the picture of "racially" non-white people may also indicate an equation between "foreignness" and difference in color. Thus, the idea of unification apart, geography could easily be a container of preexisting colonial and military discourses.

3.3.5. "Eastern Enlargement" and the advent of a Third World status: geocultural and geopolitical categories

When political and cultural regional categories are used some other spatial discourses can be observed, in particular "Eastern enlargement" and, in Karnoouh's words, the "advent of a Third World Status" ("tiers-mondialisation") (Antohi 2000; Böröcz 2000, 2001; Karnoouh 2003). This logic appears mainly on the maps of non-corporate organizations. In these cases Europe, Eastern Europe or parts of Eastern Europe are linked to areas of the Middle East, Asia or Africa.

On the one hand business corporations may divide the world into equal portions, establishing regions with more or less equally large territories and equal numbers of people. Given this approach, Europe, with its population of 660 million is too small and therefore needs an additional background. Alternatively, it can be hypothesized that African and Middle Eastern markets are so small that they cannot make up a separate category, and therefore certain territories are notionally attached to Europe instead of actually extending Europe in space. Yet again, Africa can be subsumed under the heading of Europe on the assumption of an international order, in which the world is divided into major global centers, with Africa and the Middle East coming under the control of Europe (Hewlett-Packard, Procter & Gamble).

On the other hand non-corporate actors relying on the category of Europe certainly do not equalize regions in terms of size as they extend Europe toward Asia. At first sight this logic is definitely non-Orientalist since an "undivided" Europe is linked to Asia or Central Asia. But it is worth noting that Europe in this case means only Eastern and South Eastern Europe while the other parts are excluded (with the sole exception of Ireland in the case of USAID). The World Bank, for instance, divides the world into regions in such a way that some ("Western") countries (white spots on the map) have no name, and this structure may be understood as centers of the bank's activity. Chemonics also focuses on "Central and Eastern Europe" and "Russia," specifying no project in other countries. These extensions signify an "Eastern enlargement" of former Eastern Europe, including Turkey, or simply a division of the former Eastern bloc into two areas: "European" and "Asian."

The "Eastern enlargement" or the incorporation of Eastern Europe into a wider region also appears in the case of institutions operating with the category of Central or Eastern Europe (Philip Morris), although more stick to a version of the cold-war idea of Eastern Europe, regularly supplemented by Turkey. The main tendency within this group of actors is to divide the Eastern bloc into two or three areas. The most common categorization is that of Central and Eastern Europe (Citibank), in which the latter region may or may not include the former Soviet territories. Thus in some cases we have a dichotomy of Central Europe versus a Commonwealth of Independent States (AIG), the opposition between Central and Eastern Europe and the Newly Independent States (CIPE) or the trichotomy of Central Europe versus Russia and Central Asia versus Southern and Eastern Europe and the Caucasus (EBRD). Johnson & Johnson removes Poland and Hungary from the category of Eastern Europe, placing them in "Europe." The crucial point here is a logic of dividing the Eastern Block and dividing it step by step, invoking the idea of a civilizational slope on which there exist a number of floating, indefinite borders. We can say that, in terms of visual and categorical representation, globalization has certainly not abolished the previous "denotative and territorial epistemologies" and instead rebuilds hierarchies and decomposes regions by a logic of floating, never fixed, borders.

3.4. On the slope

3.4.1.The thematic decomposition of Eastern Europe and the East–West slope

The thematic decomposition of Eastern Europe and the establishment of a descending slope can best be observed in the textual and project world of non-corporate global actors and international newspapers. This is accomplished by one major technique, the omission of certain themes in the more "Western" parts of the "East" and the appearance of new topics while moving toward the "East" or the bottom of the slope. This also means that countries or regions are not placed in eternal categories: their distance from the top sphere is changing.

There can be no doubt that thematically Eastern Europe is "othered" by global foundations and international newspapers. In their textual worlds it has the "bad" inheritance of a centrally-planned state-socialist system from which it has had to distance itself for the sake of a transition "into western-style market-led democracies with vibrant economies, open political systems, and a strong civil society" (USAID and The New York Times see: Melegh 1999). Nonetheless, although Eastern Europe has appeared on the global "developmental" map, in certain issues it is still separated from "truly" Third World countries. The former Eastern bloc is a target region with regard to democratization, market economy and some poverty issues, but among the projects and themes we do not find three related issues, "human capacity built through education and training", the "stabilization of world population and the protection of human health" and "nutrition" (USAID, World Bank). This shows that in the case of former Eastern Europe non-corporate actors see no need for doing the "basics," that is, intervening in elementary education and population reproduction, or protecting biopolitical balances between resources and population (Melegh 2002).

Not only is Eastern Europe as a whole positioned above "less developed" countries, but this descending scale is even operational within the region. At USAID, CIPE and the World Bank the projects for "Central European" Hungary are of a technical character. At the same time, Russia and the CIS region receives a large amount of aid for social stabilization, including humanitarian assistance, "learning Western values", establishing institutional frameworks and the rule of law and also, interestingly enough, funds for gender issues and anti-corruption campaigns. This shows that the link toward the "underdeveloped" world is much clearer in this latter case and thus Russia and the ex-Soviet countries are perceived further "down" the slope.

3.4.2. Liberal humanitarian utopia in the global scaling of the Financial Times

The above slope technique appears as a globalized format in the *Financial Times*, if we analyze the positioning of countries in the titles of country reports published in 2001 (See table below)

Country	Headline of country surveys in 2001	Analytical content
Luxembourg	Tiny land-locked state casts a global influence. A new monarch and a year of success for its blue-chip companies has given the EU's smallest state much to cheer about	Political stability, economic growth
Slovenia	Political stability gives economy a boost under the ruling LDS party, in power for most of the past decade, Slovenia continues to enjoy economic growth	Political stability, economic growth
Switzerland	Accolades fail to hide new uncertainties: As the corporate sector moves to keep pace with globalization, companies face the problem of how to keep in touch with Alpine roots	Ongoing globalization, some uncertainties.
Finland	High-tech haven braced for the slowdown: A strong economy, backed by strict fiscal discipline should see Finland through current difficulties	Economic problems to be solved
Sweden	Downbeat mood as telecoms sector falters. Although the economy is slowing, with jobless expected to rise, the country is not in a recession	Economic problems to be solved
Canada	Liberals strive to sharpen competitive edge	Economic problems to be solved
Germany	Economic slowdown will be a test for Schröders's nerve. The nation's economic prowess and greater political confidence have been undermined by slowing growth and rising unemployment	Economic problems to be solved, some political difficulties
Czech Republic	Heavy lifting puts a nation back on track. The next government will inherit a restructured economy, but further reform is still necessary	Economic problems to be solved, need for further reforms
Poland	Packed with promise and set for the polls. Although an ex-communist seems certain to win the elections, prospects remain bright	Economic problems to be solved, some political difficulties, further reform
Croatia	Problems of peace challenge uneasy alliance: Political and other pressures are making difficult demands on an untested system	Economic problems, political difficulties endanger the needed economic reform
Italy	Window of opportunity wide open: Silvio Berlusconi has the power to reform, but there are doubts about his willingness	Political difficulties endanger the needed economic reform
Montenegro	Free to reform – but not yet independent: A full break with Serbia is the president's wish, but a minority wants to retain links	Political difficulties endanger the needed economic reform
Greece	Challenges remain despite the reforms. Huge progress has been made with the economy, but the country's Olympian social goals mean it still has everything to work for	Political difficulties endanger the needed economic reform

Spain	Aznar strives for seat at EU's high table. The economy has been transformed recently but the government still has big issues to resolve before Spain can move from the fringes to the heart of Europe	Political difficulties which might harm movement toward the center of EU
Hungary	Politics drifts from centre: As Hungary makes its bid for membership of the European Union, moderation is in a rather short supply in its domestic politics	Political difficulties endanger movement toward the EU
Brazil	Energy crisis puts country in political spin. Power shortages have led to economic instability that many fear will not be resolved whoever gains the presidency next year	Political difficulties and severe economic problem
Latvia	Preparing for the EU. State targets stronger union with the west. Plans to join the European Union and Nato provide the momentum for the Baltic State's transition from Soviet rule	Movement into EU and political will in this transition
Lithuania	Preparing for the EU: Into Europe – with a new bridging role: Rafael Behr and Anthony Robinson on the Baltic nation's plans to join the EU and Nato – while staying good neighbors	Movement into EU, political will in this transition
Romania	Reform remains the key to a place in the sun. Severe distortions in the economy need to be removed if the country is to achieve its ambition of progressing towards EU membership	Ambitions to move into EU, severe economic problems and economic difficulties in the general reform process
Turkey	Time to face up to difficult economic and political choices: Procrastination over long overdue reform will condemn the EU candidate to further economic crises	Ambitions to move into EU, severe economic and political problems in the general reform process
China	The "Middle Kingdom" takes the world stage. Tough challenges lie ahead of China as it prepares itself for the final phase of transition to a market economy	It gets onto the map: severe economic and political problems in the general reform process
Russia	Movement if not momentum, in Moscow. The danger is that the centralizing power needed to achieve change carries the possibility of a restored authoritarianism	It is moving, severe political problems endanger the general economic reform
Egypt	Regime values stability above reform: The government's aversion to risk has stopped it from modernising institutions to adapt to the market economy	Lack of movement, severe political problems stop general economic reform
Nigeria	Treading water as the frustrations rise. With politicians under the pressure to spend their way out of the trouble before electioneering takes over, the opportunity to drive through reforms is narrowing	Lack of movement, severe political problems stop general economic reform

Kuwait	Ready to make the succession a success. With the country's current leaders unwell, Kuwaiti thoughts are reluctantly turning to the next generation	Succession, reluctant change in thinking
Kazakhstan	Geopolitics and oil focus the spotlight on Central Asia	Interest due to geopolitics and oil

The map of the *Financial Times* emerging from the headlines of country surveys published in 2001 reveals overlapping regions and regional borders. First of all, countries are mainly represented on the basis of two major issues: economic growth, or more precisely the establishment and the management of liberal markets, and the attitude of the political establishment to market economy and reforms. This is the general scale on which countries are measured in the full sense of Mannheim's liberal humanitarian utopia as introduced in chapter 1.

Surprisingly, on this scale it is not great powers such as Germany or Canada who have the best performance record but small countries like Luxembourg, "a tiny land-locked state" which "casts a global influence." In the same manner the paper praises Switzerland, Slovenia and partly Finland. This grouping raises the possibility that the ultimate civilizational achievement in this imaginative geography is the tranquil bourgeois-aristocratic life-style, which is free of the "dirt" of major industrial and world-dominating powers. We can call this the "Switzerland image," based on the well-known folklore-paradise imaginary of the affluent and "clean" "West."

The next group of countries contains Germany and Canada, which have some political and economic problems, but nevertheless bright prospects. It is important to note that these countries do not need to move on the scale, but only have a few "domestic," "local" problems. Interestingly, some countries, such as the Czech Republic and Poland, are very close to this club, but are restricted by the need for further reform (i.e. general change) and they have the shadow of the communist past hanging over them. Thus the border between the "West" and countries like Poland is a minor one.

The countries in the next large group have some substantial political difficulties in implementing large-scale reforms, or moving further up the slope. Here a more significant border is set up with the Southern and East European countries. These countries, including Hungary, Croatia and Montenegro, have an unstable polity and lack the will to make substantial political decisions to secure possible economic reforms. There is a sense of movement (pace of economic reform) which is certainly a "border" issue. The headline of the Spanish country survey is extremely revealing in this sense. The EU member and former colonial power Spain is trying to reach the "EU's high table" or the "heart of Europe" from the "fringes," but is unwilling to solve the "big issues." Spain is a college student to be educated by older and wiser fellows at the high table who are part of the establishment. That Spain is not in the heart of Europe may refer to sheer power but also suggests that the country is "truly" European. East European countries are very close to this group exemplified by the position of Hungary. In the imaginary of the *Financial Times* this group of countries shares the need for systematic reform.

An even stronger sense of border and descent on the slope emerges from the headlines for the Baltic countries. Here it is made clear that they are not part of the "West" or "Europe" and they are preparing for the EU. This theme is so strong in the case of the Baltic countries that the surveys on Latvia and Lithuania even carry the same title: "Preparing for the EU". Besides EU membership in NATO is also considered important, in addition to the issue of the "bad" neighbor and the past. The main topic is the will to cross this strong border, giving a sense of the need to move upwards on the slope.

On the map of the *Financial Times*, Romania and Turkey are also constructed around the major EU border (where application is mentioned), but in their case "ambitions" are detached from reality. There are "severe distortions" in the economy or overt "economic crises." The ambitions to move ahead are only vague aspirations due to a lack of the will to "face up to difficult" challenges. These countries may have to accept the idea of being separated from the EU and "Europe," as may China just as it appears on the "world stage" with very "tough challenges" in its transition to a market economy.

Russia almost falls into this group but possesses only movement without direction toward the "West," a market economy or the EU ("movement if not momentum in Moscow"). Europe as a destination is not mentioned and in the context of the headlines the movement may basically be away from the (communist) past while still maintaining the "possibility of a restored authoritarianism." Thus Russia may occupy a special position of her own on the map, but that position is definitely not in "Europe" or even on the way toward "Europe." On the basis of the thematic structure of the headline about Russia, she is very close to the hopeless inward-looking political standstill of Egypt and Nigeria with the sole but important difference of "movement". Egypt and Nigeria in turn seem to be at the bottom of the slope, which is invoked by the Orientalist topics of lack of movement and no change (Said 1978, 208, 241).

Interestingly, oil-producing countries are partly exempted from civilizational measurements, indicating that on a business map oil still represents a different geography and different perspectives. Both countries in our list, Kuwait and Kazakhstan, have succession problems and are not considered mature (highly Orientalist topics), but Kazakhstan's headline shows that oil in itself is enough for a country to find itself in the geopolitical "spotlight." This is a privilege of oil producers, often to their own disadvantage.

In conclusion, the map of the *Financial Times* presents several groups of countries descending step by step on a slope. Starting from global success, global impact and political stability, we arrive at a complete lack of adaptation to the market. This slope is not a smooth one but is divided by several minor and major borders. In other words, countries and spaces are understood as accumulating problems with regard to the implementation of liberal market ideas. Conversely, this also means that the borders and the differing needs for reform are not fixed and, as the case of Poland shows, the borders can be extremely fluid. This danger of floating borders seems extremely acute in the case of former Eastern Europe.

3.5. Positioning on the slope. The discursive order of the East–West slope in the era of globalization

In order to understand the mapping techniques in the process of globalization we must look at how agents further down the civilizational slope position themselves and how this positioning is related to the idea of floating borders. For this purpose we can use some texts that appeared in a public debate on Hungarian "status law" and also on EU accession in 2003 before the referendum, mainly in Hungary but also with examples from other former Eastern-block countries. The two groups of texts are related since the so-called status law was a hasty piece of legislation intended to overcome some of the negative consequences of the emerging new EU border between Hungary and its non-EU neighbors in 2004.[6] Thus both groups of texts are related examples of positioning on the East–West slope.[7]

3.5.1. Under Western eyes. Perspectives of actors down the slope

The most important feeling down the slope is that the position of the country cannot be maintained and should be changed. Public speakers almost unanimously feel that their country or their local community has been displaced for a length of time. They express feelings of having been placed "in darkness," "under a historical curse" or even in some kind of "unreal" position, to which we must and will say farewell when we join the EU or when we "return to Europe," as local discourses would have it. This feeling of displacement is eloquently voiced in a speech of the Hungarian prime minister (1998–2002) made as part of a celebration of Hungarian statehood in 2001:

> Until now Europe has been truncated, in spite of the fact that there is no reason for her to be so. She has not accepted those freedom-loving, persecuted nations who have spilt so much blood defending her, regardless of the fact that they have been ready to enter for a long time. From now on our continent, Western and Central Europe, will be reunited in a spirit of freedom and responsibility. Hungarians will participate in this European unity, protecting their independence and preserving their national pride. Even at home, everybody will understand that the European spirit does not start where our freedom and independence end. What begins there is not Europe, but once again homelessness, no man's land (translated by A. M. Prime minister's speech, 20 August, 2001, *www.meh.hu/Kormany/Kormanyfo/2001/08/010820.htm*, accessed March 10, 2002).

The need for repositioning also appeared on the poster of the liberal Hungarian Free Democrats at another point of the political spectrum. In this pro-EU campaign the party wishes all a "Happy New Life in Europe!" (*www.szdsz.hu*, accessed March 15, 2003) On the other hand, an Alice-in-Wonderland metaphor by an anti-Semitic, anti-Europe far-right publicist suggests that Europe itself can take away our "reality." The title of his essay is "Magic Europe," referring to the magic castles that trick us and remove our "normal" dimensions in most of the amusement parks in Europe (Szőcs, 2003). This feeling of displacement, enchantment or marginalization "under Western eyes"[8] is sufficient to interpret the above positioning by means of the concept of coloniality, which presupposes "inauthentic" or "real" positions with regard to the "imperial center" (Mignolo 2000, 13; Aschroft 1989, 8–9, 90; Said 1978, 5–6, 21–22, 208; Erlmann 1999, chapter 3; Calinescu 1989). As I argued in chapter 1, the crucial point of postcolonial subordination is the understanding of local experience as "unworthy" or "unreal"—a view accepted by dominant local groups. Nonetheless, the reaction to this displacement is diverse and there are many different perspectives on the slope.

3.5.2. The "othering" of local society

This is a characteristic perspective from which certain intellectual and elite groups undertake some kind of *cultural mission* to change and "Europeanize" local populations and opposing local political groups, which are seen as being further down on the slope.[9] This mostly upward-looking perspective takes most of its elements from Western Orientalist patterns and often utilizes dichotomies of cleanliness versus dirt, rationality versus emotional irrationalism and "Europe" versus "Balkans."

The reference to the civilizing mission of the European Union is the main tenet of liberal and liberal-socialist political-intellectual groups in Hungary, who continuously argue that "Europe" brings "tolerance" and "rationality" into our not truly "European" country. In other words, they see a need to push the country upwards on the civilizational slope, a Sisyphean struggle in which they face nationalists and other "oriental," "irrational" and "corrupt" forces who block the upward movement on the slope with acts such as the status law. This reasoning is particularly clear in an essay by a Hungarian liberal journalist, who falls back on the classic Orientalist dichotomy of "rational" Europe and "irrational," "emotional" non-Europe as exemplified in nationalism:

> But we are talking about something else, namely about that deep dichotomy which characterizes the entire foreign policy of the conservative government. It is about the contradiction of reason and

> emotion, choices between East and West, tension between state and nation, all of which have not been successfully harmonized or integrated.
>
> Joining the European Union is plain rationality in itself. Rational arguments constrained into the framework of quotas, funds, norms and standards, by which we might become a rational and successful state.
>
> The sense of Hungarian national solidarity, and the strengthening of this, is the very stuff of emotion. It was no coincidence that János Martonyi, the foreign minister, recently said that for the person constantly looking for domestic gains in the status law, Hungarian nationhood is an esoteric and unintelligible concept. Following his interpretation one should be spiritually involved and possess those emotions on the basis of which one should feel the pain of Trianon or the fact that there is no Hungarian electoral majority in Marosvásárhely etc.[10] The status law could only have been born in this emotional burst. It has nothing to do with the formalized and rational mental world of the European Union (Újvári, 2001, translated by A. M.).

The upward-looking perspective and the idea of Europeanization not only prescribes the rejection of "Eastern" local nationalism, but also the inferiorization of other East European countries such as Romania, which in this perspective have a less legitimate claim to "European accoutrements": "Bucharest does not hesitate to utilize the opportunity, and she takes the costume of Euroconformism—although I do think that it would suit us much better" (Heiszler 2002, translated by A. M.).

This escape from the "East" can also lead to a complete ignorance of other East European countries. In the pro-EU campaign of April 2003 this was perfectly exemplified by maps in which Hungary appeared alone as joining EU and the other accessing countries were left in complete darkness. From time to time the local intelligentsia openly called for the help of the West—in their wording—"to colonize" the local population. This is eloquently shown by a Slovakian website introducing the country to Western business people in the late 1990s, in which self-presentation pioneers are invited to exploit the advantages of the "Wild East."

> Slovakia is the Western Edge of Wild East.
> In the eighteenth and nineteenth century pioneers from all over the world restlessly fought their way through in North America, aiming to the Wild West. Feel sorry that those days have gone? Don't worry, there is still Wild East and it begins, uhmm..., do you know where? Of course in Slovakia. (*http://www.slovak.sk/business/business.htm.* accessed January 10, 2005)

The same attitude appears, for example, in a pro-Nato and pro-war, but culturally alternative leftist weekly called Hungarian Orange, in which the editors repeatedly argued that instead of bargaining for more money with the EU during the accession talks, we should focus on civilizational issues. As they put it in their editorial on the EU accession agreement: "the signature of the prime minister on the Copenhagen [EU accession] document—perish compatriot heart—was a narrow bridge over a civilizational gulf" (*http://www.mancs.hu/legfrissebb.tdp?azon=0251aszerk1*, accessed March 16, 2003, translated by A. M.).

This missionary attitude is not merely part of an "intellectual chat." It appeared in the political campaign of the liberal Free Democrats in Hungary. The main message of this rather marginal party is that we should leave most of our "non-European" and "non human" characteristics behind and start a new life when entering the EU. The imperative of social and personal improvement within local society appeared in claims like: "Do not hate otherness! Do not beat children! Do not steal! Do not evade tax! Do not stigmatize with the word Gypsy or Jew! Do not drop litter!" And, most grotesquely: "Don't be nasty!" These "European" commandments are coupled with the claim that we should not support EU accession for the sake of material advantages, which is seen as improper "bargaining" with the civilizer.

3.5.3. Modernization and a "successful nation within Europe"

This is an alternative perspective which appears in the public statements of most of the parliamentary parties, but characteristically dominates the rhetoric of the socialist parties in particular. Sharing the upward-looking perspective on the slope, the modernizationists argue that by common effort we can gradually move up the slope: "catching up and gradual ascent." See, for instance, a speech of the Polish ex-communist president Kwasnevski, delivered in front of a meeting on Polish agrarian issues in 2000. Here he argues that EU assistance will lift Poland out of her "backwardness" and rural-urban division:

> Secondly, we have to utilize EU assistance—that provided today, and that of tomorrow, within the EU family—in the best way possible. This is an opportunity to overcome the backwardness and abolish the division into urban and rural Poland. The political and ideological discussions on whether Poland is an agricultural or an industrial country belong to history. They make no sense in the reality of the 21st century. Today, the decisive factor is a given country's overall potential, its creativity. This is measured in production and material resources, but also in the cultural, intellectual and civilization-related potential; in the drive for education, and an inclination for enterprise and innovativeness (*http://www.prezydent.pl/ser/en_index.php3?tem_ID=965&kategoria=Archive*, accessed January 10, 2005).

Although it shares the idealization of the EU, this discourse or this positioning avoids stigmatizing the local society, suggesting that local traits, such as creativity—or, in the campaign of the Hungarian socialists, "ingenuity" and "stamina"—may help the local nation in its "heroic" effort to move upwards.

This perspective characteristically does not look back and forget about the actors further down the slope. If speakers utilizing this perspective nonetheless recognize them, for instance in reaction to nationalist, anti-EU claims, then they argue that "Europe" will solve these issues because those countries can also be gradually pulled up (into "Europe"). In this view the Hungarian nation, for instance, may once again be united across the borders created by the partition of the Hungarian Kingdom after World War I. Nationalist grievances with neighbors can be solved within "Europe." Prior to the point of European integration proponents of modernization blithely exclude the "Eastern flood" of labor migrants coming from the neighboring countries in order to protect the Hungarian labor markets. That was actually one of the main criticisms levelled against the Romanian-Hungarian pact related to the status law, which granted special privileges to Romanian citizens (Hegyesi and Melegh 2003).

As a result of this non-civilizatory approach the modernizationist perspective prescribes an amazingly pragmatic and flexible approach to the European Union. It seems to portray European Union accession as the most authentic form of modernization, avoiding most of the conflicts and pitfalls of "failed" socialist modernization.

It is interesting that a version of this perspective can be found in the pro-EU letter of the Hungarian Conference of Catholic Bishops, which argued that Europe was a creation of Christianity. According to the authors of the public letter, joining the EU would offer Hungarians an opportunity to live in a more just and equal society. As a small nation within the framework of the European Union, Hungary would be able to do more for the world in general and for Hungarians living in and outside Hungary in particular (*http://www.kereszteny.hu/kurir/lapszemle.php?ID=2003-03-14&LID=859*, accessed March 16, 2003).

Another version of this positive modernizationist vision is the one which argues that we should go in for "more highly developed European" social and political arrangements, but that unfortunately the different local governments have done very little to defend unprivileged groups in this process and therefore the country is not prepared for EU accession. This grotesque criticism, which appears in the public statements of the Hungarian Communist party, is also found in the arguments of the right-wing—and far-right—opposition. This perspective maintains the positive image of Europe but it does so in an anti-capitalist and anti-globalisation language. The upward idealization is complicated by criticism, a mixture which leads to statements such as that Hungary will be part of the exploiting club, but unfortunately "will only get crumbs from the pooled profit concentrated in the more developed countries" (*http://www.munkaspart.hu/eu_mp.htm* accessed March 14, 2003). Stranger still, this reaction to EU accession (the text on the website of the Communist party) could be read while listening to the music of Vangelis written for the film 1492. This in itself shows tense cognitive structures being repositioned on the slope. It is worth noting that this tension also appears in the emerging new nationalism in Eastern Europe.

3.5.4. "Being already European" and nationalism as petty imperialism.

Eastern and Central European nationalism in the 20th century has always been a frustrated political movement. A sense of frustration, decline, struggle for acceptance and, most important, "survival" have been the major discursive drives behind this phenomenon with multiple faces. It seems that our idea of the slope, which allows the analysis of "Eastern" and "Western" developments as shared stories, is able to explain this movement and can possibly help reinterpret the cognitive constructs of nationalism at least for the 1990s, very much in line with Antohi's idea of "ethnic ontology," where there is a vertical move for the purpose of "emancipating ... [the nation] from the tyranny of symbolic geography" (Antohi 2001).

The main tenet of the emerging new nationalism is that, if not hindered by the conspiracy of "liberal-communist" groups, Eastern European nations can emerge as proper European nations and leave the "terror of history" behind (Antohi 2001). At first glance one of the slogans of these groups in Hungary, "Europe is our future, Hungary is our homeland," seems to have a great deal in common with the idea of "successful nation in Europe" described above, but in essence it has a completely different dynamism. The socialist-modernisationist view is that the national interest becomes irrelevant where a step upward or closer to the West can be taken. In contrast, the new nationalist groups (FIDESZ in Hungary) argue in a so-called "eurorealist" manner. For them the Europeanness of the country cannot be questioned and only historical misfortune prevented it from joining the European club for at least half a century. This mistake was not made not by the local nationalist groups, but by the conspiracy of the great powers (Jalta agreement at the end of World War II) and/or local non-Hungarian groups (Jews and liberals, but most importantly the "Eastern" Communists looking toward Russia). This externalization of local misfortunes is very clear in the 2004 pro-EU open letter of the Polish Catholic bishops, the representatives of a Church so deeply involved in the recreation of Polish nationalism and nationalist sense of mission during and after the state-socialist period

> A sense of fundamental justice does not allow us to forget that the breakthrough year of 1989, inspired by the desire for freedom, was born in the countries of Central and Eastern Europe on the basis of primarily religious motivation. It was this religiously motivated desire for freedom that became flesh in the Solidarity impulse in Poland and in its wake led to the dismantling of the Berlin Wall and subsequently also to the collapse of totalitarian regimes and made

possible the restoration of democracy in those countries of Europe which are currently becoming a part of the European Union. This experience of the states that have only recently shaken off the influence of atheist communism sensitises them especially acutely to all forms of wrongdoing, injustice, atheisation, and elimination of religious values.

The liberation from totalitarian regimes is for those nations a token of the justice of history. It confers upon them a special moral right for the defence of endangered religious and moral values and fully authorizes them to co-create the future spiritual dimension of Europe. It should also ensure such a social order where no person is discriminated against and relegated to the second rate of citizens, and true religious freedom is not replaced by the freedom from religion.

(*http://www.episkopat.pl/?a=dokumentyKEP&doc=2004415_1 accessed* on January 11, 2005)

In this imaginary East European nations should turn away from the state-socialist experience of the past and free themselves from this "non-European yoke," claiming full membership in a "Europe" based on Christian civilization. In other words there is a fierce struggle on two fronts on the slope in the name of true Europeanness. On the one hand this struggle is carried on against groups which position themselves higher, trying to teach and civilize the local nation, and on the other hand against ex-communists who, together with other groups try to sell out the country to the Europeans and the great powers in the name of non-nationalist "modernization."

But what is sold out, what national projects are destroyed by these conspirator groups linking "East" and "West?" First of all they forget the fundamental values of nationhood and ethnic solidarity. In the Hungarian context they are seen as neglecting the Hungarian minority groups living in the neighboring countries (exemplified by the criticism of the so called status law). As the Hungarian nationalist argument goes, in order to please the masters of Europe who are too preoccupied with their previous colonies and ignore minority issues, these political forces forget about the vital support of Hungarian minorities, who cannot join us in "Europe" because their host countries are of a more "Eastern" nature. Therefore the struggle to remove these groups from their "non-European" environment and link them directly to our higher position on the slope should be intensified. But at the same time Hungarians being born in those alien territories should remain in the countries of their birth in order to fight for the higher civilizational achievements they already have. As Viktor Orbán, the national-conservative prime minister of the time, put it in his speeches on the status law aiming at the support of the extraterritorial Hungarian minorities living in neighboring countries (on this see Melegh 2001d; 2002b; Hegyesi and Melegh 2003)

> Up til now being born as a Hungarian outside Hungary in the Carpathian Basin has been a bitter fate. Second-class treatment, hatred, contempt. From now on we perform the reunification of the Hungarian nation across the borders. Because the future knows of no borders. And the fatherland will float on high as long as the border separates rather than unites us. To be born as a Hungarian means being a member of an emerging strong and respected nation capable of defending its citizens (Prime ministers speech, August 20, 2001, *www.meh.hu/Kormany/Kormanyfo/2001/08/010820.htm*, accessed March 10, 2002, translated by A. M).

In other words, Hungary has the task of defending "her freedom" and interests, and the wording, with its symbolic reference to height; is a perfect example of the nationalists' "vertical escape," a term proposed by Antohi (Antohi 2001). This perspective also aims at the virtual reunification of Hungary's former territories and the legitimate protection of Hungarians living outside Europe. Its wider objective is the specification of a Europe in which Hungary is understood as a "bridgehead" for spreading "European values." This civilizing mission is described succinctly in a parliamentary speech by Zsolt Németh, state secretary of the Foreign Ministry in the national-conservative government in 2001: "As a member of NATO and a soon-to-be member of the European Union the Hungarian Republic is committed to forming a bridgehead for spreading Western values and rules in the Eastern and South-Eastern region."

> And in this mission those belonging to the Hungarian minority are understood as a "fifth column" on an alien territory because they are

> "existentially democrats" and they always stand on the "right side". That is to say, they—whether in opposition or on the governmental side—always have close relationships with those political forces of their states which are most committed to the establishment of democratic institutions and the Euro-Atlantic integration of their countries (General parliamentary debate on April 19, 2001, *http://www.htmh.hu/plenaris.htm*, accessed March 10, 2002, translated by A. M.).

This complex perspective is best termed *petty imperialism:* looking down and playing the role of a small civilizing contiguous empire within Central Europe. In the Polish case the same idea was formulated in the much-quoted slogan of Pope John Paul II, "from the Lublin Union to the European Union," which directly refers to a historically enlarged Poland, united with Lithuania in 1596. Thus Poland once again becomes a strong nation, especially toward the "East."

According to statements formulated in this perspective, the "selling-out" exercise of the liberal-socialist elite questions our European identity. While the Polish bishops, in their letter quoted above, argue in an indirect manner, the intellectual circle supporting the Hungarian FIDESZ explicitly declared in its public statement on Europe, "we are returning to Europe, to the homeland of Christianity, culture and civilization, to which we have always belonged spiritually" (*http://www.fidesz.hu/index.php?MainCategoryID=1&SubCat=3&CikkID=8247* accessed April 25, 2003, translated by A. M.). Or in a more straightforward manner, as Sándor Lezsák, one of the leading Hungarian nationalist politicians, referring to a historical document, argued in is parliamentary speech on EU accession: Hungarians already knew in 1489 that "we Hungarians live in Europe, the Turks in Asia" (http://eu.mdf.hu/ accessed March 14, 2003, translated by A. M.). The political forces operating in this framework, then, have a completely different approach to European accession. This approach seems much more cautious, rational and deliberate in its public statements. Europe is not perfect in all respects; for instance it quickly forgets its true values. But we still need it to guarantee "European norms" and to strengthen a social framework based on the bourgeois ideals of "solidarity, effective work and individual initiative" (*http://www.fidesz.hu/index.php?MainCategoryID=54&SubCat=46&CikkID=6324*, accessed March 14, 2003). Thus this new nationalism has developed an idea of a conditional, upwardly frustrated and mainly downward-looking "Europeanness," very much in competition with the mainly upward-looking modernizionist approach, and hostile to views based on the othering of local society.

3.5.5. Against colonization or right-wing radicalism

Extreme right-wing perspectives are close to the above nationalist structures in sharing the idea of "vertical escape and ethnic ontology" (Antohi 2001). At the same time they differ in some respects, such as their open anti-Semitism or their anti-EU accession slogan "Not like this", but also in not having a downward-looking petty-imperialist vision. Here there are clear territorial claims against "successor" states, for example Romania in the case of Hungary, but we do not find any kind of civilizing mission or expansion toward "Eastern" points further down the slope.

The most important theme of this perspective is the open rejection of our "inferiority." This can be exemplified by texts on the Netherlands which, according to the extreme right-wing author quoted above, has lived "without poetry, literature, philosophy, theatre and music" but practiced colonization over the past five hundred years (Szőcs 2003). Even more directly Zygmunt Wrzodak, a member of the parliament representing the radical anti-EU League of Polish Families, argues using an anti-colonial rethoric (against the EU as a new "Tower of Babel" and against cosmopolitan Jews):

> "We are being ruined by imports from the European Union. It's a civilizational regression that can be seen by the naked eye. We are becoming a labor reservoir for Europe." Or: "This will result in the dissolving of our nation in a cosmopolitan Union" (See the commentary of Joe Lockard in Gazeta Wyborcza on Sunday, March 17 2002, under the title Debates on EU Accession, http://bad.eserver.org/reviews/2002/2002-3-17-7, accessed January 10, 2005).

In other words, the extreme right rejects the status of being "looked down" from the West, and this refusal is further based on a critical view of the West.

This critical, "anti-colonial" upward gaze is coupled with an open anti-Semitism which links the "West," the "East" (Russian communists) and the local elite. In this discourse the main problem is the domination of Jews, who are able to control even those actors in the top position of the civilizational slope, the EU and the USA. The Jewish conspiracy is rebuffed in the name of true, victimized and immaculate national life. Here the actors locate themselves at the center of the world, from where they reject domination upwards. That is why they have developed their conspiracy theory, which requires the image of powerful agents, and why they cherish the struggle for the "liberation" of the local nation from those representing "alien interests" in the name of the old Europeanness and high civilizational achievements of the local nation.

NOTES

1 Some of these arguments have been published in Hungarian (Melegh 2002a). A large section on the maps of global actors has also been published in English (Melegh 2004).

2 Berger identifies four anglophile, homogenizing faces of global culture with Western but basically American origin: Davos culture, academic-department internationalism, McWorld and Evangelical Protestantism (Berger 1997).

3 AES, AIG American International Group, Citibank, Coca Cola, Exxon-Esso, Ford Motors, General Electric, General Motors, GTE, Hewlett-Packard, Johnson and Johnson, Marriott, Nokia, Philip Morris (Kraft Food International), Procter and Gamble, SBC Communication, Volkswagen-Audi, Xerox. All websites accessed on 15 May, 2000

4 Chemonics, CIPE, EBRD, Ford Foundation, IREX, Rockefeller, USAID, World Bank

5 The GE commercial was presented by József Böröcz at a conference on "The image of Hungary", Budapest, Nov. 20–21,1998.

6 On June 19, 2001 the Parliament of the Hungarian Republic accepted the law "On Hungarians living in neighboring countries" containing rights for minority Hungarians with a status "between naturalized citizens and tourists" with the following goals, among others:

– to comply with its responsibilities for Hungarians living abroad … to ensure that Hungarians living in neighboring countries form part of the Hungarian nation as a whole and to promote and preserve their well-being and awareness of national identity within their home country (http://www.htmh.hu/law.htm)

For such purposes Hungarian nationals are entitled to certain rights, including the right to study at cultural and higher educational institutions, to obtain Hungarian state prizes and scholarships, to use Hungarian public transport with limited concessions, to have a free work permit for 3 months, to receive certain amounts of money if their children are sent to "Hungarian" classes, to receive governmental support as members of minority organizations. In addition Hungarian higher educational institutions are supported in establishing "subsidiaries" in the neighboring countries. This law has been substantially revised and labor rights have been taken out.

7 Both cases have already been analyzed in three papers (Melegh 2001; English version Melegh 2002; Hegyesi and Melegh 2003). This concluding part combines the results of these analyses.

8 This refers to Joseph Conrad's novel "Under Western eyes" on a "strange" group of Russians living in Geneva before World War 1. (Conrad 2003)

9 This is why it cannot be termed as self-colonization. The self is divided and the speaker definitely is above the other locals. For the concept of self-colonization see Tamás 1999. Thanks for the comment of J. Böröcz. In this respect Böröcz has also written a very important piece: Böröcz 1999b.

10 Trianon refers to the 1920 peace treaty concluded in France after WW1 in which two thirds of the territory of the Hungarian kingdom and a third of the ethnically Hungarian population was separated from the Hungarian Kingdom. Marosvásárhely (Tîrgu Mureş) is a city in Romania which has lost its Hungarian majority since the Trianon peace treaty.

CHAPTER 4

I am suspicious of myself. East–West narratives at the turn of the millenium

4.1. Individual narratives and East–West slope

In the present chapter I will move beyond public texts and the discourses of "collective actors" and their "collective" paradoxes in creating different perspectives on the East–West slope. I will now examine some individual narratives generated in an East–West context, which will give us additional insights into the cognitive and identity mechanisms of the East–West slope and the way power, discourses and our individual lives are intertwined. We will also be able to see further paradoxes created by this dominant pattern and how these formulate and shape our individual lives.

Narratives are texts that create temporality. They are devices through which we, individually, are able to "weave" our lives into discursive structures which are the materialization and reproduction of power arrangements. Nonetheless, narratives are not constructed by us but are social constructs which belong to the "relational" field of social life. From a given stock of narrative patterns we create our stories with regard to the social context in which we find ourselves. Thus in telling our stories we are constrained from two angles: by the given stock of narrative patterns and by the social context. Both the stock and the contexts are linked to discourses which "prescribe" a certain number of patterns, helping us to tell our stories and setting the social context through social institutions "legitimized" by discourses. Thus at an institutional or collective level the East–West dichotomy and the East–West slope not only offer patterns for identifying East–West differences (rational versus irrational etc.), but also prescribe our position on an East–West slope and thereby set the ways we utilize East–West discourses. The Orientalism of Western actors will be different from the downward perspective of Central or Eastern Europeans because they themselves are considered to be "Eastern" or to be at a lower point of the East–West civilizational slope, which in itself leads to some kind of frustrated Orientalism.[1] But individual narratives are not just imprints of discourses and discursive positions; they contain the two main elements of freedom and variability.

First of all, individuals can combine elements of different discourses as part of their "lived" and "narrated" life story. They can be creative and they can invent certain patterns. This is, for example, Said's analysis of the 'classics' of Orientalism, where he examines the invention of different intellectual careers and life stories by Sacy, Renan and "pilgrims" such as Chateaubriand and Nerval (Said 1978, 123–200). Narrators can also combine different elements and patterns, as do folk musicians or storytellers who "improvise" by linking different available narrative topics in a highly original fashion (Burke 1978). Alternatively they can simply live through epochs dominated by different discourses and therefore their lived and narrated story may reflect different discourses. Moreover, if that their life stories could be created under previously dominant discourses, traces of these may appear even in revised narratives.

Second, discourses offer rather different patterns even within the established frameworks. Rather than prescribing "subjects" in a deterministic manner, they offer alternatives which can be harmonized individually. This "freedom" of alternative identities is commonplace in the literature on identity and narrative identity, and forms part of my own analysis (among others Gergen and Gergen 1988, Baumann 1996, Neumann 1999, Kovács and Melegh 2001). Since different perspectives can be formulated in the same position on the East–West slope, liberals othering local society and petty-imperialist nationalists weave themselves into the discourse in different and in opposing ways. The only thing we have to assume is that the different "subjects" are linked to each other within the framework of dominant discourses. The existence of freedom and variability does not mean that there is no "sociology" of what narratives are offered, used and especially how they are linked. This chapter aims at describing and analyzing the stock of individual narratives in the dominant East–West discourses and changes in this respect. A key area is the type of narratives created by people crossing different discursive borders between "East" and "West" or moving across the East–West slope when asked to present narratives concerning their activities in regions they do not identify with "home." Thus the narratives cross or meet at the "border." "Easterners" speak about their activities relating to West or Central Europe and "Westerners" about their activities relating to East or Central Europe. This allows me to analyze, not only the narratives created in front of me (as an interviewing Hungarian researcher), but also the role of the locus of enunciation in this process and the individual perspectives on the slope. In addition I will also analyze the way "Westerners" and "Easterners" speak to each other in the same thematic blocks, and the possible consequences of such "interactions."

4.2. On the method

In 2000 and 2001 forty-five narrative interviews were conducted in the United States, Hungary and Russia with people involved in East–West relations. Among the interviewees were "Western" managers, representatives of multinationals or Russian business people investing heavily in the United States. There were academics working on the social and economic problems and processes of the "other" region or individuals who had simply crossed the border and taken long-term teaching assignments or scholarships. There were also employees of Western foundations and non-corporate actors involved in philanthropic activities related to Eastern and Central Europe (no reverse organization has been found). In addition, some political experts and even one senior military figure were interviewed.

A number of interviews (22 out of 45) were later selected on the basis of being complete, and methodologically sound. I also tried to balance interviews on the basis of different positions in terms of "East" and "West" and including a varied occupational or biographical background to the East–West moves. This selection procedure ensured that a large variety of narrative forms could be analyzed. Later the interviews were transcribed for hermeneutic analysis following the methodological conventions of the "biographical-interpretative method" as far as they could be applied to the present research project (Breckner 1996; Rosenthal 1991; Silverman 1993; Kovács and Vajda 1994; Kovács and Melegh 1995, 2001; Melegh 1999b). This approach involves both a special interview technique and a special type of interpretative methodology.

The interview technique employed is based on the assumption that the influence of the interviewer should be limited as far as possible in order to give the interviewee maximum freedom to construct his or her story in the context of East–West relationships. As mentioned above, the question was: "Could you please tell me the story of your activities in relation to the other region?" In these "freely" constructed interviews even the designation of the region was not fixed as I was interested in the choice of the area considered "East" or "West." The ideal interview would have covered the whole life story of the interviewee, but that was not feasible in my research. As noted, high-ranking business people, academics and even political experts were interviewed. In such a group it was fortunate that they were actually prepared to be interviewed and found time for such sessions. Due to the status of these interviewees the interviews generally had to be completed within an hour. In addition, as it turned out in trial runs, these people found it "highly inappropriate" to be asked about their life story, given both their position and the place of the interview. This defensive attitude is easily understood as interviewees were approached directly from a perspective relevant to their position. Therefore I asked them only about the story of their activities in an East–West context.

My stated interest in the activity story had the disadvantage that narratives were susceptible to being reduced to "simple" career stories. However, this fear turned out to have been exaggerated, and even when such reductions occurred at the later stages of the interviews narratives reached deeper levels of experience. In addition to the overall question and following the methodology successfully used in an analysis of migration narratives (Kovács and Melegh 2001), at the end of the interview the interviewee was asked about the story of the first day he or she had spent in the relevant region. This first-day narrative was of major help in trying to figure out the construction of East–West experiences in a narrative format.

After the main part of the narrative the first non-narrated relevant event was probed with the question: "You mentioned that you… could you please tell me a little more about it." These questions allowed the interviewee to develop his/her narrative construction within a framework chosen by him or her. This was repeated after each new part, until the major lines of the narratives (and memories) had been woven together and the narrative construction completed. After the narrative parts some predetermined questions were asked concerning the interviewee's ideas about, or perceptions of the other region.

Many of these interviews, sometimes 2 hours or 30 pages in length, have been typed out as faithfully to the oral delivery as possible. Stoppages, laughs, stresses and breaks were all marked, as were shifts in narratives (report, evaluation, summary, argumentation). The texts were then cut into "sequences." Subsequently, the interpretative, hermeneutic analysis followed two lines in accordance with the ideas of Éva Kovács (Kovács and Melegh 2001). The first tried to establish the construction of biographies, while the second was concerned with the construction of narrated life stories.

The first type of analysis was performed by collecting all the "concrete" biographical references made in the interview, which were then put into chronological order and were subjected to abductive hermeneutic analysis. The question with regard to the first "event" mentioned was: what kind of biography or course of activity might I expect on the basis of my sociological knowledge and assumptions? For example: if "he publishes a paper on the socialist economy" I may assume that he will become an economist specializing in socialism, or a comparativist, or becomes a theoretically-oriented scholar, or an area specialist covering other aspects of socialist societies, or a person who wants to reform capitalism etc. Then I repeat the same procedure with regard to the second biographical event mentioned, where "brainstorming" is extended by a review of the previous hypotheses. This manner of systematic interpretation finally results in some kind of overall pattern or patterns which reflect the elements of the life course the person concerned may have employed to organize his or her 'lived' life in front of me. Thus I arrive at some guesses or ideas concerning the patterns he or she utilizes in constructing his/her biography. It is important to note that naturally I can only move within the framework offered to me, and the "forgotten" events, that is to say those which have not been employed by the interviewee, cannot be analyzed.

As the second line of this hermeneutic analysis I try to figure out what kind of story is developed from the perspective of the present with the patterns the interviewee is using in an attempt to organize the story of his or her activities within an East–West framework. Here I reduced my analysis to the main narrative (told immediately after the introductory question) and that constructed about the first day spent in the "other" region. This reduction helped in handling an excessive amount of interview material, and it also seemed that the careful analysis of these smaller parts revealed the overall narrative patterns employed throughout in the interview as a whole. In addition, the first-day narrative also provided a useful check for the interpretation of the first narrative.

As mentioned before, both the main narrative and the first-day narrative were cut into sequences at all the "break points" of the text and subsumed under an abductive, question-and answer-hermeneutic interpretation similar to that described in connection with the analysis of "lived" life. But here the question was not what life course could be expected, but what kind of story we could imagine as a continuation of the analyzed sequence and how such hypotheses were related to those raised at earlier sequences or sections. Once again with this systematic interpretative exercise (which by definition does not erase the role of the interpreter) I arrived at a number of narrative patterns implemented in the narrated story. These patterns of the present perspective emerging from the abductive game between the interpreter and the text are then reflected against those identified in the analysis of the presented biography. These structures together form the types of narratives analyzed below. It is important to note that one text can, and generally does, contain multiple narratives, and one of the most interesting things is the way in which these narratives are woven together by concrete individuals.

In addition to the method of analysis described above there are other noteworthy procedural matters. Due to the extreme sensitivity of such narrative interviews, the interviewees were assured that from this analysis their personal identity cannot be recognized. To this end the names and real activities of the interviewees have been changed and transformed in a manner which allows readers to fully understand the narrative, without identifying any individuals. Places, institutions, dates or any other type of personal references have also been changed. Thus the people below are fictitious. One might even argue that this "cover" is important not only for reasons of privacy, but also to demonstrate that processes and mechanisms are analyzed and not individual people on some kind of operating table. East–West discourses, as almost faceless power arrangements, form "subjects" and not people who may be "well-intentioned" or "vicious," knowledgeable or ignorant. We all participate in these mechanisms and therefore the main goal of this chapter is not to expose anybody but to understand the mechanisms through which we can construct and reconstruct ourselves in the East–West context.

4.3. Forms of narrative

The number of narrative patterns with which people try to construct or reconstruct the story of their activities in an East–West context is limited. There are about a dozen major patterns which organize the narratives of the interviewees (see Table 4.1.). Among these narratives we find some which can dominate a story covering a longer period of time, while others are only brief situational narratives, which convey meaning as short stories in themselves or as subsections of other stories. Some of these narratives flow well, while others contradict each other; in both cases significant forms of self-representation emerge in the East–West context. Furthermore the locus of enunciation plays an important role in the choice of narratives and the way they are integrated in an interview. The inherent imbalance within the East–West slope clearly appears in the way people from different "loci" on the slope present themselves as persons crossing the East–West boundary.

4.3.1. Narratives of family background

One dominant narrative is involvement in East–West relationships due to some kind of family background. In Western narratives people report on parents and grandparents born in Eastern Europe and such family links in themselves provide a context for a story of "Eastern" activities. Most of these interviewees were aware of the choice of this narrative pattern. Bukovsky, an American scholar, actually started like this:

> I'll say that that I think ** like a lot of people who have become involved in this issue in my generation I think there are two two types

* one are in this country people who have * a direct link to parents, family ethnically to a country or countries in the region and there are others who for another reason got involved.

Table 4.1. Significant forms of narratives

Person	Types of narrative								
	Family background	Intimate relationship	Speaking (0) or not speaking (+) the language	Area specialist, special knowledge	Interpreter	Ideological debate	Discovery of the unknown, being discovered (+)	Global professions	Criminal, criminalized
Born in the West									
Daniel				0			0		
Bentham			+	0			0	0	
Gurnier			+				0	0	
Schmidt			+				0	0	
Kernel						0			0
Flinn		0	0	0					
Bukowsky	0	0	0		0	0			0
Smith		0	0	0		0			
Bergen	0	0	0	0		0			0
Henzel			0	0		0			
Nurick	0			0					
Karine	0	0	+				0		
Born in Hungary									
Marton			0	0	0				0
Schweitzer							0	0	
Kovács	0		0					0	
Born in Russia									
Volkov			0						0
Markatov	0		0		0	0			0
Rushkov			0	0					
Poljakov					0	0	+		0
Kovalsky				0	0	0			0
Koivista			0	0	0	0	+		
Romanov					0	0		0	0

In most of the Western narratives family background is mentioned as a reason for curiosity or language learning at the beginning, but sometimes it can be the basis of a long saga and an overall narrative of an "extraordinary" move toward the "East." Karine, a Belgian teacher, after introducing herself, told a story of moving between different parts of the family, one which emigrated and one which stayed in Russia:

> I'm thirty * no, [laugh] I'm forty-six, living here eight years in St. Petersburg. I came the first time in St. Petersburg in '91. Just at the moment of the putsch * of the putsch and of the beginning of Yeltsin. I came here like a tourist *, but not a simple tourist because part of my family is Russian, my name "Karine" is the name of my Russian husband. For Russian people better to say "Karina" but I don't like, so I'm Karine. * I came here to visit my Russian family in August '91. My grandmother, the mother of my mother, was Russian, she emigrated with half of her family in 17, and she married with a Walloon guy, and * her mother died in Belgium and * some brother and sisters too. It was a very big family, they were nine or ten children. And half emigrated and the other half stayed in Russia and they were, part of them, persecuted. I think that I will not maybe give all the details, it's a very long story, like for a lot of people of this of this period. Maybe if you have time, I could of course if if we have time, I could of course explain how we lost contact, how we * how we * got in contact 20 years after * in those stories there is always a part of * miracle * Miracle! Miracle!

In non-Western interviews this form of narrative is generated by curiosity or the search for orientation in a life course. In this case the background is not provided by a family coming from the "other" region, but by relations open to the "world." Markatov, a Russian scholar, for instance, quotes a relative who wrote extensively about Europe and described it as his "home." In another self-presentation the "Western" family background is once again a pull factor—Kovács, a Hungarian-born businessman names his aunt as his reason for leaving home and emigrating to England:

> As I say I was 14, you know, at that time, I left with my sister, my parents stayed behind in Budapest. I had no particular, at that age, no particular political opinions or whatever, it was just an adventure, it was just an adventure to leave and start a new life abroad. * You know,* it's not much I can tell you about life in Hungary, I think you know * you know more about it maybe than I do [laugh] * [unintelligible] No, no, no. But I mean, just * we had good times and bad times, and * eventually the reason we went to England with my sister is because there was an aunt, a relative who lived already in London, and was able to help us, you know, to settle into a new environment.

In a later part of the interview it turns out that Kovács once again "emigrated" for family reasons. This time he followed his sister to the United States:

> Oh, and my sister. My sister, then * in fact the reason, I mean one of the reasons why I moved to the States afterwards, my sister moved to the States maybe 6 years earlier than I, and when I was looking around in, in the '70s England was a pretty miserable place, and I was looking around for better pastures and I went to visit my sister in Chicago and I was offered a position, I was offered a job in the States, so I decided to emigrate again, a second time [laugh] to the United States.

In general the narrative of family background serves as a universal narrative which can be employed in both "East" and "West," but the locus of enunciation, the given position on the slope, leaves a specific imprint on the narrative. In the West this form of narrative arouses interest in something unknown or marginal, while in the non-West it is a pull factor for virtual or real movement from the "East." Thus the family-background narrative in the West is mainly an introduction to a career or curiosity story, while in the "East" it becomes the linchpin of narrating movement toward the "West." In cases where there is an extraordinary move down the slope for familial reasons, complications arise, and we see desperate attempts to legitimize the abnormality. This is certainly a reaction at the individual level to the upward dynamic of the East–West slope.

4.3.2. Narratives of intimate relationship

In my interviews it was "Westerners" who told of having a love affair with East Europeans. Those crossing the border form the other side did not report any love affairs. The same relationship appeared in the narratives of over sixty Hungarian migrants (Kovács and Melegh 2001; Melegh 1999) living in the "West," there was only one case of an "Easterner" reporting a love affair with a "Western" person not of the same ethnic origin. Thus we can safely conclude that the chance of telling a story of falling in love with somebody from the other side is very low in interviews conducted with "Easterners," which in itself shows a power inequality.

But discourses not only silence lovers and spouses coming from the East, they also reveal possible gender scenarios forming part of an East–West order. It was shocking to see that the scenario of "Western" man versus East European woman was dominant in all the 45 interviews, while I could find only one "Western" woman who was a wife of an "Eastern" man. Let us look at some of these examples carefully so as not to draw any hasty conclusions. At first sight these narratives reveal a clear Orientalism in the sense that the "Easterner" is a legitimate sexual object in East–West discourses and that therefore the hierarchy of an Orientalized/Orientalizing relationship can also be revealed in a narrative format.

First of all, the "Western" narratives generally contain a love affair with the daughter of an emigrant family. Interestingly, these love affairs of the sixties and seventies are not stories in which the girl is emotionally captured by a dominant "Western" man. Instead, the young men find awkward walls and twists in the relationships. In an amusing story Bergen, a "Western" scholar, had problems with a Polish-American girl, while another American scholar, Bukovsky, also courting an American-Polish girl, found himself caught in a fight between the parents. On being asked about learning Russian, Bergen replies with a story of an emotionally abusive Polish-American father and her daughter as a way toward learning about the East European region:

> And we moved, he [the father] moved, he retired to Kansas, that was the last [assignment], and I was a music student, *, piano and

> accordion, and, * one of the other students of the same teacher that I had was the daughter of another navy-retired person who was Polish-American, and he taught Russian at a Christian brothers school where my father'd actually ended up teaching after he retired, so we had this relation, this relationship with this family, and * the parents of this other student liked me very much and wanted me to sort of go out with their daughter, and [Right] they they concocted this idea that if we would study Russian together, that would somehow bring us together under un [laughs] unconstrained circumstances. I loved it, but the daughter didn't like it because she didn't want to spend any more time with her father than she had to because he was a bit of an alcoholic and probably emotionally abused her, so she didn't want to spend time with him, but I loved it, the typewriter, that, my Russian typewriter, I have, is from him, to this day, so that's actually the beginning, way back, but I have no, you know on my mother's side or my father's side, no, no genealogical reasons to be studying this region. Except for the Bavarian connection, which is a little bit farther west [laughs].

Bukovsky describes a different situation in a strikingly similar manner:

> She came just in the time when she was in Ohio I was a freshman at the University of Ohio and we met at some restaurant, she was a senior about to go off * to a * at first she was gonna go to I think * I don't remember * but then her I think partially because [laughs] she met me * you know there is this * I don't recall where mostly Polish-American kids go out, you know higher somewhere * so they ended up throwing sending her there to get her away from me and of course my parents but anyway what happened was * her father was you know a big burly guy classic image of a you know image of an American Pole who had, who was a first generation, both her parents were Polish American first generation and they often had this family dinners and they would have I mean * I would come I would take the bus or whatever from Dayton and go over and they would be speaking Polish and I could almost understand some things (special emphasis) * just from outside I would say basic stuff only and light force that would have been by that I was making second year Rus-

sian they didn't like that I would say I tell you about this [stops]all in Russian but that did not impress them because they hated the Russians but you know [laughs] you could tell [I laugh] they were from Lodz Lo.o.odz and he had gone her father was actually a very nice man he is a working-class guy, he is TV sales and repairs, I am sure they did not like the idea that his Polish daughter was going out with this Jewish guy but * this country is full of tensions like that you know (yeah, yeah) but it was her mother that I think was really a sort of, she made an effort to be nice but I am sure it was her who was really really bothered you know, she talked about her sisters and a couple of her sisters were directly from Poland (yeah) but I got the most in this, about my parents were no better, when I told to my parents that I was going out with a Polish-American woman by the name of Christine [loudly laughs, I laugh] you know you can see the same thing.

These are not stories in which weak "Easterners" are seduced by "Westerners." They are Romeo-and-Juliet narratives of being at the mercy of parents who on both sides try either to block or to arrange the marriage of their beloved offspring. Here the crucial elements are the link to the ethnicized and sometimes conflict-ridden family background and the theme of a brutal East European father. These stories are not those of Casanova in the 18th century Victor Hugo, Nerval or Flaubert in the 19th century, or Joseph Roth in the 20th century, in which the "Easterner" or "Oriental" (out of the "West" or within the West a "Gypsy") is portrayed as a sexually desirable object of "Western" phantasy, but of Malamud and Faulkner, in which aggressions between different groups are played out openly (Wolff 1994, 50–62, Said 1978 149–200; Malamud 1957, 1971; Roth 2002; Faulkner 1959).

Yet in spite of the relative balance of the representation of the lovers and their families above, severe East–West imbalances may also be detected in the love stories. Among the narratives analyzed, the story of the Belgian woman married to a Russian man reveals the "absurdity" of a "Western" woman marrying an "Eastern" man, a problem forming the main underlying logic of the whole two-hour narrative interview.

As we have seen, Karine not only had relatives in Russia, but while visiting them also fell in love with a friend of her lost relatives. This love is reported to be an overwhelming, "rich experience," and the story shows elements of "absolute" (Oriental) love comparable to the similarly arranged scenario ("Western" woman and "Eastern" man) of the film of The English Patient. But in contrast to the film, which takes place in Africa and outside the West, in this story the "Eastern" lover appears in Brussels:

> And so he came, and he spent one month, I think, in Belgium. Yeah. One month. He was 34, I think. 34, at that time. And it was a great question for me * I remember* I was*You know a little bit Brussels? Yeah? A little bit? Or more than a little bit.
>
> –Yeah. a little bit.
>
> –Yeah. And I was living in the ....Yeah. It's very pittoresque with the market outside, with a lot of people, restaurants and so on. Very interesting place. And a lot of shops, a lot of * and my first reaction was 'Oh, how he will react with those shops, this abundance, the prices and so on.' And I hoped he will arrive at night, in the evening, when the shops * not to have immediately those enormous impressions. And he came not so early, and *I remember [laughs] I was bad, I waited him, I didn't understand what happened, because I hoped that he will be the first of the people to the, and he helped some woman who had some problem with paquet, with her luggage and so on. They are like that. Russian people, anyhow, they have to help [laughs]. And so, we went to Brussels, to the flat, and I was living alone, but he is not people who is always details, so it was only my questions. And there were other questions for him. Of course he had a shock. When * when we opened the door of my flat, I had a two-room flat, and I decorated it like I like and so on, but it was pretty and for him, of course, I remember his eyes, it was a good surprise, but everything was a surprise, a new * and after that, no, the day after we * we went to walk in the street and so on, everything was very animé, and of course he looked at the prices. There was reaction. But without any enormous trouble. And I * I always say that at first we were * very protected by our love, and we were absolutely * very protected! I think we were together, very, very closed and for him, it was a protection. And for me, I think during the first moments here of course, too. But I remember that * his reaction * he liked very much technique, and technical things and so on, and he

> looked at our instruments in the street, the * the * I don't know how it is called * to work in the street, and told, 'même ça * even those things are beautiful, in good condition and so on, and not dirty', and for him it was * because it is his interest.

The tension in this moving account is between the recollected love of a man and his inferiority on civilizational grounds. The interviewee invites her beloved to her own country and tries to smuggle him into Brussels by night in order to protect him from the "abundance" of the city, a nicely decorated two-room flat and the presumed shock of a technological and consumer "paradise." This striking combination of a love narrative with a civilizational one returns later, revealing the push factor (let us leave the "East") detected in the narratives of family background. The story of her settling in St. Petersburg is described so as to suggest that the move "East" is something which should not happen and "mixed" couple should move to the "West":

> I was not especially suffering, of this * of this life, but the contrast between [stops] between the day life and the evening life was quite * difficult. And I received * because I was married * married with a Russian man, I received not very good * vibration from other people, of course. But now it's quite, of course, different, because foreigners change, too, now when the family, when the family comes to Russia, it's very different. Of course it's not so easy, and especially for children, between 10 and 20, because they are afraid to let them alone in the street, in the metro and so on. So the freedom is not so easy. But for the women it's different. They are now teaching Russian language, they want to know, they * they are much, much, much more open. But I feel that I stay some * suspect. Person suspect. Not about * I don't know* about my collaboration with the state here or something. Not about that. But ** maybe I'm suspect for myself. [laughs] I mean, I mean * this situation is quite rare here, but * but it becomes ** less and less rare, but to live * no, to imagine to live here ** without end, it's a question. It's a question for me, and for the other people.

It is "abnormal" to marry an "Eastern" man; one "side effect" of such deviant marriages is that the "deviant" becomes suspicious of herself. This indicates that the subject created by the dominant discourse comes into conflict with the actual subject of Karine, who somehow makes a wrong decision: to stay with a "drunken" Russian man in St. Petersburg. The East–West civilizational slope transforms the love narrative into a story of discomfort.

Naturally, this sense of imbalance and insecurity requires some kind of healing within the given framework. And it seems that the healing of the hierarchy and the "wrong moves" within it is racism just as in many other analyzed cases of the East–West slope. On racist grounds unequal partners can be "pulled up" by those above them in the hierarchy, or the one at a lower point of the hierarchy can claim a better position for him- or herself. . In this interview racism also becomes the ground for agreement between unequal partners Karine reports even falling in love in this manner (a text already shown among our introductory examples in chapter 1):

> It was a very, very beautiful day. And it was a discovery of Russian for me, of Russia, and I think, like everybody in the beginning, I didn't feel myself a foreigner here * I think for everybody it's the same because * especially because the people look like us * there is no difference. Of course there is un petite Slavic, but they are white, they are very different, like * like in Europe, there is black hair, there is blond hair, everything, and * we look not very different. And especially now because the clothes are the same. Ten years ago * it was all of this very soviétique, and * until now anyhow the people know in one second that you are not * you are not Russian ** Before, it was enough to look at the shoes, but you know this because you were living in Hungary. I think it is for you very familiar. They looked at the shoes and immediately they knew that you are not, and, and

Here the Russian lover is certainly an "Eastern" kind of person (as reported later: "not many initiatives, drunk" etc.), but he is at least white. A special white, soviétique, but still of the same "type." This basic whiteness is the only remedy for internal conflicts; without this remedy it is suggested that there is little hope for their life together. At one point during the interview Karine suddenly switches to French:

> It's true that it's easier to, to express certain things in French in a, in a deeper way. But since this is a * this is an endless discussion, isn't it? It's an endless discussion which is very hard to grasp and which is at the same time very rich, very rich * but sometimes my * my Russian colleague, sometimes he says to me, 'But you are [stops] how shall I put it [stops] naive! People of the East and people of the West cannot, in reality they cannot meet each other'. That's how it is. So, he says to me, when I'm depressed, when I * when I cry because my husband drinks vodka and he is very hard to tolerate, and he tells me, my colleague tells me, 'I know very well that one day you will go back to Belgium * all alone and then you will live in Belgium all alone (translated from French by Orsolya Németh).

It seems that the East–West patterns dominating Karine's narrative are based on a racist discourse of "East is East" or as the Russian colleague puts it according to Karine: "People of the East and people of the West cannot… in reality they cannot meet each other" But the organization of the text is not only a retrospective (racist) approach to lived experiences, but we also have a reference to a search in the past for "neutral" ground, even on the part of the husband. The "neutral" ground for the couple in this case was South Africa:

> He, like all Russian people, he really * like a lot of Russian people, he really not * not know very well the world other than Russia, and he spoke to me about South Africa. 8 years ago. And I was asking 'Why?' And he told me, 'Because they are * they are looking for white people!' [laughs]. But it was not, in his mentality it was not bad. It was * I think it was only because * because * he knows that for Russian people it's not so easy to live in another country. They are not asked especially. And he thought, if they need us, we could go there. And for me ** when I thought of these people I thought about the apartheid, if it is * if it is to augmenter le volume des blancs [increase the number of whites] against the black, it's not the right way.

Clearly the narrative of the marriage between a French-speaking woman and a Russian architect turns into a negotiation of racist "equalizers" between the two of them. The "superior" woman calms herself by reiterating "the fact" of the couple's shared race, while the husband is reportedly thinking about migrating to South Africa to defend his "whiteness." But the Russian husband is despised even for this as being too racist in wanting to increase the number of "whites" as opposed to "blacks." These shifts are unimaginable without the East–West slope and its inbuilt racism.

Altogether it seems that the inherent imbalance of the East–West slope appears in the narratives of love affairs. But this imbalance is felt much less by men who constructed narratives of falling in love with women of different ethnic origin in childhood or as young adults. In such cases we see internal minority conflicts, while the present perspective of the Belgian woman is definitely that of racist argumentation due to in-built inequality. Thus we are dealing with two types of love narratives: a "normal" one between "Western" men and women of East European origin and an "abnormal" one invoking racist patterns and justifications in which a "Western woman" marries an "Eastern" man and even moves to that region. It is the East–West slope that invokes racist patterns if individuals move in the "wrong" direction.

4.3.3. Language narratives

Narratives of language learning form a dominant and universal pattern in speaking about our experiences of moving between Eastern Europe and the "West." In these narratives interviewees speak about studying language or translating something related to the other region. It is a way of learning about other societies or escaping from one's own society. In narratives of learning the language of the target region the language story organizes events and experiences reported in the interview, involving communication problems, being excluded or having no contact with the "other" society.

In most of the "Western" interviews language learning was presented as the "essence" of activities related to Eastern and Central Europe. Flinn, a US political expert, starts his rather short main narrative with learning Russian: "When I was in college, my minor was Russian. Actually I had more hours in my minor than in my major."

After this introductory statement he immediately starts talking about his attempts at joining the Foreign Service. Thus language learning is introduced as some kind of "entry" into Foreign Service or, more precisely, as a way of leaving American society. Flinn learns not only Russian, which according to the narrative leads him to the Soviet Union, but also Spanish, which takes him to Mexico, Cuba and the Caribbean. This narrative appears in a more sophisticated form in the case of Bergen, who actually introduces himself as having "extra sensitivities" vis-à-vis Russian. Like Flinn, he starts with language learning:

> OK, starting at the beginning, well I I I * I actually already started learning Russian in high school * Russian language, and * that`s probably the beginning of all of this, it`s * and that was unusual because I came from a * a not very university-bound coll [the word is not finished] high school in suburban Kansas where Russian language was not normal, in suburban Denver, at least not then.

This story is later developed in a buoyant manner; language learning takes Bergen to the Soviet Union, opens up countries such as Czechoslovakia and Estonia for him, offers him job opportunities in foreign services, and as we have seen, even a love affair. Almost exactly the same story is reported by Bukovsky, who also presents himself as somebody motivated by language learning:

> And that was when I met the probably guy who had the biggest influence on me who was a Bulgarian * who was * he was in the history department but we got friendly when he heard I was slightly interested in Eastern Europe, interested in Eastern Europe ... and he is the one who kept pushing me when I was studying Russian and I was supposed to, and I thought I would take Czech * just having picked one I decided to do that over Poland probably because this Ottokar got me interested, but it turned out that there was some problem with the Czech conflicting with another course and I did not know whether to take two intensified Russian courses and he said why don't you take Bulgarian [laughs] and I decided to do it and frankly it changed my life.

It seems that learning languages can provide a series of narrative identities evoked by the "Western" locus in the East–West context. But people on the other side of the discursive wall also rely on such stories and most form counterparts to Flinn's "escape" narrative above. In most of these stories language learning is presented as a definite escape from local society in two ways. First, by emphasizing an interest in the "West" and setting up communication possibilities with "foreigners," NATO-expert interviewee seeks an entry into their group. Second, knowing a language and the related education facilitates upward mobility or obtaining a better social status. This can also foster feelings of alienation from the local society.

Most of the Russian interviewees referred to special schools in which very intensive language teaching took place during the Soviet period. In these schools, students not only had many language classes, but most of the subjects were also taught in the designated foreign language. Thus in themselves they formed institutionalized "non-local" spots and it seems that they could easily be integrated into narratives of leaving the Soviet Union and moving to the "West" or "Western" countries. Thus language learning is more than just a special interest, it is a way of transposing oneself to the other side of the wall. This is perfectly clear in the narrative of Markatov, head of a department of European Studies, whose ancestors also "pushed" him toward Europe. He introduces himself as someone who perfectly knows Paris and French culture, as a result of his studies at a special school in Moscow. With this educational background he was lifted from the local society into the "West" well before he actually traveled there:

> Well, for example, when I studied in a French language school. You know, there were ordinary schools. And one had to study language from the fifth form. But there were also 'specialized' schools, where they studied language seriously from the first form. So, already at school Paris was my native city, native. Not only Moscow, but also Paris. I knew Paris very well, without having been there. Since we studied the map, its sights, history, culture. At the school we read Hugo, Zola in French. Under the Communists. Thanks to them for having… there were such schools under Communists, elitist schools. These schools were not only for the nomenclature. We used to be a modest family. …By the way, there came educated people from, from such schools, people who know a lot. They didn't … They went on studying in eighty-five. That's why I used to be a guide for many friends of mine around Paris, without being there before, when I came to Paris in eighty-five. [I laugh] But I could find everything with my eyes closed [I laugh], cause during ten days and

> then at university ... I studied French language, I studied the map of Paris, the history of Paris. [laughs] One might say that I knew Paris, probably, no worse than Moscow... Its history, culture and map. I understood everything. The entire layout. I knew that by correspondence. So there wasn't any shock for me, neither linguistic nor cultural (translated from Russian by Y. Roman).

This first-day narrative actually ends with the story that Markatov, as a "cultured Russian," knew Paris even better than a local security guard:

> So, when I had come to Paris, I first led my team * there's a famous shop "Samaritan" on the bank of the Seine. And there's an orientation tower, orientation tower. One can see all Paris from it. All at once, at the same time. I already knew it, and I showed them the city topography. So the French, the shop guards didn't know that the tower was there. [laugh] Policemen. [my comment: it's very interesting] Nobody knew, I knew that it was, but I didn't know how to get to the elevator, where the elevator was. They say: "There isn't one." [I laugh] There is, I know! I studied Paris. I know everything. At last, we had found it and went up. There were customers passing by, and I'm sure, nobody knew about it. And there were us, who had already known. There was no shock whatsoever. We are in Europe as cultured Russians. We consider it our tradition as well, it's our common tradition (translated from Russian by Y. Roman).

The same feeling of being special or belonging to another culture appears in the narrative of Volkov, the manager of a Western consultancy company. Interestingly, he also introduces himself as a learned person: the product of a special foreign-language education. In his report he quotes Hamlet's monologue in its original wording suggesting a "proper childhood." He combines this with a report on learning Japanese and beautifully translating a Honda user's manual for a noveau-riche businessman a combination which creates a special non-local local perspective with the special English language school playing a very important role:

> About school? Hm [stops] At that time, probably now of course I don't know for sure, but at that time there were several schools in

> Moscow with very good English teachers and English lessons. And even * some of the lessons were delivered in English. For example, we started geography in English, and we had some lessons in physics also in English. So there were some special teachers. And also we started * we started English literature and American literature and, well, at that time I could say 'To be or not to be, that is the question: Whether 'tis nobler in the mind, to suffer The slings of arrows of outrageous fortune Or take arms against a sea of troubles, And, by opposing, end them?—To die,—to sleep,—No more.' You know, that is from proper childhood. So * it was a common school * but what was also very particular about that school: a lot of pupils were children of the Soviet Communist elite * Those people who later went to the Academy or to some other universities of this type, and they had peculiarly very rich parents * or rather that * not very rich, but people who had access to all the treasures of the soviet times. So these pupils, they of course were not common pupils.

In his narrative his special knowledge helps him to overcome the "great barrier" separating foreigners and Russians, to rise above the locals by allowing him to obtain the desirable job at the foreign consultancy company:

> I was hired almost from the very beginning of our Russian * of the Moscow office * and * you know, what I started with, it was a * very, very unusual thing to communicate to foreign managers, you know, in general for Russian people it was very unusual to speak * to somebody who was from abroad. Probably I was in a better position because * at that time I had already visited Hungary and Germany, so I had some experience and I had some exposure to * not to tourists, but to * other countries, also I do speak English and that helped me to communicate with foreigners but nevertheless, there was a great barrier between myself and those foreigners I had to speak to. And well, that, you know, step-by-step that barrier disappeared.

In stories employing this kind of narratives language learning is a distinct status symbol. In "Western" narratives the same mechanism can also be detected, but the "departure" from local society is less definite.

In–as–much as the process of socialization described above constitutes a form of alienation, this attitude also appears in those narratives where inability to learn the language is a dominant motif. But as with the love affairs, we can clearly recognize an East–West imbalance. "Easterners" might "forget" about ever learning the language, but it seems that they are not allowed to construct stories of not being able to speak or to learn it, which is clearly permissible for interviewees on the other side.

Some of the latter only tell a short story of not being able to learn the language. Schmidt, a German manager in Hungary, simply states that he has not been able to learn Hungarian or any of the local languages. By contrast some others develop a complete narrative based on this inability. The expat manager of a French multinational company in Hungary, for instance, finishes his main narrative as follows:

> Well, so, that's it. After that, we, I had lessons, we started, and I left. They tried to teach me a little Hungarian. At last, I could say "igen," "nem," "viszontlátásra," "jó reggelt" ["yes," "no," "goodbye," "good morning" in Hungarian]. We even had within the company, they proposed after a while, in fact, something like a little seminar lasting for two days, which was an apprenticeship of a little bit of sociology meeting people, remembering a little history, remembering a little bit of what the Hungarians had lived through. The customs, a bit of the culture: Petőfi Sándor. Well, after I had come, I immersed myself up to my ears in my job. After a little while I restarted the Hungarian courses. And I never really reached the point of speaking Hungarian correctly (translated from French by E. K.).

This story, which is repeated again later, combines the lack of success in learning the language and gaining access to local culture and local "soul." Thus language learning here is presented not as something of an "enrichment" or something lifting us out of our own community, but as a kind of tool for capturing the soul of the people surrounding us. This linkage is close in the narrative of an English manager with her own consultancy and training company in Russia. Bentham, besides introducing herself as a "culture specialist", has a long narrative of not understanding and learning the local language and not being able to understand how the "Russian brain thinks" In one part of the interview she introduces herself as a complete foreigner not able to communicate even on an airplane. As she says, she could not even read a word in the foreign alphabet:

> Q: Can you recall the very first day, here?
> B: Yeah * I sat on the runway for about 3 hours * both in London, first *. it was my first experience of Aeroflot probably the Russian air company [laughs] * that was very brave, I remember getting on the plane and thinking * what's my seat number, because they were all numbered in Russian of course * all Russian Cyrillic letters * what's my seat number, and then I thought I sat in the right seat which of course I didn't * and the hostess came down and told me in terms of her own language that I was in the wrong seat, but of course I didn't understand her, so I sort of looked at her and she mumbled and said well never mind, and put the other person somewhere else * so then we duly arrived in Russia, and so it was the 26th of December.

This lack of knowledge also appears in the description of her company structure in which there are Russians "trained by her" to educate fellow-Russians. Eventually she reports some advancement in learning Russian, but this progress seems somewhat pointless by now as more and more signs are in English. The world around her changes instead of her adapting to it: "What else can I say I mean, you know maybe my eyes are a little bit closed now because I now speak Russian, you know I can read road signs and airport signs and whatever, but it seems to me that there's more signs in English * * there's * they're becoming much more international."

Altogether language learning as a dominant narrative form serves several purposes besides the obvious one of linking people of different origin. It can be a way of narrating a career or upward mobility, while at the same time it can serve as a cause of alienation from the local society. The alienation story varies according to the position on the East–West slope. Those on the "Eastern" side distance themselves from their local community, while "Westerners" use not learning the language as a clear sign of not being able to integrate in the "other" society on the non-Western side. The imbalance in discursive power arrangements on the East–West slope not only allows the luxury of not learning the language on the "Western" side, but can also lead to clear cognitive colonial patterns of overriding local culture in developing the narrative of activities in the other region.

4.3.4. Narratives of the area specialist

In these narratives, in the biography or activity story the interviewee presents him- or herself as a person studying the development of one area or having special expertise related to certain regions. Such narratives might be reports on activities in scholarly or policy-making institutions or simply extra insights into learning about the "other" region or extensive traveling. Besides language learning, this type of narrative seems to be one of the most general formulas for the articulation of activity stories in an East–West context. Almost everybody interviewed used this pattern. But, like the narratives above, these stories are also highly diverse. The variation can again be interpreted in the light of different loci of enunciation and perspectives on the East–West slope. In a "Western" perspective, the area-specialist pattern generally works by linking knowledge of Eastern Europe with expertise on "developing" countries and areas. This shows the same linkage as the global maps termed "advent of a Third World status" analyzed in the previous chapter. "Easterners", on the other hand, construct a "mission" toward their own local society in line with perspectives "othering local society", analyzed in chapter 3 in relation to institutional actors or patterns of language learning.

Gradual involvement in regional studies appears in the narrative of Rushkov, a Russian historian specialising in the history of Poland:

> And regardless of this I thought I would like to be a historian, and this correspondence [with a Polish student] was a way of rethinking my career. At that time even they thought that I would study Russian history, but when I got to Moscow University, that was in 1982, then even at the end of the first year I had to make a decision about what I wanted, what department I should choose, what country, what period I would like to investigate. And then I thought why not Polish history since I had already learnt so much about it (translated by A. M.).

The same kind of gradual-involvement narrative is used also by Bukowsky and Bergen coming from America, who—as it turns out—present a story of "many reasons" (in other words multiple causes for moving into this field). Having a certain family background, they start their story with learning languages, meeting friends, listening to interesting professors, visiting the area and in the end becoming an area specialist.

A more straightforward entry into regional studies is told by Henzel, a German expert working for a global non-corporate institution in the United States. He starts his story like this:

> Er, thirty years ago, I decide to write my thesis for my exam at the university in Germany, about how the Soviet economy plans, organizes and implements technological progress and why they are, when it comes to technological progress, so far behind Western market economies. ** At the university that I studied there was a so-called Eastern European legal, law institute, and that's where I took this one course, and decided to write a thesis about this topic. Then I went to * the United States, and studied at the Russian and East European Institute, learned Russian, and went back to Germany, taught at the university and went, following that year to Kiev * Leningrad and Moscow for one year, to collect data and have discussions on this very topic, the planning and implementation of technological progress in Soviet industry.

In this narrative—in both the biography and the narrated story—, in addition to elements of pure curiosity there is a systematic attempt to understand a "totally" different economic system and making a career out of this. We also find a step-by-step movement linking the Soviet Union to "ordinary", developing countries, which once again can be seen as an "advent of the Third World status." At first no knowledge of the East European economy is needed when Henzel is sent to a different area of the "Third World." Nonetheless at the end of the narrative and his story he smoothly moves back into the area of "transition economies," combining the types of expertise.

This orientation toward the Third World is clearer in the case of Bentham, the English businesswomen with a consultancy and training company in Russia, who constructed an elaborate narrative about not speaking Russian. She introduces herself as a "culture specialist" with a special knowledge of Western and "non-Western" cultures, i.e. European versus African, Caribbean and Eastern European :

> Then let's begin from the base level, let me just go from the beginning of my experience of Russia * bear in mind that I had experience in, in other cultures, so I worked with African culture, I worked with Caribbean culture, I worked with European culture, but not Eastern European culture* when I arrived in Russia I was going along * what I would normally do with all those regions of the World I've always been very successful.

According to Bentham her knowledge proves to be a failure in Russia in the short term. Nonetheless she continues to organize her experience through a process of learning about different "developing" cultures. One of her questions regarding the interview was whether I was interested in cultural differences. Such a "special knowledge" is shown to be an asset on which "global" companies can be built. In this sense her story represents a case combining area-knowledge narratives with patterns of "global profession"(to be analyzed later).

The relationship between knowing a region and the aim of this cognitive act is very different in the "East." People on the "Eastern" side tend to have "missionary" and "cultural" ideals not for another region but for their own local society on the basis of their "special" knowledge of the "West." Here the function of knowledge is to change the local community of the interviewees. In most cases they are trying to correct the "misunderstandings" of local people and to show them the "reality of the West" or even to present this knowledge as a guideline for the future of their own society. Koivista, head of a Moscow-based institute on Europe, starts her story by introducing her "special" interest in the region:

> I started to analyze the activities of such European or Euro-Atlantic organizations as NATO, WEU, CSCE at that time, then OSCE, European Union and so on.

Then she comes to the conclusion that this knowledge is disseminated only to a limited number of "experts":

> As a researcher I realized what is really going on in Europe, * what is European Union * And who, who read my articles which are published in * scientific journals. Very restricted, very limited number of experts.

According to her story, she then establishes the institute with a definite mission:

> So to give a different option to our, you see, Russian people to get information

The posture whereby knowledge is granted as a process of enlightenment for "our Russian people" becomes even clearer in the narrative of the Russian scholar Markatov, who not only says that his expertise is the perception of "Europe" in Russia or in the works of the Russian emigrants, but who also clearly states that his work on "Europeanism" is a political project:

> In that sense I have been studying the history of Russian Europeanism for twenty years, which shows that there's no conflict between Russia and Europe. There's a problem, an identity problem, but it's also a possibility of synthesis, possibility of harmony. Russia could be a European country * Europe is not only a cultural problem, but also a political project in Russia (translated from Russian by Y. Roman).

Markatov's narrative seems to suggest that it is necessary to change not only the outlook of ordinary people but also the decisions of high-ranking politicians, who likewise misperceive "European reality." This pattern again forms a major narrative in the interview given by the Russian expert on security issues, Kovalsky, who throughout the interview presents his and his institute's activity as that of a political advisor or "think tank." In his story this think tank mitigates some negative decisions of the Soviet Union, for instance regarding the European Common Market. It is presented as an institution promoting "European integration" as an "objective process," without any directly political motivation.

Interestingly, from the "non-Western" locus of enunciation, not only specialized knowledge of "Europe" or the "West" can be used in narrating East–West crossings but also knowledge of the local "Eastern" region. In one case Marton, a Hungarian-born sociologist living in England, tells of learning a non-Marxist language and selling his knowledge of socialist societies to a "Western" audience and in a "Western" language. But even in this case a need for translation for the "West" is reported and the self is shown as being situated between the local society and the "West." In this sense this narrative perfectly matches the one analyzed above.

In general, then, it seems that although the narrative of being an area expert is a universal and dominant way of telling stories related to the other region, once again there is a clear division according to the locus of enunciation on the East–West slope. Those on the "Western" side either use this structure as a pattern for educating and controlling Eastern Europe, or cognitively link Eastern Europe to the developing world, while those on the "Eastern" side see a mission for themselves toward the local society and regard themselves as being special links between "East" and "West." In the above "Western" narratives knowledge of Eastern Europe or East European languages is not considered a means of changing local Western societies, while East European experts in most cases establish new "virtual" homes for themselves outside their local societies. On the Eastern side dislocation and displacement is missing only in the story of the Russian historian working on Poland, which illustrates that as a result of the small distance on the slope, knowledge of Poland can be rather neutral, while East European narratives of being an expert on "Europe" or the "West" further up the slope acquire a clear missionary character.

4.3.5. Narratives of global profession

While the above narrative pattern is a "territorial" one, where knowledge is presented with regard to an area, there are narratives in which interviewees introduce themselves as having a specific knowledge or profession in demand all over the world. Alternatively, they simply tell a story of being employed by a global organization which sends them to different parts of the world (see also Kovács and Melegh 2001; Baumann 1996).

This is probably the only narrative where a professional bias appears, particularly in relation to business, although one senior Russian military figure also used this type of structure. Take the story of the French expat manager, Gurnier, who was unable to learn Hungarian. After reporting his curiosity about Hungary, he embarks on the following narrative line:

> Afterwards, let's say, by way of my job, when I was in Paris with [the company], I had an opportunity to try to initiate a number of actions, for [the company], at the European level, it gave me a chance to go to these different countries to deal with image problems, or rather marketing problems, marketing and technical problems. So as a result in 96 they suggested that I came to take a responsible job in Hungary (translated from French by E. K.).

Gurnie's task is to adapt the global marketing strategy and global images of his multinational company to local circumstances, which is presented as some kind of background for obtaining a job in Hungary. Almost exactly the same story is told by a senior expat and ex-soldier manager of a German logistic company, Schmidt, who represents a "satellite" firm of a major German multinational manufacturing company. He starts his story by introducing the "motherhood" (sic) company:

> Okay. * The story is following the decision made by an international [manufacturing] company to go this region here and this company was also looking for a logistic-service providing company and * our company was successful in gaining * this logistic service here and therefore we had to build up an own Hungarian company * out of * our motherhood company in Germany * we built up this company in July 1997 * and because this manufacturing company is located here in Vác we also had to be here .. that's starting point of our activities in Hungary.

This line of narrative remains unbroken throughout the interview, as Schmidt focuses on how such multinational companies operate, how they can be served by "logistic" companies such as his, and how Hungarian workers can be integrated into this business. Even the story of the first day is told with this focus on the global "motherhood company":

> Okay. * The very first day was in was the 29th of September in 1999 when we get the official announcement of our client that we have been successful in offering our services * and they invited us to come here and to get into first contact and to have basic discussions * of our basic contract in cooperating with them together and it was * was a very nice day * the weather was okay I remember all. * We had first of all just general discussions to get into contact with each other * there was the very first day no contacts to any Hungarian [right] there was only by the managing director and the level below here from the client and asked that we made some general discussion and at the end of the evening we had some dinner and that's it. * That was the first day * just basic information and some positive things in coming into contact

Thus Schmidt's first day is organized entirely around the business relationship between his company and the German mother company. This relationship is contrasted with a local world completely detached from "global" business. The focus on global-local is even maintained by Bentham, who had no connection to such organizations at the time of her interview. In her main narrative she starts speaking about her work for predominantly multinational companies and at a later point she introduces a complete narrative of globalization linked to the pattern of area specialist analyzed above. In this part she criss-crosses the globe and introduces herself as being able to "invent" herself and her business wherever she ends up. She also sets herself the task of "getting into" local societies:

> Yeah um * my um, my background is hotels and I also didn't finish a degree * cause I went to * in the Third World studies, developing countries and management and that was the combination of my degree, which is still hanging in the air somewhere, but anyway, having said that um * * I had a always, outside of my own country which is England, I had always worked in developing countries, so I worked in South Africa, I worked in * Jamaica, Barbados and Saint Lucia, Russia and France which isn't a developing country. In all those situations I opened hotels, so I was always on the ground right at the beginning, building and putting policies, procedures, training * development programs for the local staff to be able to take over

> from the Western management um * and that * that teaches you an incredible amount about people, because every time you get off the plane in a new country you've got to start all over again and there's nobody with you, you know you don't have any family or your husband or whatever to go home to, so you have to get out there and you know * play a part in the society, for me that's very important, I can't live in a country ignoring everything that's around me, I have to actually get into that society and understand it, meet local people and socialize in local people * enjoy and try and understand them because that really affects the way that I train.

This "nomadic" life story together with the "universal" skills of opening hotels in different cultures and of implementing and teaching "Western" management rules to the "local" staff illustrates not only a global understanding (of cultural and social space), but also of the way knowledge of "otherness" (Third-World studies) can be utilized in such processes and global narratives can be linked to those of area specialization on the basis of ideas of mission and control.

One would think that as a result of economic imbalances only Westerners apply globalization patterns in introducing themselves in an East–West context. But this is not the case. In fact it is not only used by migrants such as the Hungarian Kovács, who has a complete narrative of serving in an early internationalized catering industry (major hotel chains) and representing the "hotel business" in areas where high standards are missing, but it can also be told by a high-ranking Russian military officer, who claims to have knowledge of universally applicable methods of "operation other than war". This method is elaborated in a "revolutionary" period of the Russian military officer's life, which he spent in the United States. Here the revolution is understood as some kind of invention made by the interviewee and his American friends:

> And fortunately in those time it was 1992, the Russian Military Authority sent me * to [a military school in the United States]. Extremely interesting. I took my wife and my children with me. It was a very famous military school. This period was revolutionary for my brain and eyes, and the world seemed to be different from I thought before. After this year I had very interesting trips around

> the USA, I organized field exercises for antiterrorism, the participation of the army under terroristic operations. When I finished my time in the academy, my contacts with them was with 62 nations, my friends were from Israel, Philippines, from Czech Republic Hungary * When I returned to the USSR, no to the Russian Federation, I knew, it is absolutely necessary to joint exercise, joint cooperation, especially peace-keeping. It was approximately 10 years ago. It was interesting time, new step in military theory, standard procedures for peacekeeping operation, peace making, humanitarian assistance peace enforcement. I am a specialist of that. It is so called: operation other than war.

Knowledge of peacekeeping operations takes the narrator to different international conflict zones, including the former Yugoslavia. In the end he leaves the "conservative" army for an American multinational company.

In conclusion, "nomadic" global narratives told in an East–West context are mainly linked to the idea of some kind of universal knowledge. This superior and deterritorialized knowledge can be claimed by actors from both "East" and "West." But the feeling of superiority it brings is also linked to missionary ideals in which the slope indicates intervention. In the case of "Westerners" that is the "other" society, while in the case of "Easterners" it is the sending one.

4.3.6. Narratives of interpretation

A narrative in which somebody poses as one who translates different cultural experiences can appear rather natural. Yet this kind of self-representation is not as dominant as, for instance, learning a language or being an area specialist, and appears mainly on the "Eastern side." Thus it seems that in the current discursive world no Westerner involved in activities related to Eastern Europe feels it legitimate to introduce himself or herself to a Western audience as somebody with a narrative of learning vis-à-vis Eastern Europe, at least in front of a Hungarian interviewer.

There was only one case in which somebody told a story of an interpreter living in communist Eastern Europe, which could be understood as some kind of model. In a story about a human-rights investigation in Eastern Europe, the political analyst Bukowsky, himself of

Jewish origin, tells a story of an interpreter moving between different cultures. It is important to note that this is linked to a common Jewish origin—suggesting a cultural background in which moving between countries and cultures is a well-established pattern of self-introduction (Kovács and Melegh 2001):

> And we were supposed to meet with * who was recently out of jail but* was placed under house arrest at that time* but we got to meet with several of the other people * and that time she was only a translator they made the ambassador here she actually turned out to be Jewish too she is * but she knew English perfectly and it but it was interesting why is she speaking American English. And it turns out she grew up in Brooklyn and then returned, her parents were lefties you know and they returned right after the war. [laughs] So she went there as fairly young girl just before, no it must have been right after world war two, a strange story she was always the interpreter for * and after that she was at [whispering] at the Foreign Ministry and they made her the ambassador to * but she died of leukemia and she passed away.

This bridge idea is missing from the other Western narratives. There, as seen in the case of global-profession narratives, only the Eurocentric implementation of "Western" and universal models or a sense of curiosity about the "East" is reported.

Analyzing the language and area specialist narratives, it seems that Eastern speakers have a great inner drive to transport knowledge of the "West" to the "locals" or to construct some kind of mission in this respect. Thus there is always the idea of interpretation, but an extremely imbalanced one since it travels one way only (Koivista, Markatov, Kovalsky).

Further analysis shows that one of the "Easterners," the Hungarian sociologist Marton, presents himself as an expert on "Eastern" society in intelligent, non-bureaucratic, non-Marxist "Western" language. But there is another Eastern narrative which, despite lacking an introduction of the narrator as an expert on the local society, Russia, is a clear-cut narrative of interpretation. This is the story of Poljakov, a Moscow-based Russian sociologist, who, according to his own narrative, makes several attempts to explain certain things to a "Western" audience, just as his Hungarian colleague does. But in this case a complete communication failure is reported:

> And then, it's interesting, my trip to Berlin showed that, generally speaking, well, I am studying something here, thinking that I'm clever, reading some books, but, as a matter of fact, I know nothing. And the West suddenly turns out to a be a sign in December 1991 as an absolutely different intellectual world I have no relation to, but which I must know. Since it's an intellectual world. Since one is engaged in intellectual labor, one must know. It was a shock for me. I probably just didn't understand what people were asking me about. ... And they didn't quite understand me. The problem's not that the language was bad, but the problem's that we happened to be conceptually different people. On the other hand, when they asked me, I didn't understand what they were asking about. I understood the words, but I didn't understand what they wanted (translated from Russian by Y. Roman).

Drawing upon these narratives, it seems that speakers on the Eastern side feel that it is legitimate to tell stories in which where the narrator is not understood and complains of a lack of "real" communication. This idea of a breakdown in communications assumes two different cultures, the borders of which cannot be crossed. Cultural closure in this context is elaborated throughout the narrative and some kind of essence is "given" to the different cultures.

The idea of two different cultures also appears in a "balanced" interpreter narrative. In this narrative the senior Russian officer Romanov introduces himself not only as somebody constantly moving between different "poles" and as a respected expert on a new global knowledge of "operation other than war", but also as a synchronizer of different cultures and as a translator of "Eastern" positions. The two seem related and lead to a certain ease in moving between "East" and "West."

The narrative of defending the "East" appears several times in Romanov's interview: when he describes his service as platoon commander in East Germany and also when he tells of standing up for the Serbian side against accusations of shelling Muslims in the Balkans (in the framework of international peace-keeping operations). In the latter story, Romanov introduces himself, not as a "Russian," but as an impartial military expert who arrives at the pro-Serbian position through careful analysis. He tells this story as a heretic within the international military community.

Later in the interview other stories of "translation" emerge, providing the main underlying logic of the whole interview. Romanov represents somebody who understands both cultures and who has a mission to bring them together. This is narrated with reference to different types of military maps:

> If I lie two maps on the table, for us, the typical Russian and an American is like abstract picture, what is the line, what is the arrow, what is the object, what is this strange boundaries, and for the Americans the Soviet map is a good picture, it is good, it is skillful. But there is absolutely no understanding what is it. What is the mission, what is the aim, what is the goal, how can we give order for that? We synchronized it. It is other culture. It is absolutely other culture. No illusion, we can't say: from today on, we use American. We can't do it. At the same time, American can take our culture. Therefore, there is more necessary step forward each other for synchronization. Our staff culture, mentality, technical standards, only for deep understanding: effectiveness, cooperation. It was the idea of my articles in the local newspapers, military newspapers.

This cross-cultural narrative leads to a self-representation of "having a flexible mind" and being able to see both sides in a situation such as peacekeeping in former Yugoslavia.

Thus it seems that the general pattern of translating and interpreting cultural knowledge is a narrative mainly restricted to the "Eastern" locus of enunciation and operates mainly as a translation for "Easterners": Western knowledge is to be transposed into the minds and hearts of the locals. The moment of self-reflection in the mirrors of different societies and cultures is missing in most cases. It seems that the East–West slope is not for cross-cultural understanding, for the weight of the "West" at the top of the slope is simply too great.

4.3.7. Narratives of ideological debates

Besides language learning and area specialism involvement in ideological debates is a general narrative employed in both "East" and "West."

Explicit cold-war type narratives are developed, where many speakers retrospectively reflect upon their life story as "children of the cold war." This reference seems to be clear in the case of "Western" speakers, while "Easterners" struggle with this perspective in their narratives.

The ideological debate on capitalism versus socialism emerges in the first main narrative of a distinguished American scholar. He reports that his original theoretical interest was redirected by the ongoing debate on socialism in the 1930s, and then he embarks on a long argument of ideological struggle in the post-depression United States in the following manner:

> But I cite this to indicate that my interests were really rather far from comparative systems * socialism versus capitalism * but this was a time you're probably too young to realize of great depression in this country and at the same time * there was in the distance * a country which was operating under a very different kind of economic system involving public ownership * central planning * very authoritarian * politics * well a whole younger people especially. There was a considerable interest in this alternative system and it was the more interesting since there were * there was some theory suggesting that maybe this is really a significant alternative to consider when capitalism fared so poorly as it did during the great depression. * So you had a debate in the * around the mid 30s. * There was a general understanding that according to Marxian views in any case the capital system would in the course of time have run its * have * would have * achieve whatever its potential was * and * capitalism would be replaced in the more advanced countries by socialism * central planning * this was a Marxian view. * It was challenged by some very distinguished economist and most important I would say were Ludwig von Mises and * Friedrich Hayek * the result was rather interesting theoretic exchange * was made more interesting by the work of Oscar Lange * have you heard of him? [Yes]* Hayek wrote a critique of central planning in which he argued that the claims were unfounded * it would * it would be system that would not function efficiently. * Lange replied designing a system which he felt * a form of planning * a socialist planning which he felt would be more efficient than capitalism and since we had the great depression in the West * this had a certain plausibility* the result was a very

> interesting discussion * on the comparative merit of this system but * I think a very interesting feature was that * it was all theoretic * that Marx * Marx's analysis was theoretic. * Mises replied with a theoretic analysis defending capitalism and Hayek did the same but there was really very little serious empirical work on the comparative functioning of the two systems. * I was someone intrigued by the * this fact I had * as I say I have working on pure theory by myself * without any real application to the debate that was taking place but I thought it might be interesting to look in what was actually happening

The scholar introduces himself as someone trying to enter an ideological socialism-capitalism debate with an empirical mind eager to see how the two "systems" actually work. But despite this "anti-ideological" standpoint the narrator organizes his life story and the ideological debate alongside a narrative identity moving into a central position. This is how he reports his first visit to Moscow in the 1930s:

> There were several Americans there in the same hotel as that where I stayed * it turned out they were rather far to the left politically * and we used to have debates on such questions as Trotsky's role in the revolution and so on * they told me later they had a meeting on the * to decide whether I was a fascist or a deluded liberal. * And they decided that I was a deluded liberal and they could still talk with me. * If I had been a fascist they told me they could not talk to at me.

Disorientation in this fierce ideological debate and fear of totalitarian repression drive the narrator to Washington as an expert analyst of foreign affairs during the war. There the activity story ends and nothing is reported on the subsequent period. We can only hypothesize that he cannot harmonize this earlier "center" or "in-between" position with later developments which push him to one side of the ideological debate.

The strength of cold-war identity is also evident in life stories starting much later, in which political analysts fight for human rights, become involved in security issues or simply take part in organized ideological debates. It seems that at least in the "West" this kind of narrative can easily be employed, as demonstrated by the following activity story, in which the narrator wants to "understand the enemy," i.e. "the communist international threat":

> Well * I got interested in the region actually when I was still in high school * I don't have any real affinities with that region ethnically * historically * Pennsylvania * none of my families comes from that area at all. * However I can just remember I was growing up. * I do remember television commercials regarding radio Free Europe [yes] with * slamming down * can also remember my grandfather talking about how the world is gonna be Communist by the year 2000 [oh right] * a lot of the things from the cold war period * and for whatever reason I don't know but I was always sort of interested in trying to understand the enemy [right] * that * that point is always growing up the enemy was always the communist * international threat. * I think it also was because now I'm 38 yeas old and I start becoming aware of the world * during the larger part of the Vietnam conflict and immediately thereafter when America * leading America pressure in the world [right, right] hear a lot of criticism from my own country and this is hard as a child to understand all that. * So that sort of got me interested trying to figure out why is a our country so bad * who are these communist * why are they threat * and that sort of what let me into * into the area *I got interested originally in political sciences

This drive "to understand the enemy" forms the main engine of such narratives, a theme which then absorbs everything else (war, Radio Free Europe, threat of war etc.), including some self-reflection in the context of American or local society. These narratives have a deliberative logic, which is "I decide who is right or who is wrong." This type of "rational-moral deliberation" is even more evident in the case of our German expert who wrote the thesis on technological progress in the Soviet Union quoted above. This is a detailed narrative which includes reports on conversations relating to car production in the Soviet Union:

> I will never forget a conversation that I had with a student there, we were living in dorms, we had always intensive discussions, a student pointed out to me, why like in the West, do you want to produce

all these different cars, all these different type of cars, you have to go through the end of the process, you produce all these different models [right] whereas we, in the Soviet Union, we at the beginning decide which one is the best car [right] and then we concentrate on producing one [right] so we don't have to do all this wasteful different cars, we know..

In this narrative the theme of the functioning of the "system" leads to an analysis of "why this didn't work." These reflections are based on a comparison in terms of worldwide competition, progress and modernities. But this perspective is combined with one linking the Soviet Union to the Third World, which may mean that such narratives are rewritten in the present perspective and the "cold-war" discourse of competing modernities is subordinated to the qualitative East–West discourses (re)emerging in the 1980s.

The process of rewriting can also be seen in the case of "Eastern" speakers, who try more dramatically to replace their "cold-war" perspective with a new one. This process is evident in the case of the Russian Kovalsky, a military and political security analysit, who tries to re-represent himself as a member of a "think tank" who has nothing to do with cold-war debates or cold-war careers:

OK: I start as my professional activity. Because after graduating from the institute where I was a student I've come to the Academy of Sciences and the field of my activity was international relations and that was a professional field, my exchange with the West. This started quite long ago, I don't remember exactly, at the end of the seventies. I was meeting Western specialists when I was a junior researcher, and then I worked in the political institution. We discussed problems that were very important at that time like East–West relations, disarmament something like that. I worked in a section which was dealing with theoretical problems of international relations so our counterpart were those dealing with theoretical issues, development of international relations, we were trying to do that on our side, we exchanged views.

In this narrative, which maintains the cold-war structure, not only the "hick-ups" and memory lapses are important, but also a stress on professionalism (see the first sentence for instance). Clearly, a career story is being formulated in which everything occurs as in the "West." Here we witness the birth of a "political scientist" emerging from the structures of a coldwar narrative.

It is important to note that some of the speakers use the narrative of ideological debate, but this time not as a "cold-war" debate but as a new division between Russia and the "West." This is a fragmented and only partial narrative and only partially employed; as yet no complete career stories have been invented. For example, the Russian sociologist Poljakov not only found it difficult to communicate with his Western colleagues, but actually tells stories of "ideological" debates on issues such as Yugoslavia, provoking long Slavophile arguments on the different nature of the "West" and Russia. The same type of report can also be observed in the case of the Russian officer quoted above, who frames his story in the format of an ideological debate when asked about the first day. This narrative perfectly combines a cold-war narrative with a new ideological debate. There is a well-developed thematic line combining the struggle between "East" and "West," i.e. the conflict with Germany, the bombing of Yugoslavia and "betrayal" by former friends such as Hungary:

> It is a mixed feeling. My personal position is that now I know this, and I know this way is right. Each man and woman lived in that life, it was flexible, it was permanently swinging. According to this real law, there wasn't any flexible way. Now, when I think about my changing position, from extraordinarily negative. My father was a fighter of the Second World War, his position about Germany for example, was absolutely clear. They are the aggressor, we fight them, there is no doubt, we are going to stay in the same position throughout history. I don't know what was the reason for changing my understanding. Factoral research, external war, mass media, my flexible mind, friends around me. I think this altogether. I changed my position from left side to right side. But now I can't say I am hundred percent orthodox approval of the Western politics, mentality. From time to time, when I meet someone similar, for example the former Yugoslavia bombing, I understand it was demonstration of power, it was not war. When I participated in radio discussion, or TV, the Russian TV, every time I said: it is not war, absolutely not. It is demonstration of power. It

> was pressure on the Milošević regime in Kosovo, etc. In that time I had a lot of attack against me. Are you a western spy? No, I said, it is my sincere opinion. But on the other hand, I can't understand with a lot of steps from the Western world, about Russia, or about Eastern Europe, about our former friends, like Hungary, Czech Republic, Bulgaria. I am not sure whether the whole step is hundred percent right. It's a flexible line. In my mind I have so many mistakes. But this is a topic for separate discussion.

Thus cold-war ideological debates have not gone away and still organize career stories set in East–West contexts. This is especially true of those speaking from a "Western locus"; those on the "Eastern" side are very much in the process of rewriting, with the East–West slope enforcing a suppression of the "bad" Eastern inheritance. Nonetheless, it is worth noting that this rewriting operates not only on the basis of "Western norms," but also according to older patterns of one's community being "spiritually different" from the "West" pushing one into political and civilizational debates. Here we see that just as in the case of collective actors, individuals in the same locus also weave themselves onto the East–West slope by way of different perspectives. In telling conflict stories between "East" and "West," nationalist rejection is just as valid as the "othering of local society" or even the othering of cold-war selves when confronted with the "West."

4.3.8. Narratives of the discovery of the unknown

The cold-war narratives are about understanding the enemy and being engaged in some kind of "debate" with him. In such "debates" the main question is which system is "good" or "progressive" in the competition of modernities. The narratives of discovery are quite different, since activities are narrated, not as part of a debate, but rather as a one-way discovery of something "unknown." These narratives include self-representations in which somebody is trying to get closer to the "soul" or the "brain" of the unknown person. Alternatively there is a story of traveling with such intentions. Conversely, these narratives can include stories in which somebody is "discovered" or treated as an unknown "barbarian". These two versions vary according to the different loci of enunciation, but we should not regard this as a natural fact, since actors further down the slope can also apply it to perspectives "looking down" further "East."

In terms of unequal cross-cultural contacts, the cognitive attitude of discovering the unknown has become a central theme in the criticism of imperialism, colonialism and Orientalism (among others Böröcz 2000; Erlmann 1999; Said 1978, 1994; Williams and Chrisman 1994; Wolff 1994). This well-established 18th and 19th century pattern also plays an important role in present discourses. In Éva Kovács's words, what we are looking at is a deeply embedded cultural pattern, a supernarrative readily offering itself to individuals as a well-established framework in an East–West context. We should not be surprised to find it in the material thus far examined (Kovács and Melegh 2001).

Narratives of the unknown generally come up rather early in interviews indicating that they can be rather dominant and elaborate patterns through which whole careers can be organized and told. Daniel, a newly-employed East and Central Europe specialist at an American foundation, started his narrative on Eastern Europe by introducing friends and family members involved in wild-water canoeing who helped him to discover an unknown area:

> As a matter of fact, this is a one-turn story, but I try to make it short. Originally I visited Yugoslavia, and Croatia, in the late eighties, it was still Yugoslavia, and that was predicated upon to see family members, and to see canoeing friends of my father and uncles, who have been serious wild-water canoeing in the sixties or seventies and this indicates they had a number of Slovenian friends and I was supposed to visit his son. They opened my eyes to an area what I have misinterpreted about something very close and dark.

The feeling of excitement and wildness in the narrative is not only shown by the references to "wild water" and a "close and dark" region, but at later points the interviewee still comes back to how insecure he felt when he was traveling there. This feeling of strangeness is partly related to visiting a cold-war enemy, but the main source of "wildness" is the coming war in Yugoslavia.

The theme of discovery also appears in the narrative of the French expat manager in Hungary, but once again the stress is less on cold-war fears than on visiting and observing changes in an "unknown" area. This narrative perspective focuses on the way these "unknown" and previously "lost" people adapt liberalism after communism, closely following the mental patterns described by Larry Wolff with regard to the 18th century[2]:

> Hungary? Or not? OK. So in 1990, it was more of a region, because I had not been to Hungary, I'd been to the Czech Republic and Poland for nonprofessional reasons, just to discover the countries opening a little bit to East Europe. That's just to say that I was interested in what had been happening and I was ready to meet people; I knew a number of Hungarians, Poles who lived in France and who I talked to, For example, there was a Hungarian who had emigrated in 56 and who talked to me as if he were seeing Hungary today, afterwards, at the pesent time, from all that he knew in the previous years. And it was interesting for me to see how it could evolve and how it could be, well, how countries which were in fact very close to France, or culturally at a certain moment, yes, maybe to Austria, or to the countries which I knew better, how they could evolve then, after such a period of communism which had been very close, in any case, as we perceived * by us. So, it was possible to meet people who had been enthusiastic for these insights and for the capacity to change, to change life and change their way of looking at things. And at the same time I had something like an impression, when I was there, of finding a country that was kind of as my parents told me about France forty or, well, fifty years ago.... That's it, and on the contrary, on the other hand, we also saw, we met people we had less contact with, because they didn't speak any other languages, but the way as the population lived in general gave impressions or brought back memories of * It was interesting to watch the difference. Well, or else, then, it was the first stage, which is the stage of curiosity, in fact (translated from French E. K.).

Encounters with these strange people emerging from the "past" and open reflections on making contact with them physically and spiritually recur throughout the story. In the first-day narrative the French expat reports not only his lack of ability to learn Hungarian, but also deep cultural differences between the French and the Hungarians. The narrative even breaks down at one point and a very interesting conversation about the working attitudes of Hungarians takes place between the manager and the interpreter:

> Even if it's clear that like what was said to us was either by the Hungarians living in France or even by the French we could meet here, they, there was obviously a way to work or comprehend commerce which was different in any case, or not seen in the same way, I was struck as were the others. In particular, but it's, I probably got it later, the attitude, it quite struck me at the beginning, not so strongly during the first days, but this attitude to work and to this position in life, which was—on the whole—not true for everybody, for sure—but on the whole it was different from the way, the way they have in France, I had such an impression. Maybe, and it was, and it struck me as well, it's the number of people who have, who had, who invested outside their work, maybe more than in other countries, in France or in other European countries, into cultural aspects, music, singing, sport, which finally occupied a great deal of time and place. We had that impression, at least.
>
> Interpreter: [turning to me]: I do not know if he is trying to say that work is secondary to us.
>
> Gurnier: You have added something.
>
> Interpreter: I was just thinking whether work is of secondary concern to us.
>
> Gurnier: At certain points I thought I had this feeling. Not in terms of time but in attitude even among people in important and responsible positions.[turning to me] Don't you have such an impression (translated from French by E. K.)?

By the end of this discovery process, a major difference is emphasized vis-à-vis working attitudes, later subsumed into an ethnicized argument about the "unhappy" Hungarian "soul."

The spirit of Russia formed a focus in the "discovery of Russia" by the Belgian woman Karine, whose "illegitimate" love affair directly reflected the way she understood Russian behavior. This discovery and the concomitant encounters were expressed in visual terms referring to "regard" or "eyes" as entries into the collective spirit and as signs of differences. For instance she was told that she could be recognized as not being Russian by her way of looking:

> We know that you are not Russian by your regard. Your eyes. And * Well, I understood that a lot of eyes, maybe not so much now, but at that time, were anxious. No? Were not free, and so on, and I don't have those eyes. That's true, that's real, and so it was a big difference. Yeah.

In the interviews such differences are also discovered by the speakers, not only in terms of the soul and the eyes, but also of the "brain", which Bentham, the professional globalized consultant from Britain, tried so hard to understand. Speaking about her discovery of the Russian collective mentality, her otherwise easy-going narrative breaks down:

> * I came to Russia and it was a complete disaster, and I couldn't understand and I was like why, why are people not responding to this, and um. * I of course started to analyze it, and it took me about 6 months to actually understand that the Russian brain thinks a different way and * I I can't actually tell you how they think, cause I'm not sure that I know myself, but I do know that I * changed my training approach, and I can access the Russian brain but I'm not sure that I can tell you what the difference is * um * *. * certainly, um * * certainly having done that I was much more successful and I was, and I am successful, so are my staff but they're Russian to Russian, which has its own complications actually, which is perhaps another story.

This "other" story is never told, but throughout her narrative she focuses on essentialist differences between cultures, not only for the purpose of understanding and discovery, but also of "invading" in order to be more efficient in business training (see her airplane narrative cited earlier in the discussion of her global profession). This colonial and Orientalist perspective of capturing the "Russian brain" is well illustrated by her description of her training technique:

> I mean my approach is that we all have an opportunity to learn from you and I help you to learn from me.

Thus in this cultural exchange there is a need for teaching the trainees how to learn from the teacher, who represents some kind of "global" knowledge. She can learn by herself; others are not able to do this by themselves. The "Russian brain" is thus in need of tutelage—a pattern of semi-Orientalist control again amply demonstrated in the European civilizational map of the 18th century (Wolff, 1994).

We cannot, therefore, be surprised that on the "Eastern" side of the discursive wall we have several stories of being treated as "barbarian." When asked about her first day, Koivista, the head of a Russian institute on European affairs, suddenly launches into a story of "physical" discovery on her way to Triest:

> But the second session was in Triest. So I traveled from Moscow to Milano and then from Milano to Triest by train. Very interesting experience. You know, I came to Milano and * it was April or May, something like that, and then I immediately from the* from the airport I * I went to the railway station and I * so, I used normal train to go from Milano to Triest. And * there my * you see, the people who were en face were Italian students from Brescia, Brescia University and we spoke a lot and I was the first Soviet that they met in their lives, and then they told everybody, in this, you see, in this wagon, that there is a Soviet young woman and people * you see, the majority of them they were coming to our, you see, to our places and they would like to, even to touch me. Even to touch me. And then they realized that I speak fluently French and English, they touched my hair, my hands, yes, and they, probably they expected to meet a bear or I don't know [she laughs] what was that, you know, it was * they were changing of course, and by Triest, all the way from Milano to Triest, and we came from the wagon and see little, little cities like Bologna, Brescia and so on, and when I came to the hotel in Triest and the next day, next morning, I got, you see, very nice flowers from one * with a business card and it said that 'it was a great pleasure to meet you and this a sign of my * I don't know * my gratitude for, you see, for these 2–3 hours that we spoke together in the train. In the train.' So it was so.

The encounter between a Soviet woman and the Italians is told almost as if the narrator were an animal in a zoo being stared at by children.

The discovery of the woman is physical, but the story ends with a flattery that lifts her from a position of being the target in an anthropological inquiry into one of being accepted as a cultured woman. The ambiguity and contradiction of being treated as a "barbarian" and at the same time being fluent in several languages and "Western" culture can be one of the major structures of East European self-introduction in an East–West context. This constant play with "race," "physical outlook" and "culture" serves to lift the subject out of a local, "provincial" context, which reminds the interpreter of pre-World War I patterns in German and Central European territories.

In the narrative of Poljakov, the Moscow-based sociologist not understood by "Westerners," there are several smaller narratives of being treated as a strange phenomenon to be classified, showing a certain interplay between the "West" and Russia. Here the "West" is also represented by Hungary. Poljakov's name is fed into a computer in 1989 in Hungary at an opposition rally, which apart from invoking-cold war memories and a criminal narrative identity, may be further understood as an act of categorization:

> It's at the office, at the foreign department of the Party CC [Central Committee], he put me into the computer straight away, it was written there: Poljakov, Alexander, Russia, Soviet alternative. So, well, I was put into some computer, that's for me it was * some person put me in, he was an expert or something (translated from Russian by Y. Roman).

The story then continues with Poljakov talking about a Hungarian political activist who explains to him that leaving Hungary he is going to a "totally different country."

> He was interested, he asked: 'So, you came here by train, I've bought you a return ticket for the plane. The train, it was slow coming here, and you'd find yourself suddenly from Hungary by plane into Russia just at once, in a totally different country. It'll be a sort of shock for you' (translated from Russian by Y. Roman).

The story ends with the creation of a dichotomy of alien cultures in which the "West" and Russia confront and regard each other as "savage":

> So, it was my first collision with the West, thereafter came talks with some people, and trips. Well, on the whole, the West initially existed, to put it correctly, as a political thing. Then it went on acquiring some cultural traits. The West as a certain culture. Because * it's clear, that when it's for the first time in the other country, in Hungary * there're many details, which seem to me absolutely savage. As if another man, a Hungarian, or German, or Czech coming here—he'd find something savage (translated from Russian by Y. Roman).

We may conclude that in certain "Western" and "Eastern" narratives of discovery, the idea of civilized versus barbarian and the related culturally essentialist cognitive patterns are played out rather directly. This can be seen as the (re)appearance of historical patterns in which "Eastern" speakers seek cultural or racial compensation for being "under Western eyes," as they understand it, i.e. for being regarded as inhabitants of the "unknown" or " lost" lands of Eastern Europe. Once again, due to the inbuilt inequality of the East–West discourses, the "Eastern" personality is seen as problematic and not really existing within the offered framework. This type of coloniality is has often been described with regard to "proper" colonial encounters (Ashcroft 1989, 8–11; Said 1978, 207–208). With regard to East European speakers the interesting point is that here "Easterners" are eager to present themselves as being treated in this way, which can be seen as a protest and a claim for fairer treatment. With their demand to be taken out of "abnormal" categories they only partially question the categorization itself.

4.3.9. Narratives of criminality

The analysis of migration in a Central European context suggests that border crossing, in today's cultural structures, frequently invokes narrative patterns of criminality, in which migrants portray themselves as involved in an illegal passage between countries (Kovács and Melegh 2001). The crossing of imaginary borders such as those between "East" and "West" also carries an intrinsic illegitimacy in population discourses and individual narratives. Roma people, being "more Eastern" than the majority of an "almost" Western nation, are not allowed to go to the "West" to criticize the majority, as exemplified by the Zámoly case analyzed in chapter 2. Alternatively, "Western" women should not marry "Eastern" men since this move destabilizes the power constellation of the East–West slope. Therefore it is no surprise that we also find narratives in which the interviewee presents himself or herself as being involved in "criminal" acts or, even more importantly, as being treated like a criminal. Subjects appear as "spies" or as "smugglers" or as simply "problematic." This type of narrative, linked to Foucauldian forms of discipline and control, seems to follow another universal pattern employed in all loci of enunciation on the East–West slope. Thus people on either side can be "suspects."

The most common narrative is that of being treated as a spy or somebody moving too freely in or between closely controlled societies. All these patterns are related to a cold-war scenario, but it is important to note that in most cases such narratives are only episodes, that is to say, they organize shorter sections in the narrative. Nevertheless, they reveal East–West divisions. In the East such narratives are more highly developed. Thus, for instance, Bergen, Kernel or Bukowsky from the "West" speak about episodes of border guards knocking on the door when the interviewee hurries into the toilet after many hours of travel or starts talking to "frightened" sailors on a Moscow bus, on the "Eastern" side we sometimes have complete sagas in which the subject is seen as some kind of criminal.

Marton, the Hungarian sociologist, builds a massive narrative on publishing books and articles in the "West" without official approval during the state-socialist period. This is presented as an act for which some of his friends were persecuted or even executed. Explaining his first trip to Belgium, Kovalsky, the Russian security expert, develops a complete narrative about being refused a passport to the "West" in the Soviet period for unknown reasons, while his fellow-travelers received it immediately. This narrative, crucial in retrospectively establishing the image of a "dissident" type, is a long self-investigation of a high imaginative quality, which includes the following passage:

> You know when * there is no passport, wait, wait, maybe there is a procedure your passport, you were not given a passport and this could be because there might be some complaints of KGB in your case, there might be some secret files or there is some information that you were not loyal or you allowed some statements which are not permitted, some statements which were considered as challenge of the Soviet sys-

> tem or maybe there was something else or maybe you have divorced, for this reasons, because there are some problems with your moral integrity, or maybe there is something else we do not know we just do not know why this happened because we are not, there was no decision.

This Dostoevskyan narrative of being at the mercy of power and of externally conditioned self-control and self-doubt concludes with the "solution" of Kovalsky obtaining the passport after waiting one more day. But the success does not end the story of self-criminalization; after obtaining the passport there are problems with foreign currency. But let us leave this almost endless crime narrative of Kovalsky and arrive in the "West" with Volkov, who also presents a multi-layered criminal narrative. Now the "West" is Hungary. Volkov describes the hours of arrival on his second trip to Hungary as follows:

> OK. The second time when I came to Hungary I came with my wife. We arrived to the * railway station in Budapest, we had a lot of luggage because we brought some more gifts * gifts to, you know, the people who invited us to Hungary. [Right] At that time it was impossible just to go, you had to have some invitation from some person, and * yeah. So we had gifts, very strange gifts for everybody, they were vacuum cleaners. Vacuum cleaners. Vacuum cleaners? Not that strange! [I laugh] At that time we had very good vacuum cleaners in Russia. So if they can cope with it, it's a very good gift, vacuum cleaners. So we * we brought * I think two vacuum cleaners, I don't know. Well. And, well, it was necessary to call by phone those people. I don't remember why they didn't meet us at the railway station, so anyway, we had to call by phone, and you know, I had to try to call with Hungarian words and Russian words, and I spoke on the phone in Hungarian. With the help of a book. [Right]. But the person * asked me also in Hungarian. That was incredible! So * it was impossible to speak! My wife, she speaks German and then she tried to speak German with those people. Finally * we agreed that we * and when we came, with all the luggage and all the gifts, it happened that these people were not there to meet us. Just a problem of language. We didn't understand pretty good by phone and * we didn't understand and * and there was some problem with the telephone set on the street. It didn't connect us properly. [Right] It

> just didn't connect, but we spoke with some other people and they said, 'OK, come' and we came. The * the husband of that lady who said 'Come', it happened that he was a policeman. And he had a brother, in high rank in the criminal police. And when we came he had a feeling that we are criminals. Because he used to * to be with criminals! You know? Some strange people from Russia come and say that you have invited us! [Laughs]. So it was a very difficult, you know, negotiation process. Finally he himself called those people who really invited us. And he had the chance to speak Hungarian with them, and eventually everything was understood. But it was very late at night. Eventually we arrived at night. So it was very late and they were so kind that they didn't let us go.

This French-farce narrative—somebody phones a wrong person, actually a policeman, after "smuggling" two vacuum cleaners into Hungary—demonstrates the "operation" of East–West taboos. Crossing the East–West border is "forbidden" and extra efforts in terms of both language and gifts are needed. These difficulties in organizing the move lead the narrator into trouble and into a situation in which he appears to be a criminal. But in Volkov's narrative not only have real borders been presented as taboos, but talking to foreigners in itself may be seen as something illegal. Volkov, who becomes the manager of a consulting company working for multinationals, builds his whole narrative on overcoming this subordinate position. In the end he lifts himself out of this "uncivilized" state by establishing everyday links to the "West." Here we cannot miss the similarity to the story of the Russian scholar who was treated by the Italians on the train as both a real human being and some kind of animal. The East–West slope not only invokes the image of forbidden borders, but actually creates it also, as Volkov's and Koivista's narratives serve to distance the interviewees from their local society and to transpose them into the "Western" sphere.

4.4. Combinations of different East–West narratives

The different types of narratives are not normally told on their own and almost all the interviews analyzed contain multiple patterns of storytelling. Despite the limited number of narratives a variety of stories can be told and retold. Many combinations are possible and "strong" individuals can create striking biographies, East–West careers and even extremely persuasive and original stories told in a literary style. Regardless of discursive restrictions people can make us laugh and cry. We may be dominated by grand narratives, but individual creativity is still alive. It seems that there is a definite need for narrative internal reflections and meditations in trying to understand ourselves as we move between "East" and "West."

In addition to individual combinations, certain regularities emerge, defining which narratives complement or exclude one another. By analyzing these combinations (a correlation between vertical lines in the table below) we can trace different supra-cognitive patterns which organize East–West stories and East–West encounters, although in so doing it is important to consider the different loci of enunciation, since the same narrative might become radically different in a different "locus." Through reflecting narratives told from different discursive positions, we can formulate ideas about the "dialogue" between "East" and "West" or different positions on the East–West slope. The differences may be great according to the different loci, but reflecting upon or presenting ourselves in the same narrative field means that somehow we are in communication or in conversation with each other. In other words, we may find partners in the "other" world with whom we can communicate (by virtue of sharing the same thematic fields) regardless of whether this communication takes the form of a debate or some kind of agreement. But as we will see, the organizing patterns and the dialogues are not straightforward; different combinations of narratives and structural positions (horizontal and vertical axes in the table) are often incongruent and containing a great deal of flexibility. Most importantly, we can formulate such narrative combinations as have not necessarily been "suggested." The analysis below should be read merely as a scenario or a possibility. There are no laws for creating narratives and for the ways we weave ourselves onto the East–West slope. But there is some kind of order, which is certainly an important consideration in the sociology of the East–West slope.

4.4.1. "Cold-war" self-representation and the othering of local society

Table 4.2. Combination of 'cold-war' individual interviews

Person	Types of narrative						
	Speaking (0) or not speaking (+) the language	Area specialist, special knowledge	In ideological debate	Criminal, criminalized	Family background	Intimate relationship	Interpreter
			Born in the 'West'				
Kernel			0	0			
Flinn	0	0				0	
Bukowsky	0		0	0	0	0	0
Schmidt	0	0	0			0	
Bergen	0	0	0	0	0	0	
Henzel	0	0	0				
Nurick		0			0		
Karine	+				0	0	
			Born in Hungary				
Marton	0	0		0			0
Kovács	0				0		
			Born in Russia				
Markatov	0		0	0	0		0
Rushkov	0	0					
Poljakov			0	0			0
Kovalsky		0	0	0			0
Koivista	0	0	0				0
Romanov			0	0			0

The analysis of the individual narratives shows that the cold-war associational field has been very strong in the construction of stories, be they spy stories, crossings of the iron curtain or monitoring the military and economic capabilities of the "other" side. Some narrators even described themselves as "children of the cold war." Thus we have a pattern connecting certain narratives into a metanarrative of cold-war type encounters.

This metanarrative contains several individual narratives, the most important of which are the learning of languages, area specialization, ideological debate and criminal stories. These patterns may be accompanied by family-background and love stories predominantly in the "West." In the "East," self-representation may be strengthened by the interpreter narrative, which rarely happens in the "West." These latter East–West narratives may thus be understood as some kind of subnarratives, but they can also be separate patterns of storytelling not linked to the rest.

Crucial to this overall pattern of self-representation is the involvement in an ideological debate. The main task is to position ourselves according to different moral, political and social values. Here we have two different "real" poles with their own power arrangements as reference points for our biographies and careers. This "reality" of the poles is evident in the narrative of involvement in a debate, which cannot be constructed without two opposing poles. Language learning is also relevant in this respect, as this narrative illustrates that the speakers feel it important to present themselves as having "access" to the social and cultural life of the other pole. Speakers on all sides had a range of stories which described going into theaters or visiting cultural attractions.

But there is also a pattern which keeps people at home and makes crossing borders very difficult. That is why we have narratives of criminality within this combination of narratives. Interviewees find it important to present themselves as persons transgressing "uncrossable" borders and being treated as criminals or spies. This introduces anxiety and tension into the overall pattern. Learning about the "other" is linked to "illegitimacy" and this combination of curiosity and fear gives a special flavor to the overall narrative identity.

As mentioned above, such narratives may (although not necessarily) be linked to narratives of family background and love affairs. This combination also forms a link with the "reality" of the two poles. Being real and being separate may allow us to fall in love or increase the value of family relations. Thus by starting a cold-war story, we not only look for linguistic links and debates, but are also anxious to find real people linked to the "other" region.

While there is some balance in the cold-war idea, there is an imbalance if we look at communication between "East" and "West." It seems that in today's perspective "Eastern" speakers present their dealings with the "West" as being in some way pro-Western.

Individual "Eastern" narratives present this pattern of self-representation, language-learning and interpreting narratives as a means of moving out of the local community or obtaining a privileged position within, from which local people can be taught about the "West." In this overall pattern of self-representation "Eastern" interviewees find it important to narrate the role of "special schools" or their early educational background which taught them foreign languages. Among both those born in Russia and those born in Central Europe.

There are well-established and easily related mythologies of schools and educational facilities as a means of "upward" mobility on the slope. In this sense the cold-war pattern is certainly a mechanism of pushing people up on the slope through the acquisition of "Western" values and knowledge of "Western" culture and social life. Perfecting or civilizing ourselves and educating others in the local society could be one of the results.[3] Narrators simply present themselves as "interpreters" who can communicate special knowledge to their own societies. They have a mission of "Europeanization." All the interviewees implementing this pattern were "angry" with their own people. Markatov built his story as a fight against "savage" Russian tourists, who spoil the image of Russians in the West. Koivista wanted to teach her Russian fellow-citizens a new way of thinking, while Romanov berated his fellow-officers for not learning new military techniques. In this way the cold-war metanarrative pattern is in congruence with the perspective of "othering the local society," which was analyzed with regard to the positioning of institutional actors in chapter 3.

Thus it seems that upward-looking perspectives or identities othering the local society do not come directly from colonial discourses but are post-communist and post-cold war reformulations and reinterpretations of cold-war narratives. This can be a trick of history, as the breakdown of a power arrangement of competing modernities and the struggle to overtake the "West" ends in a pattern whereby "Eastern" cold-war narratives turn out to be "missionary" versions of "westernizing" local society. The linchpin of this reformulation is certainly a utopian type of thinking in which communist ideals are replaced by ideals of the "West" (Melegh 1994; Böröcz 2003 84–85; Chakrabarty 2000, 30). Ironically, in this way "Easterners" with a cold-war narrative identity become the best partners of "Western" missionaries speaking in another metanarrative pattern of globalization and colonization, analyzed below. It is no surprise that the former communist elite has been the best client of the "West" in dismantling East European state socialism (Karnoouh 2003).

4.4.2. Global self-representation and colonization

Besides cold-war self-representation it seems that the next consistent combination of different narratives is the introduction of oneself as either global, nomad, or local as opposed to those always "on the road."

The global-nomad meta-self-representation is rather distinct from the cold-war version and the narrative patterns are rarely brought together by the interviewees. The global nomadic structure combines narratives of global professions, the inability to learn languages and undergoing a process of discovery. The key point in this complex self-representation is possession of knowledge or a profession convertible in different parts of the world. In contrast to "territorial" cold-war self-representation, in which the borders between "East" and "West" are well defined, this narrative is a deterritorialized one in which the hero of the story moves with great ease between different countries and

Table 4.3. Global self-representation

Person	Types of narrative		
	Speaking (0) or , not speaking the language (+)	Discovery of the unknown	Global profession
Born in the West			
Daniel		0	
Bentham	+	0	0
Gurnier	+	0	0
Schmidt	+	0	0
Karine		0	
Born in Hungary			
Schweitzer		0	0
Kovács	0		0
Born in Russia			
Romanov	0		0

towns. In his story Kovács, a Hungarian-born hotel manager, goes to England, the Netherlands, Switzerland, the United States and Russia, while his children by a Dutch wife are even more geographically mobile. Romanov, the Russian officer, also moves between East Germany, the Russian Far East, the United States and the Balkans without any significant break in the narrative. Schmidt, an ex-officer German expat manager in Hungary, is also on the move throughout his life. This combination of narratives produces "on the road" patterns, in which the storytellers hardly have time to pack.

Wandering can be one reason for not learning languages—the other defining characteristic of this type of self-representation. The point is not lack of time but "pride" in presenting such stories. This pattern is not about finding links to local societies (regardless of any such claims), but not possessing such links. The mission is not trying to understand "the enemy," but to implement global patterns of management, logistics or military procedures, and in such a project speaking the language is not necessary. In the perception of the interviewees everything becomes international. As we remember from our previous analysis, airport signs can easily be read without learning the Cyrillic alphabet.

It is important to keep in mind that these people do not speak about themselves as free agents. They are the "servants," or on the Western side the "missionaries," of their companies. They have a duty to introduce certain techniques, procedures and images into local spheres. They have the task of ruling and transforming local social, political or cultural arrangements in a colonial or semi-colonial manner. In order to illustrate these points let us examine some additional quotes from two stories. The first shows a link to the cold-war situation, but if look at the story carefully it turns out that in essence this is not a cold-war story, but a civilizational narrative of discovery and domination. Here one of the interviewees, Schmidt, after formally finishing the narrative interview, starts speaking about his experiences of the transformation of the East German army:

> Okay when because of the end of the cold war there was * there was a Western Germany force and there was an Eastern German force and there was a Western German state and an Eastern German state and when the reunification was done * and decided in 1989. * They

> said okay * now we have one one big area * East and West it belongs together * and that means we have to build up one German forces * from East and West together and ** because of the much higher development, the technical development of the equipment * of the situation * of the barracks * and all these things and the decision was absolutely clear from the beginning that the development of the forces could only be guided * by the Western part of Germany and because also this Warschau, Warsaw Pact thing they were quitted and * West Germany was a member of NATO so we had to build up the NATO structure in the Eastern German part but * there were about 300 thousand East German soldiers * still within East German * clothes of the East German clothes and * with all these things of the Eastern German army and my job was to * first of all to collect ammunition * from the different areas to a central point * the second job was to train * Eastern Army officer in the first step in the basic democratic and political things and the basic military things of the NATO and all these things. * I * builded up there * a new storage area* a logistic service point ** out of the system from West Germany * so there was my storage area that was in Western Germany was finished and we said okay we have to deploy this one over * to east Germany [right] and that was my job what I did there * therefore I spent * and I was also going to Poland because of the decentralization of their logistic point the Eastern Germans had that was my job [whispering] half a year.

Here, missionary self-representation appears in the fact of referring to civilization as an argument for dissolving the East German army and incorporating it in the West German in the name of unification. But there is also a story of teaching "basic democratic and political things" alongside a story of expansion involving certain systems and services to the other territory ("out of the system of West Germany"). These three aspects, the civilizational and technological superiority, the teaching of "essential" and superior values and being engaged in the process of expansion, add up to a complete colonial-type narrative (Comaroff and Comaroff 1992).

The same mentality of ruling, discovering and transforming also appears in Bentham's story, as the continuation of a shorter episode of getting off the plane alone in Moscow and finding ways of accessing the "brain" of the people there. Bentham, perceiving the situation in "developing" countries, interprets her role as follows:

> I have to actually get into that society and understand it, meet local people and socialize with local people *. Enjoy and try and understand them because that really affects the way that I train, because I have a deeper understanding of what they face when they run a 5 star hotel, and the luxury that that brings, and the difficulties they face in trying to * shower * you know people living in wooden shacks and they have no water, and yet we expect them to come showered and smelling fresh and beautiful * so even that's a very simple, level. * But when battling with an education system which has again you know missing parts that you require for your business, so it's up to me to identify what is the missing part and to build that into the training to compensate for that, so that the business is able to * to move forward * and that they're able to, to grow with the business and get that base of understanding * each country has its own * history, its own culture, its own approach, the sort of any common area is for me working with hotels * and that was it really.

She not only sets the standards and the need to have people showered and smelling good, but she also points out the "missing" elements in their education and corrects them during the training process. In other words, with this narrative she aims at overriding local epistemes and providing an introduction for the local people to the "modern" system. The globalization narrative is thus clearly established on colonial patterns of looking down the civilizational slope and intervening at the lower points.

Altogether, on the basis of self-representation and narrative identity, the East–West dialogue seems to be a rather unequal process of "communication" with interesting twists. The-cold war metanarrative on the "Western" side is a deep, territorialized investment in the culture and society of the former cold-war enemy, in which curiosity, language learning and familial or romantic links are very important elements. Paradoxically, without transferring this knowledge back to the home society, this narrative is a rather "honest" preoccupation with another region of the world, with the ideas of which it is worthwhile entering into an ideological debate. This approach, and the deep interest in the culture and society of the Other, is reciprocated on the "Eastern" side, but with an idealization of the "West" establishing a "utopian" basis for missionary projects towards local society. The inequality is much greater in the structure of global self-representation in which this "interest" is lost on the "Western" side and only discovery and direct intervention remain. The cold-war and the global structures are mutually reinforcing and form a peculiar alliance for the domination of "Eastern" societies, regardless of the fact that the "Eastern" missionaries would be much happier with a "West" which respected the local culture. But this cold-war type interest was based on the idea of a powerful "Eastern" block which have collapsed. This can be the tragedy of "Eastern" missionaries as they are idealizing a "West" which is changing its face with the reappearance of old colonial patterns of dominance in the form of the "global" metanarrative. In this respect, global narratives told from a "non-Western" position seem more global, especially as people in Central Europe have cultural patterns to introduce themselves as global nomads or simple wanderers without missionary ideals (at least in narratives told to a Hungarian researcher when asked about the "West").

The "Western" dominance is rarely counterbalanced on an individual level, although, as has been observed regarding the narratives of ideological debate, there are "fundamentalist" answers from Eastern Europe which simply reverse the "Western" narratives of looking down on the slope by upgrading "Eastern" civilization understood in an essentialist manner. This perspective falls under the shadow of the combined forms of "Eastern self-othering" and Western tutelage, but certainly has the potential to radically reject all other major forms of East–West identities. As soon as the cold-war narratives really disappear and we enter a period increasingly dominated by global-nomad identities and the othering of the local society, then surely the star of hostile "nationalism" will rise again. The East–West civilizational slope seems to be digging its own grave or, to put it better, preparing its final outcome by constructing the cradle for new "fundamentalist" power arrangements in which there is no place for ideals of gradual civilization, but only for conflicts fought in the name of civilization.

Notes

1 This is also true in the case of the teleological pattern inherent in Eurocentric discourses. With regard to this see Böröcz's analysis of teleology from the "sidelines" (Böröcz 2003, 76–89).

2 Wolff vividly describes how Eastern Europe on the map of Enlightenment represented a previously "lost" area inhabited by unknown Christians who have been only recently liberated from an "alien" yoke, which gives a particular urgency to mapping and observing these people (Wolff 1994, 144–194).

3 With regard to self-perfection understood as the defining characteristic of modern biography see among others: Baumann 1996, Comaroff and Comaroff 1992, Erlmann 1999.

CONCLUSION

The Sociology of the East–West slope and the recomposition of Eastern Europe

The role of the East–West discourse and the East–West civilizational slope is to set the terms and rules of global and local positioning and to formulate cognitive perspectives and maps in which different actors can locate themselves, each other and their own societies in the late-modern capitalist world system or modern/colonial systems. In other words, the East–West slope is a dominant discourse for the articulation of identities and political programs and the creation of institutions in the struggle for control and/or social or political recognition. It appears in almost all areas of social and political life: individual careers, family life, institutional frameworks, scholarly works and major global political programs, and it creates a web of discursive arrangements "normalizing" our lives in the latest phase of world capitalism. Eastern Europe has proved to be an especially fruitful field for analyzing the mechanisms of the East–West slope not only because this region and the actors in it have been (re)imagined into an intermediate position, but also because this region has been decomposed as a separate and competing block and (re)folded onto a hierarchical slope during the fall of state socialism and the (re)establishment of liberal capitalism. In this way the East–West slope has played a vital role in the recent history of Eastern Europe, with several functions in the dramatic changes affecting the lives of more then 300 million people.

1. The fall of state socialism

Without the discourse of an East–West civilizational slope there would not have been a rapid and "consensual" burial of socialism and reintegration of centrally planned socialist economies and societies into a hierarchically organized world economy. Evidence of the discursive effect of the East–West slope in the fall of socialism can be found at both a political and a structural level.

1.1. The East–West slope and the return of elites

The fall of socialism was decided as soon as the ruling socialist elite throughout Eastern Europe fell back on Eurocentrism, "normalization" and the idea of "peaceful coexistence" during the 1960s. It was at that time that the rulers finally abandoned the idea of challenging the West on the grounds of social progress and looked instead to consolidate their own power in Eastern Europe. This ideological reorientation of the East European socialist elites was not a political mistake but a social and political reconfiguration deeply embedded in Marxism itself and state-socialist experimentation.

From the beginning East European Marxism wanted to "overtake" the West in historical progress and push "backward" nations into the forefront of historical development, without challenging Eurocentrism and the idea of East–West slopes.[1] It was only a competing modernity in the struggle for the primary position in historical progress. It can even be argued that Marxism's focus on the European working class as a vanguard of history provided a critique of capitalism, but this criticism could rapidly be absorbed into a civilizational East–West slope. The "Westernization" of the working classes in Western Europe through generous welfare systems (established in fear of communism) "invalidated" the proletarianization thesis, the cornerstone of Marxist criticism and "socialist" superiority. After 1968 nobody could expect the radicalization of the Western working classes and a subsequent socialist revolution. Even Trotskyites maintaining the possibility of a socialist revolution in the capitalist centers till the 1950s opted for a "Western" type of "civilized" humanization of the labor process and completely turned away from any kind of "real" socialist experiment in Eastern Europe or the Third World (Callinicos 1990, Castoriadis 1988, 3–106).

The shift from a modernizationist competition to a civilizational discourse could be utilized by a local East European intermediate groups (professionals, middle peasants, intellectuals etc.) who, after considerable oppression in the early phase of state socialism, found a way (back) to power after 20–30 years in social "parking orbits" (Szelényi 1988, Konrád and Szelényi 1979). Even under more repressive East European socialist regimes this return was prepared during the "velvet," "silent" and "negotiated" revolutions. This march toward class power needed some ideological constructs, which could be the found in the East–West slope, understood in cultural and civilizational terms, which could give the reemerging elite a higher status and later even a missionary role with regard their local society. This could clearly be seen above both in the case of individual narratives in which the East–West slope functioned as a complex way of creating identities based on differences and exclusions of the local "non-enlightened" society, communists, the lower classes and "Oriental" elements inside and around the countries concerned.

During the fall of state socialism the new/old elites formulated different perspectives on the East–West slope and conflicts arose between them. But they all used ideas of "Europeanization," "Westernization," "return to Europe" and "true Europe" to consolidate their power in late modern capitalism. In fact this was their only ideological asset, which was certainly not very original and extremely narrow in focus (Tamás 1999a). In this sense there is nothing more important than to understand the social conditions of the (re)emergence of civilizational East–West discourses around the late 1970s and early 1980s in order to give an accurate account of the collapse of state socialism.

2. The East–West slope as the imaginary of the world economy

The basic social and economic condition of the East–West slope is the existence of a capitalist world economy. For the last three hundred years the world economy as a hierarchical economic system lacking a unifying political structure has found its ideological framework in the universalist idea of a single "civilization". This idea has been a key element of capitalist expansion and colonization since the 18th century (Wallerstein 1991, Césaire 1972; Amin 1989; Wolff 1994) Therefore the story of state socialism can be told as a gradual reintegration of planned economies into the capitalist world system under the East–West civilizational ideological umbrella. To begin with, financial and international debt links were established between state-socialist systems and the "world economy" in the context of the energy crisis of the 1970s, which then led to market-oriented reforms and the "dual dependency" of smaller East European countries on both the "West" and the "East" (Böröcz 1999). In this respect the parallel change in discourses and in the global political economy (from a modernizationist political economic scenario based on the nation state to globalization and the dominance of financial aspects) provides the proper context for understanding the fall of socialism (Chase-Dunn 1999; McMichael 2000). The civilizational discourse was a vital "fifth column" of the world system for defeating socialist modernization as a challenge. It reestablished the idea of Western superiority. It facilitated the shift in elites and the (re)legitimization of social and political agents reestablishing links between socialist planned economies and the world economy. Among these people we can find East European technocrats, East European World Bank experts, economic institutes in Eastern Europe, "Western" consulting agencies, intellectuals looking for class power, East European migrants in the "West" and groups of politicians in the communist parties. In the light of this massive structural reintegration process the inability to offer any kind of a response could be the real historical failure of the Marxist and Communist political parties in Eastern Europe, which only tried to strengthen their monopoly on power and to find ideologically correct Marxist-Leninist ways to "reform" socialism in the international context of "normalization" and "peaceful coexistence."

3. The East–West slope and the recent social and political order in Eastern Europe

3.1. The East–West slope and the consolidation of a new international order after the collapse of state socialism

The "task" of the East–West slope was not only to reintegrate the so-called "Eastern bloc" into the capitalist world economy in the 1970s and 1980s. This civilizational discourse shaped and gave meaning to all the dramatic changes that reformulated the everyday experiences of more than 300 million people during the late 1980s and the early 1990s. I must emphasize that reformulation in this sense is best described as world-economic restoration and not as a series of revolutions.

After the restoration the discourse of the East–West slope remains firmly rooted in late-modern capitalist social and political life in Eastern Europe. The order of the discourse has been, and will be, a major cognitive structure in the processes initiated by or linked to the late-modern capitalist world economy. We can hardly imagine ourselves outside this discourse in the near future and as analyzed in this book there are several additional functions and mechanisms which will maintain this power arrangement. On a structural level, then, some of the major events after the collapse of state socialism can also be seen as the products of the reintegration of Eastern Europe into world capitalism.

In terms of international politics the break-up of the Soviet Union, Czechoslovakia and Yugoslavia and the subsequent civil war in Yugoslavia would not have happened without the East–West slope. Sorin Antohi rightly claims that the mimetic competition for integration into Western political structures at the expense of other non-Western competitors led to "fragile identities," bringing about political disintegration and a subsequent reorganization of state structures (Antohi 2000).

In the mental maps of gradual civilization, nested Orientalism ("Easterners" finding more "Eastern" actors to exclude them) inevitably turns out to be one of the main mechanisms of the (re)emerging East–West slope. This exclusion in itself can break down existing non-homogenous state formations. In such states the elites of minorities or autonomous or semi-autonomous entities may capitalize on the ideological constructs offered by the East–West civilizational slope. They can always claim that their status on the civilizational slope is higher than that of the ruling majority. This can amply be demonstrated with regard to the Baltic republics, the Czech and Slovak debate and the Hungarian minorities living in Yugoslavia and Romania. Bakić-Hayden has also correctly observed that "nested Orientalisms" and the related change in power arrangements were key elements in the Yugoslavian civil war:

> As a political entity, the former Yugoslavia encompassed traditional dichotomies such as east/west and their nesting variants (Europe/Asia, Europe/Balkans, Christian/Muslim) largely neutralizing their usual valorization. With the destruction of this neutralizing framework, the revalorization of these categories, now oppositions rather than simply differences has resulted in the destruction of the living communities that had transcended them (Bakić-Hayden 1995, 930).

Nor would there have been the "Eastern enlargement" of the European Union in the way it was implemented. The "Eastern enlargement" was a creative way of establishing a new second tier around the West European core states, a process in which the East European states and societies (even those not joining the EU in 2004) underwent a massive transformation almost completely reformulating the legal, political and social configurations they had lived in for several decades. This new hierarchy and its ideological, cognitive mechanisms have been abundantly demonstrated by József Böröcz in his work on the contiguous imperialism of the European Union in relation to Eastern European candidates (Böröcz 2000, 2001; Böröcz and Kovács 2001, especially the introduction by Böröcz).

In this process the East–West slope has been the basis of an alliance between Western-oriented local elites (mainly liberals and ex-communists focusing on the gradual civilization of the local society) and Western investors and policy makers formed to dominate and discipline East European societies caught in the immense uncertainty of late-modern capitalism. This alliance and the East–West dialogue at an institutional and individual level is not without tensions, twists and conflicting interests, but there is general agreement on promoting "European" and "Western" ideals or, more precisely, on promoting a move toward such ideals.

This has served the "imperial," downward perspective of the American and West European political elites in controlling the region and using it for a variety of global political and economic strategies. "Half-civilized" and "half educated" East European countries can be silenced, played off against each other or used for major power games between the United States and the European Union. The lack of solidarity among countries further down the slope within the discursively set "orders of Europe" allows considerable room for maneuver for European and North American powers to intervene and to use these countries for various geopolitical and geocultural strategies, as exemplified by the subsequent wars in our new world order. Eastern Europe has become the background of European and North American political and economic power games, which can be demonstrated by the selective "Eastern enlargement" of the European Union and the extension of NATO for the purpose of controlling areas such as the Balkans or the Middle East. Or during the Iraq war in 2003 the American administration could rely on "new Europe" against an "old Europe" which rejected the Anglo-American military intervention, while "old Europe", being in temporary conflict with the USA, could also show its muscles to the "infantile" East European states (Melegh 2004a). These types of disciplining are among the major functions of constructions such as the East–West slope and they create a perfect terrain for war-mongers East and West who want to engage in conflict in the name of civilization.

3.2. The East–West slope and the consolidation of social and political order in Eastern Europe

Local elites, although sometimes protesting against subordination to the EU and the United States, receive a great deal of legitimacy and discursive material from the "West" which they regularly use to enhance their local political position. It helps them to silence opponents or to convert domestic problems into a debate on the status of the local societies on the slope. This immediate translation could be observed every time local elites have been forced to introduce financial austerity measures and cuts in social spending during the 1990s or in the present decade. As they have argued, such measures were inevitable for the sake of European integration and therefore the "development" of the country. Alternatively, political opponents have continually accused each other of not finding a "European" solution for the emerging problems and of harming the advancement of local East European societies on the slope, as could also be seen in my analysis of the EU referendum. Upward-looking liberals and modernizationist socialists blame local "Eastern" "corrupt" nationalists and from time to time "uncivilized" local populations for blocking "Europeanization." At the same time nationalists imagining themselves as "true Europeans" and thus ontologically (vertically) rising to the highest level of civilization (Antohi 2001) blame liberals for the failure of petty-imperialist projects such as that concerning the "status" of Hungarian minorities in "Eastern" neighboring countries. This conflict over the status on the slope disguises many of the hidden and not so hidden internal power struggles over resources, capital accumulation and distribution of government revenues.

The slope directly serves and facilitates class projects. That is why one of the most important functions of the East–West slope is the recreation and maintenance of racism and other forms of exclusion inherent in hierarchical Eurocentric constructions (Amin 1989; Chakrabarty 2000). Sociologically the slope controls, or to put it better, filters movement between different areas of the world or between social groups. This could be demonstrated in several spheres of social life in the preceding chapters.

In the 1980s population discourses in both East and West changed in such a way that the "quality" of the population became the focus, allowing new forms of exclusion directed against "low-quality" populations. "Eastern" floods of migrants can be stopped or made illegitimate, as exemplified by recent Western policies on migration with qualitative "point" systems to filter incomers, as for instance in Canada and Germany. It also allows Western migrants (so-called "Western" experts with their extra prestige) to join the upper spheres of local East European societies, while migrants coming from further "East" are forced into the lower segments of the same societies, thus creating an East–West slope in labor migration (Melegh et al. 2004). Such exclusions are the result of the co-operation of capital and state under the cognitive umbrella of the East–West slope.

In another variant East European Roma minority can be regarded as "unworthy" of being allowed into "Europe", as exemplified by the Zámoly case, or to receive social benefits because of their inherent "unhealthiness." In the same framework "pro-Western" "Jewish" conspirators can be excluded from the local elite, as exemplified once again by the Zámoly case. In this sense the liberal paradoxes of gradual "Westernization," which includes the (re)emerging ugly characteristics of the "Eastern" half of Europe side by side with its European integration, are no paradoxes at all. They are the everyday means of domination in an Eastern Europe (re)ensnared in the machinery of late modern world capitalism and its cognitive patterns experimented with and developed in the modern/colonial systems or the world economy since the 18th century.

4. Possibilities of critical sociology

This book is not simply a description of the 'East–West' mechanisms of power at different levels and in different spheres of social life. It is also an attempt to escape from the prison of this dominant discourse. As a locus of enunciation Central and East Europe in the current social and epistemological world order offers unique possibilities of deconstructing and rethinking theories of social history, while at the same time providing materials for the creation of new concepts and new narratives. It seems that the major challenge today is to develop a type of critical thinking which has been called "border thinking" (Mignolo 2000). This intellectual practice involves the questioning of the "universalist" Hegelian Western episteme of historical development, "provincializing Europe" and at the same time deconstructing essentialist nationalist and other "Eastern" perspectives which partly oppose and partly reinforce such overwhelming discourses (Chakrabarty 2000). The idea of border thinking or border gnosis involves looking for a border point which can be reached by deconstructing cognitive patterns, ideas and theories of social development constructed along the dominant civilizational East–West slope. Contrary to popular intellectual practice, the border point is not a geographical localization and fixation, because that type of specification is an act of limiting discourses and therefore an act of sheer political power and exclusion. Rather, exploring border points is being critical in all possible directions on the slope. On the one hand we must focus on the spread, the dominance and the social mechanisms of the liberal-humanitarian utopia of the "West," while on the other hand we must scrutinize the discursively linked and subjugated "Eastern" reactions trapped in a love or hate or love/hate relationship with it. Simultaneously observing both from a border point is not an act of moving into their epistemological and conceptual spheres, but a critical perspective which helps us combine these different stories in a framework controlled neither by "Western" nor by "Eastern" gazes. And what could be more important in our global world East and West, North and South?

Notes

1 My views on the Eurocentrism of Marxism and Trotskyism owe a great deal to József Böröcz, who organized a seminar on "Socialisms" at Rutgers University, in spring 2004. See also: Chakrabarty 2000, 29–30; Amin 1989, 77, 118–124; Wallerstein 1991.

Bibliography

Adamik, Mária. "Család versus népesség" (Family versus population). *Replika* no. 40 (June 2000): 197–202.

Amin, Samir. *Eurocentrism*. London: Zed Books, 1989.

Anderson, Benedict. *Imagined communities*. London: Verso, 1992.

Andorka, Rudolf. "A születésszám gazdasági és társadalmi tényezői" (The economic and cultural factors of fertility). *Valóság* no. 3 (1969): 26–39.

———. "Az ormánsági születéskorlátozás története" (The history of fertility control in the Ormánság region). *Valóság* no. 6 (1975): 45–61.

———. "Az európai nagy pestisjárványok"(The great European plague epidemics). *KSH NKI Történeti Demográfiai Füzetei* no. 2 (1985): 47–70.

———. The use of direct incentives and disincentives and of indirect social/ economic measures in fertility policy and human rights. In: United Nations (1990) *Population and Human Rights. Proceedings of the Expert Group Meeting on Population and Human Rights*. Geneva, New York, 1990.

Ankerl, Géza. *Nyugat van, kelet nincs. Értől az Óceánig (There is West, but no East. From the river Ér to the Ocean)*. Budapest: Osiris, 2000.

Antohi, Sorin. "Habits of mind. Europe's post–1989 symbolic geographies." *Between past and future. The revolutions of 1989 and their aftermath.* eds Antohi, Sorin, and Vladimir Tismeanu. (Budapest: Central European University Press, 2000), p. 61–77.

———. "A kilencvenes évek románsága. Szimbolikus földrajz és társadalmi identitás" (The Romaniannes of the 1990s. Symbolic geography and social identity) *Café-Bábel* (Special issue on "East and West", Spring-Summer 2001): 53–63.

———. Romania and the Balkans. From geocultural bovarism to ethnic ontology. *Transit-Europäische Revue* no 21 (2002) (*http://www.iwm.at/t–21txt8.htm. accessed on 12/18/2003*).

Appadurai, Arjun. *Modernity at large. Cultural dimensions of globalization. Public Worlds* 1. Minneapolis, London: University of Minnesota Press, 1996.

Arendt, Hannah. *The origins of totalitarianism.* New York: Harcourt Brace Jovanovich, 1975

Aschroft, Bill, Gareth Griffith and Helen Tiffin. *The Empire Writes Back. Theory and practice in post-colonial literatures.* London, New York: Routledge, 1989.

Ash, Garton. Does Central Europe exist? *New York Review of Books*. (October 15, 1986, *http://www.nybooks.com/articles/4998*. accessed 15 December 2003)

———. "Zehn Jahre danach" (Ten years after). *Transit* no. 18. (1999–2000).

Bakić-Hayden. "Nesting Orientalisms: The case of former Yugoslavia" *Slavic Review* 54, no. 4 (Winter 1995): 917–930.

Bandarage, Asoka. *Women, population and global crisis. A political-economic analysis.* London. New Jersey: Zed Books, 1998.

Barber, Benjamin R. *Jihad vs. McWorld.* New York: Ballantine Books, 1995.

Baumann, Zygmunt. "From pilgrim to tourist – a short history of identity." in: *Questions of cultural identity.* eds. Hall, Stuart and Paul Du Gay (London: Sage,1996), 18–37.

Beck, Ulrich. *What is globalization?* Malden, MA: Polity Press, 2000.

Bence, György. "Piszkos kezek: rezsimváltás előtt és után" (Dirty hands before and after the regime change). *Századvég* (Special issue on Politics and Ethics, 1993): 7–16.

Berger, Peter L. "Four faces of global culture." *National Interest* no. 49 (Fall 1997): 23–30.

Bibó, István. *Democracy, revolution, self-determination: selected writings.* Highland Lakes: Atlantic Research Publications (East European monographs; no. 317, Atlantic studies on society in change ; no. 69, 1991)

Bideleux, Robert and Richard Taylor *European integration and disintegration East and West.* New York, London: Routledge, 1996.

Bíró, Zoltán Sz. "Moszkvától Zámolyig" (From Moscow to Zámoly). *Népszabadság,* (March 4, 2001): 7.

Bojtár, Endre and Attila Melegh, eds. "Mi lesz veled Közép-európa? Hogyan is lehet valaki közép-európai?" (What will happen to Central Europe? How can one be Central European?) *Századvég* (special issue, 1989): 55–182.

Bornschier, Volker. "The civilizational project and its discontents: Toward a viable global market society?" *Journal of World-System Research http://csf.colorado.edu/wvsystem/jwsr.html.* no. 5 (1999):160–175.

Bozóki, András. "Rhetoric of action: The language of the regime change in Hungary." In *Intellectuals and politics in Central Europe.* ed. Bozóki, András (Budapest: Central European University Press, 1999): pp.142–166.

Böröcz, József. *Leisure migration. A sociological study on tourism.* Oxford, New York: Pergamon, 1996.

———. "Térkép e táj" (This land is a map). *Kritika* (April, 1998).

———. "From comprador state to auctioneer state: property change, realignment and peripheralization in post-state-socialist central and Eastern Europe." in: States and sovereignity in the global economy. Eds. Smith, David A., Dorothy J. Solinger, and Steven C. Topik (London, New York: Routledge, 1999), pp. 193–209.

———. "Magyarország a médiumok tükrében" (Hungary in the mirror of the media). Paper given at the Conference "The image of Hungary" (Budapest: Nov. 20, 1999a.) *Transcript of the proceedings.*

———. "Reaction as progress: Economists as intellectuals." in *Intellectuals and politics in Central Europe*. ed. Bozóki, András (Budapest: Central European University Press, 1999b), pp. 132–150.

———. "The fox and the raven: The European Union and Hungary renegotiate the margins of 'Europe'." *Comparative Studies in Society and History* 42, no. 4 (October, 2000): 847–75.

———. "Döntés és indoklása – avagy miként szivárog a szubsztancia a formális jogba az Európa Unió keleti bővítése kapcsán" (Rationales for a choice: How substance enters formal law in the "Eastern Enlargement" of the European Union). *Replika* no. 43–44 (June, 2001): 193–220. *ttp://www.rci.rutgers.edu/~jborocz/ration2.htm*

———. Social change by fusion: Understanding institutional creativity. *Doctoral dissertation submitted to the Hungarian Academy of Sciences, defended January 6, 2004.* Budapest: Hungarian Academy of Sciences, 2003.

———. "Goodness Is elsewhere: The rule of European difference." Forthcoming in *Comparative Studies in Society and History.* (2005).

Böröcz, József and Melinda Kovács, eds. *Empire's new clothes. Unveiling EU enlargement.* E-book: Central Europe Review. (2001) *http://www.ce-review.org/ebookstore/rutgers1.html*

Breckner, Roswitha. "The biographical-interpretative method – principles and procedures." in *Social strategies in risk societies*, SOSTRIS Working papers 2, Centre for Biography in Social Policy. Sociology Department, University of East London, 1996.

Brezinski, Zbigniew. "Visszatérés Közép-Európához" (Return to Central Europe). Lecture in memory of Hugh Seton-Watson. London Centre for Policy Studies, January 28, 1988.) *Századvég* (special issue, 1989): 82–86.

Burch, Thomas K. "Icons, straw men and precision: reflections on demographic theories of fertility decline." *The Sociological Quarterly* 37, no. 1 (1996): 59–81.

Burgess, Adam. *Divided Europe: The new domination of the East.* London, Chicago, Ill.: Pluto Press, 1997.

Burke, Peter. *Popular culture in early modern Europe.* London : T. Smith, 1978.

Caldwell, John. "Malthus and the less developed world: The pivotal role of India." *Population and Development Review* 24, no.4 (1998): 675–696.

Calinescu, Matei. "Hogyan is lehet valaki román" (How can one be a Romanian). *Századvég* (special issue, 1989): 110–118.

Callinicos, Alex. *Trotskyism.* Minneapolis: University of Minnesota Press, 1990.

Castoriadis, Cornelius. *Political and social writings. Volume 1. 1945–1955: From the critique of bureaucracy to the positive content of socialism.* Minneapolis: University of Minnesota Press, 1988.

Ceizel, Endre. "A két-három gyermekes családért" (For families with two or three children). *Élet és Irodalom* (August 19, 1972).

———. "Eugénika?" (Eugenics?) *Világosság* no. 2 (1976): 108–106.

Césaire, Aimé. *Discourse on colonialism.* New York: Monthly Review Press, 1972, 2000.

Chase-Dunn, Christopher. "Globalization: A world-systems perspective." *Journal of World-Systems Research* 5. no. 2 (Spring, 1999): http://csf.colorado.edu/wsystems/jwsr.htm

Chakrabarty, Dipesh. *Provincializing Europe. Postcolonial thought and historical difference.* Princeton and Oxford: Princeton University Press, 2000.

Chirot, Daniel, ed. *The origins of backwardness in Eastern Europe: economics and politics from the Middle Ages until the early twentieth century.* Berkeley: University of California Press, 1989, 1991.

———. "Who is Western, who is not, and who cares?" *East European Politics and Societies* 13, no.2. (Spring, 1999): 244–248.

———. "Returning to reality: culture, modernization, and various Eastern Europes. Why functionalist-evolutionary theory works." *Transit* (2002) (*http://www.iwm.at/t-21txt2.htm.* accessed: Dec. 18, 2003).

Cliquet, Robert L. "The second demographic transition: fact or fiction?" *Population Studies* no. 23 (1991).

Coleman, David A. "Converging and diverging patterns in Europe's Populations." *Paper presented at the European Population Conference* (Cracow, 10–13 June 1997. Plenary Session).

Comaroff, John and Jean Comaroff. *Ethnography and the historical imagination.* Boulder: Westview, 1992.

Conrad, Joseph. *Under Western Eyes.* Mineola, N.Y: Dover Publications, 2003.

Csizmadia, Ervin. "Diskurzus és diktatúra. A magyar értelmiség vitái Nyugat-Európáról a késő Kádár-rendszerben" (Discourse and dictatorship. The debates of Hungarian intellectuals on Western Europe under the late Kádár regime). Budapest: Századvég, 2001.

Dancsi, Katalin."Kelet-Nyugat fogságában: Közép-Európa helye szövegek térképén" (In the prison of the East–West dichotomy). (The position of Central Europe on the map of texts) in *Szürke zónák. Összehasonlított regionális másságok.* (Twilight zones. Regional otherness compared) ed. Melegh, Attila. *Replika* no. 43–44 (June, 2001): 109–192, 139–156.

Dányi, Dezső. "Demográfiai átmenetek (Valóság, tudomány, politika)." (Demographic transitions. Reality, science and politics.) *Demográfia* 43 no. 2–3 (2000): 231–251.

Demény, Paul. "Social science and population policy." *Population and Development Review* 14, no.3 (1988): 451–79.

Dussel, Enrique. Beyond Eurocentrism: The world-system and the limits of modernity. in: *The cultures of globalization.* eds. Jameson, Fredric and Masao Miyoshi (Durham, London: Duke University Press, 1998), pp. 3–31.

Elias, Norbert. The civilizing process. Oxford, Cambridge, Mass.: Blackwell, 1994.

Erdei Ferenc. "A magyar paraszttársadalom" (Hungarian peasant society). in: *Erdei Ferenc Összegyűjtött Művei. A magyar társadalomról.* (The Works of Ferenc Erdei. On the Hungarian society) ed. Kulcsár, Kálmán (Budapest, Akadémiai, 1942), pp. 83–252.

———. (1976) "A magyar társadalom a két világháború között. I–II" (Hungarian society between the two world wars). in: *Erdei Ferenc Összegyűjtött Művei. A magyar társadalomról.* (The Works of Ferenc Erdei. On the Hungarian society) ed. Kulcsár, Kálmán (Budapest, Akadémiai, 1976), pp. 291–346.

Erlmann, Veit. *Music, modernity and the global imagination. South Africa and the West.* Oxford, New York: Oxford University Press, 1999.

Fábián, Zoltán."Vélemények a cigányokról és az idegenellenesség" (Opinions on Gypsies and xenophobia). In: *Idegenek Magyarországon.* (Aliens in Hungary) eds. Sik, Endre and Judit Tóth. (Budapest: MTA Politikai Tudományok Intézete Nemzetközi Migráció Kutatócsoport Évkönyve, 1998), pp. 153–74.

Faragó, Tamás. Different household formation systems in one country at the end of the eighteenth century: variations on John Hajnal's thesis. Paper: *General Population Conference*, Beijing, China. (1997).

Faulkner, William. *Light in August.* New York: Vintage Books, 1959.

Fisher-Galati, Stephen. Eastern Europe in the twentieth century: "Old wine in new bottles". in: *The Columbia history of eastern Europe in the twentieth century.* ed. Joseph Held (New York: Columbia University Press, 1992), pp.1–16

Foucault, Michel. *The archeology of knowledge and the discourses on language.* New York: Routledge, 1972.

———. *The order of things. An Archeology of the human sciences.* London: Routledge, 1974.

———. Right of death and power over life. In: Rabinow, Paul (ed.) *The Foucault reader.* (Penguin: London, 1991), pp. 258–273.

———. (1991a) "A diskurzus rendje" (The order of discourse). *Holmi* no.7: 868–889.

———. "Életben hagyni és halálra ítélni" (Allowing to live and sentencing to death). *Világosság* no.1 (1992): 45–52.

———. "A tudományok archeológiájáról" (On the archeology of knowledge). in: *Nyelv a végtelenhez. Tanulmányok, előadások, beszélgetések.* (Language for infinity. Essays, lectures and conversations). Foucault, Michel (Debrecen: Latin Betűk, 1999), 169–201.

Fülep, Lajos. *A magyarság pusztulása.* (The destruction of the Magyars). Budapest: Magvető, 1984.

Gergen, Kenneth J. and Gergen, Mary M. (1988) "Narrative and the self as relationship" Advances *in experimental social psychology Vol. 21* ed. Berkowitz L. (California: Academic Press), pp.17–56.

Glenny, Misha. *The fall of Yugoslavia. The third Balkan war.* London: Penguin, 1992.

Goldberg, David Theo. The social formation of racist discourse. in *Anatomy of racism.* ed. Goldberg, David Theo (Minneapolis: University of Minnesota Press, 1990.)

Goldsworthy, Vesna. *Inventing Ruritania. The imperialism of the imagination.* New Haven, London: Yale University Press, 1998.

———. "The last stop on the Orient express: The Balkans and the politics of British in(ter)vention." *Conference paper*: South-Eastern Europe: Concepts, Histories, Boundaries conference at the School of Slavonic and East European Studies, University of London (19 June, 1999) *http://www.ac.wwu.edu/~kritika/VgoLaStop.html*

Greenhalgh, Susan. "The social construction of population science: An intellectual, institutional and political history of twentieth-century demography." *Comparative Studies in Society and History.* 38 no.1. (January, 1996): 26–66.

Gross, J. T. "The burden of history." *East European Politics and Societies* 13, no.2 (Spring, 1999): 285–287.

Hablicsek, László. "Népességelőreszámítások, demográfiai előrebecslések" (Population projections and demographic estimates). in: *Demográfia.* (Demography) ed. Kovacsicsné. Nagy Katalin (Budapest: KSH, 1996), 375–410.

———. Az első és második demográfiai átmenet Magyarországon és Közép-Kelet-Európában" (The first and the second demographic transition in Hungary and Central-Eastern Europe). Budapest: KSH Népességtudományi Kutató Intézet Kutatási Jelentései no. 54 (1995).

Hajnal, John. "European marriage pattern in perspective" in: Population in history: *Essays in Historical Demography.* ed. Glass and Eversley (London: Arnold, 1965), 101–143.

Hajnal, John. "Two kinds of preindustrial household formation" in: *Family forms in historic Europe.* eds. Wall, Richard et al. (Cambridge: Cambridge University Press, 1983), pp. 65–104.

Hannaford, Ivan. *Race. The history of an idea in the West.* Washington: The Woodrow Wilson Center Press, 1996.

Havel, Vaclav et al. *The power of the powerless: citizens against the state in Central-Eastern Europe.* London: Hutchinson, 1985.

———. "The thin veener of global technological civilization." In *Excerpts from Vaclav Havel's Harvard Commencement Address. June 8, 1995. http://www.jimhopper.com/havel.html#thin*, accessed: April 1, 2002

Hegyesi, Adrienn and Attila Melegh and forever. "Immár nem mi vagyunk a szegény rokon a nemzetközi világban". A státustörvény és az Orbán-Nastase-egyezmény vitájának sajtóbeli reprezentációja és diksurzív rendje" (We are no longer the world's poor relation. The media representation and the discursive order of the status law and the Orbán-Nastase pact). in: *Kampánykommunikáció* (Campaign communication), eds. Sárközy, Erika and Nóra Schleicher (Budapest: Akadémiai, 2003), pp.135-171.

Heiszler, Vilmos. "Mégis kinek az élete?" (Whose life is it anyway?) *Magyar Hírlap.* (January 5, 2002).

Hodgson, Dennis. "Demography as social science and policy science." *Population and Development Review* 9 no. 1. (March, 1983).

———. "The ideological origins of the Population Association of America." *Population and Development Review* 17 no. 1. (March, 1991).

Huntington, Samuel P. *The clash of civilizations and the remaking of world order.* New York: Simon & Schuster, 1996.

Jones, E. L. *The European Miracle: Environments, Economies and Geopolitics in the History of Europe and Asia.* Cambridge: Cambridge University Press, 1981.

Judt, Tony. *A grand illusion? : an essay on Europe.* New York: Hill and Wang, 1996.

Kamarás, Ferenc. "A termékenység alakulása és befolyásoló tényezői" (The development of fertility and its determining factors). in: *Népesedés és népesedéspolitika.* (Population Development and Population Policy) ed. Spéder, Zsolt (ed.) (Budapest: Századvég, 2001), pp. 13–41.

Karnoouh, Claude. Van-e erkölcs a posztmodern politikában? (Is their morality in postmodern politics) *Századvég* (special issue on Politics and Ethics, 1993) 17–24.

———. Eastern Europe at the Time of Disenchantment (From the fall of Communism to the Advent of a Third World Status) *Social Justice: Anthropology, Peace and Human Rights* 4, no. 3–4 (2003): 228–267.

Keane, John, ed. *Civil society and the State: new European perspectives.* London: Verso, 1988.

Kideckel, David A. What's in a name. The persistence of East Europe as a conceptual category. *Replika,* (special issue on Colonization or partnership? Eastern Europe and Western social sciences, 1996). *www.c3.hu/scripta/scripta0/replika/honlap/*

Kiss, Balázs. "Foucault, White és Bätsch-Kehasie a diskurzusokról" (Foucault, White and Bätsch-Kehasie on discourses). *Manuscript.* (1996)

Kligman, Gail. *The Politics of Duplicity. Controlling Reproduction in Ceauşescu's Romania.* Berkeley, Los Angeles, London: University of California Press, 1998.

Kodolányi, János. *Baranyai utazás.* (Journey in Baranya county). Budapest: Magvető Könyvkiadó, 1963.

Kohn, Jerome. "Totalitarianism: The inversion of politics." in: *The Hannah Arendt Papers: Totalitarianism: The Inversion of Politics. Part 6.* (2001). *http://memory.loc.gov/ammem/arendthtml/essayb6/html.* Accessed August 15, 2001.

Konrád, György. *Antipolitics : an essay*; translated from the Hungarian by Richard E. Allen. San Diego: Harcourt Brace Jovanovich, 1984.

Konrád, György and Szelényi, Iván. *The intellectuals on the road to class power.* New York: Harcourt Brace Jovanovich, 1979.

Koselleck, Reinhart. *Futures past : on the semantics of historical time.* Cambridge, Mass, London: MIT Press, 1985.

Kovács, Éva. "Megszállók, vendégek, szomszédok. Az amerikai IFOR-Misszió Taszáron és Kaposváron" (Invaders, guests and neighbors. The American IFOR mission in Taszár and Kaposvár). *2000.* (February, 2001): 13–27.

Kovács, Éva and Attila Melegh. "Az identitás játékai. Kísérlet Erdei Ferenc a magyar társadalom a két világháború között című tanulmányának tartalmi kibontására." (Games of identity. An attempt to unravel Ferenc Erdei's study of Hungarian society between the two world wars). in: *Vera (nem csak) a városban.* (Vera /not only/ in the town) eds. Tóth, Zoltán and László Á Varga (Salgótarján: Hajnal István Kör, 1995), pp. 487–505.

———. "Whose social history is it? New discourses in Hungarian social history." *Sources-Travaux Historiques.* no. 40 (1997): 29–45.

———. "It could have been worse, we could have gone to America. – Migration Narratives in the Transylvania-Hungary-Austria Triangle." in: *Diasporas and Politics.* eds. Nyíri Pál et al. (Budapest: MTA Politikai Tudományok Intézete Nemzetközi Migráció Kutatócsoport, 2001), pp. 108–138.

Kovács, Éva and Júlia Vajda. "Leigazoltam a zsidókhoz. A 'társadalmi zsidó' identitás kialakulásának élettörténeti gyökereiről" (I have signed for the Jews. The biographical roots of "socially Jewish" identity). *Thalassa. Pszichoanalízis – Társadalom – Kultúra* no. 1–2. (1994): 228–245.

Kovács, Imre. *A néma forradalom* (The silent revolution) Budapest: Tevan, 1989.

Kovács, János Mátyás. "Turbulenzen im Vakuum. Anmerkungen zur kulturellen Globalisierung in Osteuropa" (Turbulences in a vacuum. Notes on cultural globalization in Eastern Europe). *Transit* no. 17 (Summer, 1999): 33–45.

———. Praising the hybrids: notes on economic thought ten years after. *East European Politics and Societies* 13, no. 2. (Spring, 1999a): 313–322

———. Rival temptations – passive resistance. Cultural globalization in Hungary. in *Many globalizations: cultural diversity in the contemporary world.* eds. Berger, Peter and Samuel P. Huntington (Oxford, New York: Oxford University Press, 2002).

Krasznai, József. "Valamit megmozdítok vele" (I make a difference). *Amaro Drom.* (October. 3–7, 2000)

Krémer, Balázs. "A népesedéspolitika nyelve – avagy a rasszizmus legitim nyelvi közege" (The language of population policy as a legitimate context for racism). *Replika.* no. 40 (2001): 189–196.

Kuczi, Tibor. *Szociológia, ideológia-közbeszéd.* (Sociology, ideology and public discourses) Budapest: Scientia Humana, 1992.

Kundera, Milan. "The tragedy of Central Europe." *The New York Review of Books.* (April 26, 1984)

———. "An introduction to a variation." *Cross Currents* no. 5 (1986): 469–476.

Laslett, Peter and Richard Wall. *Household and family in past time.* Cambridge: Cambridge University Press, 1972.

———. Family and household as work group and kin group: areas of traditional Europe compared. in *Family forms in historic Europe,* ed. Wall, Richard et al. (Cambridge: Cambridge University Press, 1983), pp. 513–563.

Laslett, Peter and Melegh Attila. "A múlt hangjai és együttélés a jövőbeli énjeinkkel. Interjú Peter Laslett" (Voices of the past and living with our future selves. Interview with Peter Laslett). *Aetas* no. 3–4 (2001): 279–290.

Lengyel, György. "The ethnic composition of the economic elite in Hungary in the interwar period." in *A social and economic history of Central European Jewry*. (New Brunswick: Transaction Publishers, 1990), pp. 229–248.

Lesthaeghe, Ron. "The second demographic transition in Western countries: An Interpretation." *Interuniversity Programme in Demography, Working Paper* no. 2. Bruxelles, 1991.

Macfarlane, Alan. *The origins of English individualism: the family, property and social transition* Oxford: Blackwell, 1978.

———. *Marriage and love in England: modes of reproduction, 1300–1840*. Oxford, New York: Blackwell, 1986.

———. *The culture of capitalism*. Oxford, New York: Blackwell, 1987.

Macura, Miroslav, Yumiko Mochizuki Sternberg and Jose Lara Garcia "Europe's fertility and partnership: selected developments during the last ten years." *Manuscript*. (1998).

Malamud, Bernard. *The assistant*. New York: Farrar, Straus and Cudahy, 1957.

Malamud, Bernard. The tenants. New York: Farrar, Straus and Giroux, 1971.

Malthus, Thomas. *An Essay on the principle of population*. HTML format ed. Stephan 10 Aug 1997, (1798) *www.ac.wwu.edu/~stephan/malthus/malthus.0.html*

Malthus, Thomas, Julian Huxley and Frederick Osborn. *Three essays on population*. Introduction by Frank W. Notestein. President. The Population Council. New York: Mentor Books, 1960.

Malthus, Thomas Robert. *First essay on population 1798*. London: Macmillan; New York: St Martin's Press, 1966.

Mannheim, Karl. *Ideology and utopia*. New York: Harvest Books, Harcourt, Brace & World Inc, 1936.

McLaren, Angus. *A History of contraception from antiquity to the present day*. Oxford: Blackwell, 1990.

McMichael, Philip. "Globalization: myths and realities" in *From modernization to globalization. Perspectives on development and social change,* eds. Roberts, Timmons and Amy Hite (Malden, MA, Oxford: Blackwell, 2000), 274–292.

Melegh, Attila. "A nyugati modell" (The Western model). *Hiány* (July, 1992).

———. "A Nyugat bűvöletében" (Under the spell of the West). in Értelmiség és politika, (Intellectuals and politics) ed. Martin, József (*Széchenyi Füzetek* no. 8, 1994): 8–15.

———. "Le Model Occidental" (The Western model). in *L'Engagement des Intellectuels a'l'Ouest,* ed. Catherine Durandin (Paris: L'Harmattan, 1994a).

———. Új téglák, régi falak. Kelet-Európa a New York Times civilizációs térképén. (New bricks, old walls. Eastern Europe on the civilizational map of the New York Times, 1999) *2000*. June 17–28.

———. "Gail Kligman and Ceauşescu's Reproduction Control Policy." *Books* (Summer, Fall, 1999a): 113–117.

———. (1999b) "Amerikás élettörténetek" (American life histories). in *Migráció és társadalom,* (Anthology on migration and society) eds. Tóth, Pál Péter and Sándor Illés (Budapest: KSH, 199b), pp. 27–42.

———. "Ki mitől fél? Kommentár a népesedési körkérdésről" (Who is afraid of what? Comments on a survey of population issues). *Demográfia* 42, no.3–4 (1999c): 339–350.

———, ed. "Népesedési körkérdés" (Survey of population issues). *Demográfia* 1999. 42. no. 3–4 (1999d): 1–338.

———. "Az angolszász globális népesedéspolitikai diskurzusok alakulása a 20 században Lépések a pro-és antinatalista népesedéspolitikák összehasonlító vizsgálata irányában" (The development of Anglo-Saxon discourses on population policy in the 20th century: steps toward a comparative study of pro- and anti-natalist population policies). *Replika* no. 39. (Spring, 2000): 157–178.

———, ed. "Szürke zónák. Összehasonlított regionális másságok" (Twilight zones. Regional otherness compared). *Replika* no. 43–44. (June, 2001): 109–192.

———, ed. "Válság vagy átmenet? Régiók és népesedés" (Crisis or transition. Regions and population development). *Regio* no.1 (2001b): 111–212.

———. "A Kelet-Nyugat beszédmód" (The East–West Discourse). *Népszabadság*. (Dec. 12, 2001c)

———. "Mondialisation, nationalisme et petit imperialisme." (Globalization, nationalism and petty imperialism). *La Nouvelle Alternative* 16, no.55 (2001d): 130–142.

———. "East–West exclusions and discourses on population in the 20th Century." *Working Papers on Population, Family and Welfare.* no.3. (Budapest: Demographic Research Institute, Hungarian Central Statistical Office, 2002).

———. "Mozgó kelet. Globális térképek és a státustörvény." (The East in motion. Global maps and the status law) in Zárva várt nyugat. Tanulmányok a kulturális globalizációról. (Awaited/resented West. Studies on cultural globalization) ed. Kovács, János Mátyás (Budapest: 2000 Sík Kiadó, 2002a), pp. 103–135.

———. "Globalization, nationalism and petit imperialism." *Romanian Politics and Society*. 2, no.1 (2002b): 115–129 .

———. "From Reality to Twilight Zones. The Change of Discourses and the Collapse of State Socialism." *Regio* English edition (2003): 170–186.

———. "Maps of Global Actors" in *After Communism. Critical perspectives on society and sociology*, eds. Carol Harrington; Ayman Salem and Tamara Zurabishvili (Bern: Peter Lang Publishing, 2004), pp. 63–95.

———. "La liste d'aptitud." *Outre-Terre. Revue francaise de géopolitique.* (Special edition: Attention Europe!) no. 7 (2004a): 273–85.

Melegh, Attila and Péter Őri. "A második demográfiai átmenet" (The second demographic transition) in *Család és népesség itthon és Európában* (Family and population at home and in Europe). ed. Spéder, Zsolt (Budapest: Századvég, 2003), pp. 495–523.

Melegh, Attila, Elena Kondrateva, Perttu Salmenhaare, Annika Forsander, László Hablicsek, Adrienn Hegyesi. "Globalisation, Ethnicity and Migration. The Comparison of Finland, Hungary and Russia." *Working Papers on Population, Family and Welfare. No. 7.* (Budapest: Demographic Research Institute, Hungarian Central Statistical Office, 2004.)

Mester, Dóra Djamila. "Medvetánc. Oroszország angolszász sajtótükörben" (Bear dance. Russia in the mirror of the Anglo-Saxon press). in "Szürke zónák. Összehasonlított regionális másságok" (Twilight zones. Regional otherness compared) ed. Melegh, Attila *Replika* no. 43–44. (June, 2001): 113–132.

Mignolo, Walter D. "Globalization. civilization process and the relocation of languages and cultures." in *The cultures of globalization*, eds. Jameson, Fredric and Masao Miyoshi (Durham, London: Duke University Press, 1998), 32–53.

———. *Local Histories and global designs. Coloniality, subaltern knowledge, and border thinking.* (Princeton Studies in Culture/Power/History.) Princeton, New Jersey: Princeton University Press, 2000.

Monigl, István, ed. "Népesedési viták Magyarországon 1960–1986" (Population debates in Hungary 1960–1986). *A Népességtudományi Kutató Intézet Kutatási Jelentései* no. 37. (Budapest: KSH, 1990).

———, ed. A *népesedés és a népesedéspolitika a hosszú távú tervezés összefoglaló dokumentumaiban. 1968–1985* vol. I.–II. (Population and population policy in the documents on long term planning. 1968–1985). (Budapest: KSH NKI, 1990a)

———, ed. "Az 1952–53. évi népesedéspolitikai program Magyarországon. Dokumentumgyűjtemény" (The Hungarian population policy program of 1952–53. Documents). Budapest: KSH NKI, 1992.

———, ed. *Népesedéspolitika és fontosabb dokumentumai az 1960–as évtizedben Magyarországon. Dokumentumgyűjtemény.* (Hungarian population policy and its major documents in the 1960s. Documents) Budapest: KSH NKI, 1992a.

MTA Demográfiai Bizottság, *A demográfiai tudomány helyzete Magyarországon.* (The status of demographic research in Hungary) Budapest: KSH NKI, 1982.

Nádas, Péter. (2001) "A szabadság tréningjei" (The trainings of Freedom). *Magyar Narancs http://www.mancs.hu/legfrissebb.tdp?azon=0051publ2*, accessed 2003.03.21

Némedi, Dénes. *A népi szociográfia, 1930–1938.* (Populist sociography) Budapest: Gondolat, 1985.

Neumann, Iver B. *Uses of the other: "The East" in European identity formation.* Minneapolis: University of Minnesota Press, 1999.

Notestein, Frank W. "Population – The long view." in *Food for the world,* ed. Schultz, Theodore (Chicago: Chicago University Press, 1945), pp. 36–51

———. "Demographic sources of power. Lecture: 20 September" *Manuscript* (Princeton: Office of Population Research, 1949)

Okólski, Marek. "Migration pressures on Europe." in *European populations. Unity in diversity,* eds. van de Kaa, Dirk, Henri Leridon, Giuseppe Gesano and Marek Okólski, Marek (Dordrecht, Boston, London: Kluwer Academic Publishers, 1999), pp. 141–194.

Orwell, George. *1984*. New York: New American Library, 1983.

Osborn, Frederick. "On Population." in *Three essays on population*. Introduction by Frank W. Notestein. eds. Malthus, Thomas, Julian Huxley and Frederick Osborn (New York: Mentor Books, 1960), pp. 83–138.

Őri, Péter. "A demográfiai statisztika összehasonlító története" (A comparative history of population statistics). *Demográfia* 41 no. 1 (1998): 116–128.

———. "Paradigmaváltás a francia történeti demográfiában?" (Change of paradigm in French historical demography?). *Demográfia* 41, no. 4 (1998a): 414–455.

———. "A Conscriptio Animarum mint demográfiai forrás." (Conscriptio Animarum as a source of demography) *Lecture at KSH NKI*, (Budapest, April 1999).

Petersen, William. "Marxism and the population question: theory and practice." in. Population and resources in Western intellectual traditions. Eds. Teitelbaum, Michael S. and Jay M. Winter *Population and Development Review*. (Supplement 14, 1988): 77–101.

Pongrácz, Tiborné. "Élettársi kapcsolatok és házasságon kívüli szülések Nyugat-Európában." (Partnerships and extra-marital births in Western Europe). in Házasságon kívüli szülések. (Extra-marital births) *KSH Népességtudományi Kutató Intézet Kutatási Jelentései* no. 61. (Budapest: KSH NKI, 1998): 45–53.

Quine, Maria Sophie. *Population politics in twentieth century Europe*. New York: Routledge, 1996.

Racevskis, Karlis. *Michel Foucault and the subversion of intellect*. Ithaca, N: Cornell University Press, 1983.

Ramet, S. P. "Eastern Europe's unfinished business." *East European Politics and Society*. 13, no. 2 (Spring, 1999): 345–352.

Rätzhel, Nora. "Gender and racism in discourse" in *Gender and discourse,* ed. Wodak, Ruth (London, Thousand Oaks, New Delhi, 1997), pp. 57–80.

Richards, Jeff. "Old wine in new bottles: The resurgence of nationalism in the new Europe." in *Ethnicity and nationalism in Russia, the CIS and the Baltic states,* eds. Williams, Christopher and Thanasis Sfikas, Thanasis D (Aldershot, Bookfield USA, Singapore, Sydney: Ashgate, 1999): 11–23.

Rosenthal, Gabriele. "Élettörténet-rekonstrukció. A történet-alkotás szelekciós alapelvei narratív életút interjúk során." (Life history reconstruction. The basic principles of story building in narrative life-course interviews) *Manuscript*. (1991).

Roth, Joseph. *Weights and measures*. London: Chester Springs, PA : P. Owen, 2002.

Rupnik, Jacques. "Újraértelmezett totalitarizmus" (Totalitarianism redefined). *Századvég* no.1 (1990).

———. "In search of Central Europe: ten years after." in *Central and Southeastern Europe in Transition. Perspectives on Success and Failure Since 1989*, ed. Gardner, Hall (Wesport, Connecticut, London: Praeger, 2000), pp. 5–20.

Said, Edward. *Orientalism*. New York: Vintage, 1978.

———. "The problem of textuality. Two exemplary positions." in *Michel Foucault. Critical assessments*, ed. Smart, Barry (London, New York: Routledge, 1994) (1978a) 117–118.

———. *Culture and imperialism*. New York: Vintage, 1994.

Saito, Osamu. "Historical demography: achievements and prospects." *Population Studies* 50, no.3 (1996): 537–553.

Schneider, J.C. and P. T. Schneider. *Festival of the poor. Fertility decline and the ideology of class in Sicily 1860–1980*. Tucson: The University of Arizona Press, 1996.

Schopflin, George and Nancy Wood, eds. *In search of Central Europe*. Totowa, N. J.: Barnes & Noble, 1989.

Sen, Amartya. Population: delusion and reality. *New York Review of Books* 41, no. 15 (Sept.22, 1994).

Silverman, David. *Interpreting qualitative data. Methods for analyzing talk, text and interaction*. London, Thousand Oaks, New Delhi: Sage Publications, 1993.

Simon, Julian L. ed. *The Economics of population: classic writings*. New Brunswick, NJ, London: Transaction Publishers, 1998.

Sklair, Leslie. "Competing conceptions of globalization." *Journal of World-Systems Research* 5, no. 2 (Spring 1999) *http://csf.colorado.edu/wsystems/jwsr.htm*

Smith, Richard M. ed. *Land, kinship and life cycle*. Cambridge: Cambridge University Press, 1984.

Spivak, Gayatri Chakravorty. *The post-colonial critic: Interviews, strategies, dialogues*, ed. Sarah Harasym, London: Routledge, 1990.

Stoler, Ann Laura. *Race and the education of desire. Foucault's history of sexuality and the colonial order of things*. Durham, London: Duke University Press, 1995.

———. "Sexual Affronts and Racial Frontiers." in *Theories of race and racism. A reader*, eds. Back and Solomos (London: Routledge, 2000): 324–353.

Szelényi, Iván. *Socialist entrepreneurs: embougeoisement in rural Hungary*. Madison, Wis.: University of Wisconsin Press, 1988.

Szentgáli, Tamás. "A demográfiai átmenet elmélete. (The theory of demographic transition)" in Demográfiai átmenet. *KSH NKI Történeti Demográfiai Füzetek*. no.1: (Budapest: KSH, 1991): 21–34.

Szentiványi, István. "Jogodban áll gyűlölni" (The Right to Hate) *Népszabadság*, (August 17, 2001. Translated by A. M).

Szőcs, Zoltán. "Elvarázsolt Európa" (Magic Europe). *Magyar Fórum* (March 6, 2003. Translated by A. M.).

Szreter, Simon. The idea of demographic transition and the study of fertility change: A critical intellectual history. *Population and Development Review* 19, no. 4. (December, 1993): 659–701.

Tamás, Gáspár Miklós. "Törzsi fogalmak I.–II." (Tribal concepts) Budapest: Atlantisz, 1999.

———. "Paradoxes of 1989." *East European Politics and Societies.* 13, no. 2. (Spring, 1999a): 353–357.

———. "A botrány botránya" (The scandal in the scandal). *Népszabadság* (March 29, 2001): 21.

Teitelbaum, Michael S. and Winter, Jay. *A question of numbers. High migration, low fertility and the politics of national identity*: New York: Hill & Wang, 1998.

Thompson, Warren S. "Population." *The American Journal of Sociology* 35, no. 6. (May, 1929): 959–75.

Tismaneanu, Vladimir. "Introduction to the revolutions of 1989." *East European Politics and Societies* 13, no.2. (Spring, 1999): 231–235.

———. "Hypotheses on populism: The politics of charismatic protest." *East European Politics and Societies.* 15, no. 1 (Spring, 2001): 10–18.

Todorova, Maria. *Balkan family structure and the European pattern: demographic developments in Ottoman Bulgaria.* Washington, D.C.: American University Press, 1993.

———. *Imagining the Balkans.* Oxford: Oxford University Press, 1997.

Vajda, Mihály. "Who excluded Russia from Europe?" *East European Reporter* no. 4. (1986).

Valkovics, Emil. "*A demográfiai átmenet elemzésének néhány gyakorlati nehézségéről*" (On some practical problems in analyzing demographic transition). Budapest: KSH NKI, 1982.

van de Kaa, Dirk. "Anchored narratives. The story and findings of half a century of research into the determinants of fertility." *Population Studies* 50, no. 3 (Nov. 1996): 389–432.

———. "Europe's second demographic transition." *Population Bulletin* 42, no.1 (1987): 1–57.

———. "The second demographic transition revisited: theories and expectations." *Paper presented at the Symposium on Population Change and European Society 7–10 December 1988, Florence.* (1988)

———. (1999) "Europe and its population: the long view." in *European populations. Unity in diversity,* eds. van de Kaa, Dirk, Henri Leridon – Giuseppe Gesano and Marek Okólski (Dordrecht, Boston, London: Kluwer Academic Publishers, 1999), pp. 1–50.

———. "Without maps and compass? Towards a new European transition project." *European Journal of Population* 15, no.4 (1999a): 309–316.

Wall, Richard et al. eds. *Family forms in historic Europe.* Cambridge: Cambridge University Press, 1983.

Wallerstein, Immanuel. "The modern world-system as a civilization: *Geopolitics and geoculture*" in *Essays on the changing world-system,* ed. Wallerstein, Immanuel (Cambridge: Cambridge University Press, 1991), pp. 215–230.

———. "Eurocentrism and its avatars: The dilemmas of social science." *New Left Review* no.226. (Nov/Dec, 1997) 93–108.

Williams, Patrick and Laura Chrisman. *Colonial discourse and post-colonial theory. A reader.* New York: Columbia University Press, 1994.

Wolff, Larry. *Inventing Eastern Europe. The map of civilization on the mind of enlightenment.* Stanford: Stanford University Press, 1994.

Wrigley, Anthony and Richard Schoefield. *The population history of England. 1541–1871: A reconstruction.* Cambridge, Mass.: Harvard University Press, 1981.

Index